SMALL TOWNS, SPRAWL AND THE POLITICS OF POLICY CHOICES

The Florida Experience

Gary Armes Mattson

University Press of America,® Inc.
Lanham · New York · Oxford

Boca Raton Public Library, Boca Raton, FL

Copyright © 2002 by
University Press of America,® Inc.
4720 Boston Way
Lanham, Maryland 20706

PO Box 317
Oxford
OX2 9RU, UK

All rights reserved
Printed in the United States of America
British Library Cataloging in Publication Information Available

ISBN 0-7618-2464-2 (paperback : alk. ppr.)

∞™ The paper used in this publication meets the minimum
requirements of American National Standard for Information
Sciences—Permanence of Paper for Printed Library Materials,
ANSI Z39.48—1984

Contents

Acknowledgments		vii
Chapter 1	*Community Sprawl in Postwar America*	1
	The Rise of the Urban Place	2
	Our Sprawling Suburbs	4
	How Sprawl Came About	6
	The Themes of Sprawl	8
	Taming Sprawl by Growth Management	12
	The Organization of the Book	14
Chapter 2	*Community Sprawl and the New Urbanism*	15
	Three Planning Scenarios	16
	Florida's Sprawl and Neo-traditional Planning	19
	Neo-Traditional Planning and the Civic Community	22
Chapter 3	*Florida's Economic Roots*	25
	Florida's Traditional-Individualism	26
	Reconstruction and Its Aftermath	29
	The Bourbon Ascendency	30
	Populism, Progressivism and Jim Crow	33
	The Great Depression and the New Deal	36
	The Making of Modern Florida	40
Chapter 4	*Florida's Changing Political Culture*	45
	The Solid South No More	45
	Secular Realignment and Wedge Issues	48
	Civil Rights and the End of Jim Crow	49
	Citizen Stakeholders and Political Participation	52
	Policy Implications	60

Chapter 5	*The Politics of Florida's Growth Management*	61
	Sprawl and the Dynamics of Multi-Cultural Parochialism	61
	Florida's Entry into Growth Management	64
	Environmentalism and Local Parochialism	65
	Phase One—All Thumbs and No Fingers	68
	Phase Two—Both Thumbs and Fingers	71
	Phase Three—Weak Thumbs and Strong Fingers	73
	New Laws and New Guidelines	74
	The Locational Lottery into the New Millenium	75
	Jeb Bush and the New Millennium	80
	Concluding Remarks	82
Chapter 6	*Civic Engagement and Governance*	85
	Civic Commitment and Post-war America	85
	Building a Civil Community	86
	Small Towns, Political Culture and Civic Core Values	87
	Traditional-Individualism and the Civil Community	89
	The Dimensions of Personal Freedom	90
	The Micropolitan Policy Community	93
	Policy Implications	95
Chapter 7	*Small Town Planning in Florida*	97
	Three Tasks of Small Town Planning	97
	Civic Culture and the Growth Machine	104
	Politics of Small Town Planning	105
	Policy Implications	107
Chapter 8	*Decision Rules and Community Development*	109
	Administrative Rules and Federal Block Grants	110
	The CDBG Program	110
	Grant Getting and Small Towns	112
	The Policy Research Design	113
	Florida DCA and Small Towns	114
	Factors For Grant Getting	115
	CDBG Policy Allocations	117
	Block Grants and Growth Management	121

Chapter 9	*Financing of Florida's Public Projects*	123
	Shifting Florida's Tax Bite	123
	Red Ink and the State's FY 2002 Budget Crisis	126
	Municipalities With Few Tax Options	134
	Financing Florida's Public Facilities Under Sprawl	138
	Fiscal Policy Planning	140
	Capital Facilities Planning	143
	User Charges, Dedications and Impact Fees	145
	Discussion	151
Chapter 10	*Municipal Services and Small Florida Towns*	155
	Public Goods and Fiscal Stress	155
	Public Services and the New South	161
	From Progressivism to the Depression	164
	Civic Engagement and Municipal Service Outputs	168
	Sprawl and the Cost of Municipal Services	169
	Privatization and Public Services	171
	Policy Implication	180
Chapter 11	*Small Towns And Economic Development*	181
	Corporate City Planning and Small Towns	181
	Two Economic Policy Strategies	183
	Small Town Economic Policy Priorities	185
	Florida's Tax Increment Financing Program	189
	Policy Implications	193
Chapter 12	*Think Regionally, Acting Locally*	195
	Sprawl and Florida's Policy Shift	196
	A Southern Strategy, A Southern Solution	198
	Smart Growth and the Local Community Options	199
	Social Solution—Pedestrian Friendly Communities	202
	Environmental Solution—Crisp Edges and Greenbelts	209
	Fiscal Solutions—Financing Public Services	221
	Concluding Observations	228
Bibliography		231
Index		259

Acknowledgments

This book may be a forecast of local policy issues in America in this twenty-first century. We have always been a restless people. Economic opportunity seems to be tied to mobility. Florida is at the forefront of this mobility, with most of its citizen-taxpayers coming from somewhere else. No doubt small town Florida's changing civic and political culture is a consequence of the tensions and conflicts that emerges with such population dynamics. Yet, small towns often lack the fiscal and administrative capacity to cope with this social change. Florida towns appear to be no exception. The thoughts and ideas in this book represent my ten years as a practitioner, and countless discussions with former colleagues and students. Many of the thoughts were tossed out in seminar discussions. Several former graduate students, now practitioners of either the art of city planning or city management, were not afraid to take issue and deserve special recognition. Among them are: Anthony Burke, Shelli Barr, Angela Donaldson, Larry Garza, Gary Greenberg, Dave Pavilich, Jerry Lee Yoder, Russ Ewy, Catherine Clark, John Worsham, Lawrence Kiefer, Amy Collett and Laura Lutz-Zimmerman.

Among those academic friends who deserve some credit in keeping me intellectually honest are: Howard Foster, Marc Holzer, John Keller, Vernon Deines, Jim Seroka, Bob Wolensky, Henry Thomas, Al Keithley, Tim Barnekov, Robert Warren, Roger Caves, David Darling, Tim Borich, Steve Padgitt, Fred Lorenz and William J. Wilson. Stan Reigger and Phil Twogood, each of whom assisted in UNF's Center For Local Government's original investigation, deserve a special thanks. I deeply appreciate the technical support from Linda Rice at Kansas State University on an early draft. With sadness I wish to acknowledge a third generation Floridian and son of a Cortez fisherman who kept me in stitches with his sketches of a nearly forgotten small town. A former planning student and then colleague—Brian Bailey—will be missed by all those who had the opportunity to cross his path, especially by me. I cannot forget my editor Ms. Diane Avery, another former Floridian, who encouraged me to pursue this book to its finish. And, Janet Cooper who helped make this camera ready. Last but far from least, I am totally indebted to my wife, Elosia, who spent countless hours turning my scribbling into a readable manuscript which I hope the reader will enjoy. Of course, any factual errors or theoretical missteps are mine, and mine alone.

Chapter 1
ಶಿಂಌ
Community Sprawl in Postwar America

Sprawl's subtleties are easily recognizable but difficult to define. Like pornography, we know what it is when we see it. For most Americans, sprawl is not simply a pattern of development, but rather the lack of planning for such development. It is haphazard development, where a former farmer's field has turned into fancifully named subdivision full of new houses or where rural crossroads are turned into interchanges overnight. Sprawl has been defined by Florida's Department of Community Affairs to be: "Scattered, untimely, poorly planned urban development that occurs in urban fringe and rural areas and frequently invades lands important for environmental and natural resource protection."

Unbridled sprawl is seen as an intrusion of "franchise outlets amid a sea of parking lots and a forest of signs" on the countryside (Daniels, 1999: 137). Typically it manifests itself in one or more of the following pattern: (1) leapfrog development; (2) ribbon or strip development; or, (3)a large expanse of low density, single dimensional development (Pelham, 1995: 106). Sprawl is most keenly felt on the urban-rural fringe where adequate roads and public facilities simply do not exist. Commonly referred to as exurban development, it is most noticeable along our transportation corridors, which is defined as the "area between urban/suburban and the rural landscapes" (Davis, et. al. 1994: 45). For anti growth advocates, sprawl is the byproduct of a host of public policy decisions that are tied to our love affair with the automobile. That is, housing choices, job opportunities and the demand for infrastructure improvement are imposed onto the rural landscape (Nelson, 1992). Indeed, the emergence of the automobile gave us greater mobility. Once the highway network was completed, any city dweller could seek his or her piece of Eden, causing the scattering of dwellings throughout the countryside. The automobile gave us the freedom "to live, to work and to play outside the metropolis." Accordingly, public policy solutions for mitigating the problems associated with sprawl require policy choices that illustrate initiative, imagination and political will. Yet, the history of sprawl containment often lacks all three elements. It is the focus of the book to look at Florida and its efforts to meet the challenge of sprawl.

The Rise of the Urban Place

In our first national census (1970) only 5 per cent of Americans lived in an urban setting. Defined as having twenty-five hundred or more people, there were only 24 such communities. America was an agrarian nation—culturally, socially and economically. Until 1950, this definition for urban area remained. It was then that the Census Bureau reclassified the concept of an urban setting. Acknowledging the suburban population spillover, an urban place was redefined as a central core city that had at least the density of a thousand people per square mile, and a total population of 50,000 persons, within a surrounding metropolitan area containing at least 100,000 people.

At the beginning of the Twentieth Century, urban America accounted for only 25 per cent of the nation's population. Yet, the forces of decentralization had already appeared. In 1890, the electric motor and improved power transmission technology encouraged the widespread adoption of electric street cars, replacing the slower and more expensive horse-drawn trolley. This newer electric streetcar/trolley technology stretched transportation corridors and transformed our pedestrian central cities. In one short decade, the effective radius of the average American city doubled. In addition, other modern technological innovations (the elevator, the telephone, steel-framed construction, electric dynamos, pneumatic pumps, etc.) allowed for the feasible construction of skyscrapers and the improved distribution of water/sewer systems. By the dawn of the Twentieth Century, cities became spatially larger and socially segmented. With the rising cost of centrally located space, the typical early Twentieth Century single family-home became too expensive to be near the downtown. Instead, multi-family dwellings for the middle-class and tenements for the working-poor had begun to replace the single family urban residence as the predominant form, increasing densities in the central core (Warner, 1995; Teaford, 1993; Mohl, 1985; Klein and Kantor, 1976). But the streetcar and the subway were probably the most important transportation technology to alter the spatial urban landscape before 1920. This new form of transportation allowed many young middle-class households to relocate beyond the central cities while maintaining business and social ties within them (Muller, 1981).

This central core city dominance was to be short lived. The mass production of the automobile gave greater mobility and greater opportunity for the middle class to adopt lifestyle choices that had been previously restricted to only the most wealthy. For the next eighty years, the automobile "made it infinitely easier to commute in direct perpendicular to the trolley tracks" (Jackson, 1985: 183). Improved roadway networks gave impetus for the home building industry and land speculators to redirect development activity "away form the densely settled streetcar corridors to the more profitable and newly accessible interstices." Since then, the suburban proportion of the population has expanded every decade. During the 1920s the suburban population expanded a modest 17 to 20 percent. Between 1930 and 1950, suburban expansion again was modest, increasing to 23.3 per cent of the nation's population. Since the 1950s, suburbia began to overtake the central city, and has never stumbled. Indeed, between 1950 and 1990, the suburban population had doubled to 46.6 per cent, and by the fiscal year 2000 it became 51.1 per cent of the nation's population (Goldsmith and Blakey, 1992: 118-123; Muller, 1981: 41-57; *New York Times*, December 29, 2000).

Florida has mirrored the nation's post World War Two trends. In 1950, 65.5 per cent of the state's 2.77 million residents were located within its central core cities, principally within Jacksonville, Tampa, St. Petersburg, Miami, Tallahassee and Pensacola. Between 1950 and 1990, Florida's population grew almost five folds to 12.9 million residents, with 56.7 per cent of its people spreading beyond these central core cities into 20 designated Metropolitan Statistical Areas. Even with the emergence of new edge core cities such as Orlando, Fort Lauderdale and Sarasota, there was considerable population dispersal to the suburban-rural fringe, where this sprawls simply lack any sense of place. For instance, in 1980, about 4.5 million people lived within Florida's unincorporated areas; this figure rose to 6.5 million in 1990 (Dortch, 1995; Shermyen, 1991: Table 1-10; Purdum and Anderson, 1988). A decade later, the 2000 Census had Florida officially the fourth most populous state, and the nation's seventh fastest growing with 15.98 million people. This computes to about 845 new residents per day or about 314,500 new residents per year throughout the 1990s. Although equivalent to a new Wichita, Kansas each year, almost 45 per cent of these new residents had scattered beyond the formal jurisdictional boundaries of existing communities (*The New York Times*, December 29,2000: A15; US. Bureau Census—State Census Tapes, Count Aa; *Miami Times Herald*, December 29, 2000: A15). Suburban sprawl has invaded Florida's urban-rural fringe with each subdivision merging "into the next without noticeable landmarks or hints of different street layouts, architectural types, or land use patterns." These new subdivisions do provide "living space, greenery and convenience for auto users," but they seem to drain the Florida landscape of "its vitality and distinctiveness." (Stephenson, 1997: 120).

Our Sprawling Suburbs

The 1950 U.S. Census, as the first post Second World War census, is used as an analytical baseline by anti-sprawl advocates. Pre-war comparisons noted that America had entered a pattern of changing land use development. The pre-war attractions of open space and home ownership were reinforced by the pull of newer dispersal forces. Besides the pent up demand for housing, the widespread availability of easy term financing of housing loans guaranteed by federal programs and the adoption of mass production techniques for housing construction both made it feasible for inexpensive suburban housing tracts. In contrast to the pre-Second World War household formations, a majority of the baby-boom households subsequently formed could easily relocate beyond the nation's existing metropolitan central cities. Jobs also began to flee to suburbia, accelerated by easy access of high speed, federally funded freeways. In an Urban Institute study of the sixty largest pumas from 1970 to 1986 using postal district boundaries indicated that the central city postal zones contained 52 per cent of all metropolitan jobs in 1976, but only 47 per cent by 1986. Moreover, two-thirds of all the new jobs added to these metropolitan areas after 1976 were in the outer postal zone. That is, outer suburbia captured 93.5 per cent of the relocated manufacturing jobs, and all the newly created manufacturing jobs added from 1976 to 1986 (Downs, 1994: 46-47). Or as Muller (1985: 52) points out, metropolitan road building with its emphasis "on radial and circumferential limited-access superhighways in the 1960s quickly destroyed whatever remained of the tenuous prewar balance between the central core city and its surrounding suburbs." Not only jobs fled the core city but also the higher income households, further segregating minorities and the urban white poor, causing greater concentration of households in poverty within the central core city (Goldsmith and Blakely, 1992: 46-55; Downs, 1994: Ch.5).

By 1990, 115 million folks were residing beyond the 522 central cities within the nation's 320 metropolitan areas. These folks were mostly white and are middle to upper-middle class households (Goldsmith and Blakely, 1992: 108-132). In six of the ten most populous states (California, Pennsylvania, Ohio, Michigan, Florida and New Jersey), a majority of their state population and employment activity were by then located within suburbia, with nineteen of the twenty-five fastest job growing cities being "edge" cities (Rusk, 1993; Schneider, 1995). Such a demographic population shift means a decline in a central core city's tax base, further eroding a central city's ability to compete within the region.

With the exception of Jacksonville which is a consolidated city-county government, half of the Florida's job growth rate has been beyond the existing municipal jurisdictional boundaries (*Florida Trends Annual*, 1998). For instance, Orange County's unincorporated areas have had a job growth rate three times that of its central city, Orlando, Florida. By mid-decade, about 63 per cent of the county's total population was located within unincorporated areas, likewise with 45 per cent of the jobs (*Florida Trends Annual*, 1998; *Planning*, March, 1996: 4; Shermyen, 1991: Table 1-31). Charlotte County provides a similar perspective. Punta Gorda, which population has nearly doubled in the past decade, is still largest city within Charlotte County. Yet, sixty percent of the county's estimated 137,000 folks reside in the unincorporated areas. As the planning profession knows, where population resides, jobs soon follow. Within non metropolitan northern Florida, this population and job dispersal has been similar, ranging from 49 per cent in Gulf County to 95 per cent in Wakulla County (*Florida Trends Annual*, 1998; Dortch, 1995; Shermyen, 1991; Purdum and Anderson, 1988: 16). Or as John Herbers (1986) observes, since the 1970s, much of our population and job shift has occurred within the "politically amorphous" areas on the suburban-rural fringe, which he coined as America's "New Heartland."

We are now a suburban nation of 281 million people. Since 1950, two trends has dominated our national population growth rate. First, the 2000 Census found that there is a continual migratory shift of people from the Frostbelt to the Sunbelt, with four Sunbelt states—Arizona, Florida, Georgia and Texas—each gaining two congressional seats and political power at the expense of the Frostbelt states. Second, there is a continual population shift to suburbia, meaning both rural areas and the central cities have fewer people, fewer jobs and less political clout (*USA Today*, December 29, 2000:

6A; *The New York Times*, December 29, 2000: 15A). For most states, these two trends imply a shift in legislative political power. With political power shifting to suburbia, it is unlikely that the central cities or the rural areas will be able to exert the type of political clout both had once enjoyed.

How Sprawl Came About

The political economist Charles Tiebout (1956) has provided one of the earliest scenarios for the rise of suburban sprawl. After observing the policy behavior of suburban communities, Tiebout wrote that households and firms were simply responding to the land use marketplace forces. Accordingly, the central city and its surrounding towns and villages were in competition with each other to improve their respective economic/tax base standing within the region. "Cities, like all social systems, seek to improve their position in all three systems of stratification—economic, social and political—characteristic of industrial societies." Unlike the Greek or Renaissance "walled" city-state, the modern cental core city is completely vulnerable to the social and economic forces beyond its jurisdictional boundaries (Long, 1972). As opportunities for annexation become less likely, it becomes increasingly clear that households were more fluid. Subsequently, the central city and its surrounding municipalities were in competition with each political jurisdiction devising a policy planning strategy to improve its "marketplace position," its attractiveness "as a locale for economic activity" (Peterson, 1981: 22).

There are only two land use policy choices directly under the control of any municipality—its spatial area arrangements [land use regulation] and its ability to provide public services [a tax package bundle of public goods and services]. Subsequently, each municipality within the region, in an effort to attract "high-end" households and businesses, will devise a local land regulatory and public service tax bundle policy scheme that improves its attractiveness to individual households and firms. Based on a series of posited assumptions pertaining to perceived attitudes and beliefs of the individual households and firms, Tiebout and his colleagues asserted that individual households and firms are consumers of spaces who act rationally when demanding locations for homes or business sites. Therefore, a dynamic local government will respond to these demand preferences by devising a municipal tax-package bundle and/or constructing ideal land site opportunities. Failure to do so will lead to citizen dissatisfaction, causing an individual household or firm to "vote with its feet." Households and firms within the region will "comparison shop" and more likely relocate to a community that best fits their market preferences. Thus, much of the policy behavior of local community officials is tied to the socio-economic preferences of households and firms (Lyons, et.al., 1992; Schneider, 1989; Sharp, 1986; Peterson, 1981).

If Tiebout's Model is appropriate, then the blueprint for sprawl began in the 1950s, when American veterans demanded a single family home with some "quality of life" elbow room. The "suburban mystique" replete with its wood framed ranch homes, curved streets and backyard barbeques asserted itself. It is true that the American suburban dream was actively sold to the potential home buyer by developers. But, real estate developers and builders responded to the "tastes" or "preferences" of these home buyers. The Post-War period there was considerable pent up demand to move away from the crime and the grime of the big city. In 1944, there were only 142,000 housing starts nationally; by 1946, housing starts shot up to 1,023,000 housing units, eventually climbing to its peak of 1,952,000 units in 1950. Every year between 1947 and 1964 the number of annual housing starts topped the 1.2 million units. Levittown became the prototype for the modern suburban community. With financing by low-cost government loans, an ex-service man could become a Levitt homeowner. For $90 down and $58 a month for twenty-five years, a former veteran could own his suburban home with a picket fence close by to shopping, parks and schools (Teaford, 1993: 100-107). The builder William Levitt took his design cues from Frank Lloyd Wright and built his Cape Cod and Colonial housing styles, allowing his urban customers to flee from the confines of bleak, boxlike apartments and the gritty streets of the urban core (Stern, 1986: 151-59; Fishman,1987). Besides most central cities were too politically diverse to hear the civic voice of the individual households and be able "to provide public services tailored to the needs of particular segments of their populations"(Mills and Oates, 1975).

Florida's housing boom mirrored the national trends. Modern technology made Florida sprawl a reality. Air conditioning made its climate tolerable. The automobile and a modern highway system encouraged migration from the North. Between 1940 and 1960, the number of housing units in Pinellas County alone jumped from 40,250 to 165,823 units, or about 400 percent, with three-fourths of these units constructed in the 1950s and bought by former northern Yankees (Stephenson, 1997: 119). Broward County shared a similar growth pattern. Carved out of Dade and Palm County in 1915, its population growth between 1950 and 1960 grew by 298 per cent, then dropped to 86 per cent for the next decade. It indicated a moderate growth rate of 64 per cent between 1970 and 1980, largely due "to infilling." By 1990, Broward County became the second most densely populated county in Florida, with 975 persons per square mile (Purdum and Anderson, 1987: 12; Vogel, 1992: 27). Simple percentages belie the true impact. Broward County gained more than 250,000 people between 1950 and 1960, another 286,000 between 1960 and 1970, and almost 400,000 between 1970 and 1980. In the past two decades, Broward County's population had grown by another 416,000, causing citrus groves and large tracts of scrub pine to become incorporated into 18 new municipalities, fragmenting an already "weak" countywide growth management plan (Vogel, 1992: 27-30; Purdum and Anderson, 1988: 12). Throughout Florida yesterdays orchards and tree plantations are today's shopping malls, apartment complexes and housing subdivisions. Land has become more profitable for commercial development. For Florida, people and firms are nationally "voting with their feet" by moving to the Sunshine State.

The Themes of Sprawl

The 1970 Census bore out the Tiebout Model, with households and firms spreading out into the metropolitan hinterland. Sprawl had come of age. The suburbs were not new. They had been in existence since the mid-Nineteenth Century (Jackson, 1985; Stern, 1986: Ch. 4; Fishman, 1987). What was new, was its form. A half century ago, the downtown was still the community's town center. Main Street was the common thread. It was the place where we shopped, worked, worshiped and entertained. Today, the common thread is the highway. Our interchanges are our new town squares, linking our office parks and our shopping malls to our residences. Smart Growth advocates claim that suburban sprawl lacks a Sense of Place—a town center. This lack of a Sense of Place is a consequence of three limitations of the existing market forces.

Sprawl is characterized by its landscape of a spaghetti-like network of highways, parking lots, shopping strip malls, and endless assortment of soulless residential enclaves. It is a form that "so separates, segregates and isolates us," that we become "pockets of hostile aliens." Our garage door "has replaced the front door, the parking lot the public steps of City Hall, and the underground garage the office building lobby" (Gratz and Mintz, 1998: 33-34). Subsequently, we have increasingly purchased scaled-down Mac Mansions, located in isolated communities that are increasingly walled, gated, and guarded to protect us from the social interaction of others whom we perceive as unworthy of our attention. Smart Growth advocates (2000: xiii) write that our sprawling suburbs are not of our own choosing. Rather, they were "imposed upon us, by local zoning and the demands of the automobile." Because of a patchwork federal policies that encouraged the construction of our modern highways, we were encouraged to purchase subsidized, low-density, detached single-family homes (Freilich, 1999: 2; Downs, 1994: Ch.5). For no fault of our own, we moved to communities that consume "land at an alarming rate, while producing insurmountable traffic problems and exacerbating socially inequity and isolation." (Duany, et.al., 2000: 4).

Apparently, the culprits of sprawl are not we or our choice of lifestyles; rather, the culprits are three key factors—the automobile, developers who manipulate a fragmented regional system of governance, and a rigid, antiquated local planning model tied to local parochialism. Each are intertwined and helped establish a set of rules for the modern land use development game (Kunstler, 1993,1996). These development rules send "a clear signal to employers, householders, builders and political leaders: build out on open, un-urbanized, in some cases untouched land, and by-pass older areas." (Katz and Bradley, 1999: 28). In other words, a set of rules have been devised by someone,"which reflect the desire for an rural lifestyle coupled with an urban income." (Freilich, 1999: 16). Accordingly, the real culprits of sprawl are the automobile and fragmented, non-innovative government.

Local Parochial Governance

For decades, rural local officials, with a desire to improve the local tax base has made policy choices based on the presumption that any development was appropriate (Rudel, 1989; King and Harris, 1989; Hibbard and Davis, 1986; Hahn, 1970). In rural America, sprawl takes the form of **rural lot splits**, which is the process of "dividing off" large tracts of land into smaller parcels with minimal provision for public services and utilities. As a former rural planning director, I was often faced with rural lot split development. Located off an existing road network, the parcel contains its own water well and septic system. The impetus for this residential choice is a desire to avoid the crime, grime and crowdedness of the city but still be within its commuting distance. It is a rational choice, given the market forces. The household can enjoy the benefits of a diverse lifestyle in a reasonably priced home.

Typically, an urban fringe municipality or county professional staff is small or nonexistent (Baker, 1994). Because of scale, local politics is highly personalized, making it difficult for the professional planner to establish a non-political framework for decision-making (Mills and Davis, 1963; Gamberg, 1968). Besides, it seems to be unfair to penalize " a landowner by refusing to approve such a "rural lot-split," especially if his neighbor has been allowed to do so (Cullingworth, 1993: 123).

Most local governments believe that an effective mechanism to protect the rural way of life is by local autonomy. Municipal incorporation is a form of governance known as **local parochialism.** By becoming a separate political jurisdiction, the community can decide: (1) what municipal services to provide, (2) what its local tax base, and (3) what shape its landuse will be. Local parochialism means shaping one's own destiny. Even faced with sprawl, relinquishing local autonomy is a difficult undertaking for most citizens. The people of Sanibel Island discovered this. A low-lying barrier island just off the City of Fort Myers, it was governed by Lee County. Under its comprehensive plan, Sanibel Island's unique topography was classified as if similar to Lee County's mainland. Once a causeway was built in 1963, a building boom followed resulting in condominium on its frontal sand dunes and golf courses on its wetlands. Felt neglected by Lee County officials, its residents demanded incorporation from the legislature. Even though their consultant urge the adoption of cluster and performance zoning techniques tied to a state advisory plan (Clark, 1986), Sanibel Island residents fearful of the loss of new gained autonomy adopted traditional zoning and subdivision land use planning tools. It was an opportunity lost to local parochialism.

Fragmented Land Use Regulations and Leapfrog Development

Under Florida state enabling law, towns and counties are allowed to devise zoning, housing, building, health, and subdivision codes to control the proliferation of rural lot splits. Zoning codes, first adopted in 1939, is the most frequently adopted land use tool. As Delafons (1962: 23) points out, towns quickly saw zoning "as a means of strengthening the institution of private property." Moreover, in the South, zoning became a legitimate means of racial segregation (Mohl,1995; Silver, 1984; Harris,1977). Even to this day, fiscal zoning has been used to preserve the social composition of suburban communities. That is, communities regulate the uses of land within their jurisdiction to exclude "undesirable" uses (Mills and Oates, 1975). Besides, zoning is free to the town. "No compensations need to be paid to property owners for reductions in property values caused by limitations imposed by the zoning ordinance on the type and intensity of use permitted." (Levy, 1994: 112). Once the town council adopts its map and codes, it is a quasi-judicial policy instrument that entails a very precise set of decision rules pertaining to site layout, compatible use of lot sizes, set-backs, building heights and the density of structures per acreage (Levy, 1994: 111; Cullingworth, 1993). In *Growth Management in Countryfied Cities*, Doherty (1991: 119) explains that rural towns and counties are, however, rarely innovative, often focusing on locally unwanted or incompatible building design issues. In other words, local parochial zoning emerges as a reactive planning style, which simply focuses on site-specific problems such as rural-lot splits.

By contrast, subdivision codes are tied to the legal process "of dividing land into smaller units called 'lots' for future sales and development." (Daniels, et.al., 1995: 194). It bestows legal ownership standards upon the purchaser and ensure that existing design standards are compatible. A subdivision code provides an opportunity for the community to assure that safe and convenient circulation traffic patterns, and the proper facility capacity of water, sewer and storm drainage exists. Florida's subdivision statute requires public access to each lot by a street layout, and requires the seller of more than five lots to provide curbs and gutters, internal sewers and water lines, sidewalks, and street lights and street signs. Subdivision codes are frequently utilized by rural county planning agencies to avert blight and deterioration by requiring that development proceed in a carefully specified manner that is consistent with the public's health, safety and welfare (Freilich and Shulz, 1995: 25).

New Urbanism or Smart Growth proponents claim both traditional land use tools, as presently used, encourage sprawl. Neither zoning or subdivision regulations allow for the timing and sequencing of big scale housing and commercial projects. As reactive planning tools, both regulatory instruments encourage "discontinuous development" (Kelly,1993: 12-25,135; Cullingworth, 1993: Ch.10). Generally known as **leapfrogging** policy behavior, this form of land utilization allows for the skipping of higher priced, improved urban land for cheaper priced, under improved rural property by the developer. Generally, land prices tend to fall as the distance from the central business district (CBD) increases. Most potential buyers are competing for ideal scarce sites that are tied to the city's utilities, with most of these ideal sites located in close proximity to the tranquility of the countryside. **Leapfrogging** allows household and firms to make tradeoffs associated with their municipal service tax-package, site location, and transportation network. Both households and firms will tend to **leapfrog** over higher price land near the core, and relocate to the urban-rural fringe. In this way, **leapfrogging** contributes to sprawl, suggesting that many state mandated growth management strategies are "explicitly motivated" to prevent this type of site location behavior (Fischel, 1991: 342).

Municipal land use and public service delivery policy behavior appears too assisted by fragmented regional governance. As the **Tiebout Model** claims, households and firms are "the buyers" of local municipal services in the form of "tax package-amenity bundles." With each town in competition with other towns, it is rational policy behavior for each town to offer municipal services that will attract "high-income" households and "non-polluting" firms. Subsequently, **like-minded** households or firms become the " buyers" of ideal sites by "shopping around" among the communities, seeking the best "tax package-amenity bundle" of public services. In the long run, household and firms will **leapfrog** over inefficient jurisdictions (stiff land use regulations) and locate to a place with "tax-package bundles" is more affordable. Too often, a developer with deep pockets can avoid those town's that are sincere with growth management and leapfrog to those communities which are "sellers" of affordable sites. Without a regional scheme, a builder can play one community against another. The outcome, according to Smart Growth advocates, is the construction of high rise office towers, shopping plazas and ordinary, boorish subdivisions, each development endangering certain quality of life factors within the community that had made the community attractive in the first place.

Taming Sprawl by Growth Management

The national debate over growth management is focused **not** on the question of goals, but rather on the issue of **who** should be undertake the responsibility for local land use management (Innes, 1992; Fischel, 1989). "Central to all growth management programs, regardless of location," according to Gale and Hart (1992: 192), is the belief that "land development and population increase" can be balanced with "the desire to conserve natural, historical and/or cultural resources." Politically, however, growth management proposals too often defer to local parochial interests, focusing on the: (1) the enhancement of a town's tax base; (2) the expansion of its job pool; and, (3) the protection of its residential, commercial and infrastructure investments (DeGrove and Miness, 1991).

Florida was an early entry into the **growth management** game. As noted, an underlying premise of growth management advocates is that our love affair with the automobile has discouraged the adoption of quality of life planning principles. To accommodate the automobile, local zoning and subdivision standards have ignored the former type of compact development of the preautomobile, southern small town. Thus, "auto-oriented" planning—strip malls, big box stores, ugly parking lots and friendless subdivision—has wreaked havoc on the surrounding countryside. For Smart Growth, Neo-Traditional Planning advocates, the only solution is to devise a planning management framework that emphasizes New Urbanism principles within a regional setting.

In 1972, Florida's legislature adopted the most innovative and progressive regional growth management policy plan in the nation (See Ch. 5). By doing so, the Florida legislature expanded the state statutory authority over local land use planning, forcing cities and counties to become more accountable in their local land use activity (Healy and Rosenburg, 1979; DeGrove and Turner, 1991). Like the other growth management states of the period (Vermont, Oregon and Hawaii), the Florida legislature hoped to get a handle on three specific policy issue: (1) protection of the state's unique natural environment; (2) the containment of the cost of municipal service delivery due to sprawl; (3) maintenance of the state's economic development momentum without sacrificing the first two objectives.

After one decade, the Governor and the state's legislature felt the plan had not worked. Population growth had not slowed or been managed. Proposed revisions were made. Known as the **Growth Management Act of 1985**, it was hailed as the most innovative growth management policy in the nation. A key theme was its regional planning component. By making municipalities responsible for devising local comprehensive plans that are "consistent" with regional, county and adjoining jurisdictional plans [Section 163.3194, Fla, Stat.], each comprehensive plan would take into account the issue of urban compactness in their subdivision design standards so that the "carrying capacity" of the local infrastructure would not be overburdened and/or be incompatible with adjoining governmental entities—counties or municipalities [Section 163.3177, Fla. Stat.]. The Florida legislature also recognized the failure of its earlier 1970s initiatives to designate a state coordinating agency, staffed with non-elected bureaucrats, to assure that the state's goals of growth management are implemented. Accordingly, Florida's Department of Community Affairs was assigned this compliance responsibility. As an agency directly under the Governor's control, it was given the authority to impose sanctions, if necessary, to those municipalities and counties which failed to submit comprehensive plans "that meets state standards, or in other ways choose not to comply with program requirements." (Gale, 1992: 435). The threat of sanction at the state level would undergird this innovative, reform growth management initiative. Yet, Florida's 1985 growth management policy plan was not without its critics. For many of Florida's local officials, the state mandated growth policy plan was perceived as a threat to their very political existence, and their Traditional-Individualistic political cultural model (see Ch. 3). Indeed, Florida's land use politics with a variety of stakeholders appears to mirror the nation's struggle with sprawl, making it an excellent laboratory for examining the tensions derived from state directed policy planning choices that will likely continue into the 21st Century.

The Organization of the Book

This book tends to acquaint community planners and other practitioners with the Traditional-Individualistic political cultural model. It will be asserted that the local parochial tendencies of Traditional-Individualism have influenced how policy was implemented at the small town level, often contradicting statewide initiatives, suggesting potential conflict and tension between state bureaucrats and local political leadership. An appreciation of this civic cultural model is essential for understanding how public policies are being carried out within urban-rural fringe communities.

The book is organized into two parts. Part One consists of a discussion of Florida's social and economic developmental history as it relates to the shaping of Florida's political cultural model. Part Two explores the overriding theme that Florida's urban-rural fringe towns are spatially fixed with limited economic and organizational capacity. A town's land area is one of the few economic "stakes" or political "goodies" available for policy choices. Since towns are in constant competition with each other, the Florida Growth Management Act (1985) with its emphasis on regional cooperation had altered this policy planning game. It is asserted here that rural towns simply lack the professional skills to make needed adjustments, and are placed in further economic jeopardy, making the policy planning game much harder for Florida's smaller, rural communities.

Chapter 2
⚜
Community Sprawl and the New Urbanism

As of Fiscal Year 2000, there were 10 states that had initiated some sort of state comprehensive planning programs to tackled sprawl. By then, nationally, the citizen debate centered on efforts to fit a particular policy strategy for tighter land use regulatory control guidelines that did not jeopardize a community's unique economic, environmental or quality of life. As Florida can testify, a suburban sprawl was no longer the problem of the metropolitan centers of Tampa or the Miami-Dade; by then, it had reached the Panhandle communities of Pensacola, Panama City, Tallahassee and Apalachicola. Throughout Florida, yesterday's farms, citrus orchards and tree plantations are today's shopping malls and housing subdivisions. Land has become more profitable for housing tracts than for raising trees to produce turpentine, lumber or oranges.

Florida's Traditional-Individualistic tendency has assured a long history of alliances between state governmental leaders and the business community to exploit its landscape (See Chapter 3). For instance, the support from state governmental leadership had allowed both Henry Plant and Henry Flagler to build their railroads, and Governor Bloxham's sale of state trust land had allowed Hamilton Disston to drain the Kissimmee River basin. To maintain a post World War II momentum, the state's legislative leadership known as the "Porkchop Gang" created a pro-growth coalition with the state's financial and business community. This pro-growth alliance passed a series of state constitutional and legislative enactments designed to ensure a real estate boom. Before the 1985 growth management law, land development was a principal factor for Florida's economic post-War boom. Since 1950, a relentless population surge has taken hold, with the state's population nearly doubling each of its preceding decades. Many of Florida's former sleepy villages, such as Fort Myers, Panama City or Melbourne have been transformed into sprawling communities. In 1985, New York Times columnist Jon Nordheimer (*New York Times,* July 15,1986: 5) observed, while many Frostbelt communities were in a recession, the "sprawl shrine" became "the altar" before which many Floridians had worshiped. And, for many Floridians, this mantra of "growth is good" had helped they "to prosper" in these lean times.

Three Planning Scenarios

Planning schools teach that there are three scenarios for land use management. The first scenario is "to do nothing," and let the marketplace determine land use arrangement. Known as the **"Pro-growth Strategy,"** this approach allows for "more people and more jobs and the construction of houses, offices, factories, malls and commercial strips." For developers, this scenario is most desirable. It presumes that sprawl is inevitable; therefore, towns should accommodate the sprawl by emphasizing "more housing, better transportation, such as highway access; and economic development in the form of new commercial and industrial areas." (Daniels, 1999: 71-73).

A **"Balanced Growth"** alternative is the second scenario. Most favored in the planning profession, it presumes that sprawl can be guided. Balanced Growth advocates accept the inevitability of land use change associated with the sprawl. Like the pro-growth machine boosters, Balance Growth advocates try to accommodate the sprawl by devising "growth containment" boundaries (Knapp and Nelson, 1992). The bottom line is to "channel growth to appropriate locations and minimize negative impacts associated with on-going growth" (Zovanyi, 1998: 37). Also known as the **growth phase strategy**, planning implementation emphasizes the regulation of the "location and timing of new development, generally based on the availability or presumed availability, of public facilities." (Kelly, 1993: 48). Sprawl follows sewers and freeways. Infrastructure financing is a critical component of containment. Advocates contend that the comprehensive plan is held captive by special interests. Therefore, the solution to sprawl is the slowing of growth by the timing and phase-development of infrastructure.

Two early examples are the Petaluma, California and Ramapo, New York policy plans. In each case, local government attempted to guide their respective growth patterns by influencing the supply and quality of public financed facilities, believing that housing subdivisions and malls can be accommodated without sacrificing the community's sense of place (Porter, 1997: 21; Freilich, 1999).

The **Balanced Growth** strategy is not as simplistic as many advocates suggest. Balance growth does provide a game board by which implementation conflict between landowners and land regulators can interact. Under the agreed rules it appears the primary game players can all be viewed as winners. That is, the developers are able to build, the landowners are able to sell their land at a profit, and the local politician can devise a comprehensive plan that avoids drawn out conflicts. Indeed, the town politician may be the biggest winner. He or she is seen as a "broker" between the two disputed camps who has accommodated development without sacrificing the community's image. At least this is what Balanced Growth advocates would like us to believe (Zovayni, 1998). Performance threshold standards are quite common in the plan. For smaller cities, which lack professional expertise, schedule improvement delays is also quite common, allowing developers opportunities to obtain waivers and ignore "in-fill" or "build-out" requirements (Porter, 1997: 123-129). The **Balanced Growth or Phased Growth** strategy simply means "an ongoing equilibrium between development and conservation, between various forms of development and the concurrent provision of an infrastructure, between the demands for public services generated by growth and the supply of revenues to finance those demands, and between progress and equity." (Chinitz, 1990: 6).

The **Smart Growth** model is the third planning scenario. It is the most controversial. It draws a "line in the sand" on the fortunes of suburban sprawl. This planning management strategy is a radical departure because it purposely limits a community's population level, reorders zoning and subdivision requirement priorities and encourages containment by urban growth boundaries (Utt and Shaw, 2000; Anderson, 1999). By utilizing some sort of land use **activity caps,** smart growth advocates claim to guide growth, and in many respects, limit the expansion of sprawl. Both the concepts of **carrying capacity** and **regional coordination** are part of the Florida growth management plan.

The Cape Cod Plan provides us with a useful illustration. Barnstable County, better known as Cape Cod, is situated a day's drive from two major metropolitan centers—New York City and Boston. Like Florida, it is a very popular spot for vacationers and weekend home dwellers. But, the onslaught of vacationers and weekenders has placed serious pressure on the Cape's fragile eco-system. Roger Caves (1992: Ch.4) wrote the carving up of many former farms had created traffic congestion, waste disposal and ground water contamination problems that spilled beyond the boundaries of individual townships. The Sprawl became the "plague" that was infecting the entire Cape Code landscape. The Sprawl soon became a regional problem, which required a regional solution. Consequently, Massachusetts' legislature created a regional solution known as the Cape Cod Regional Commission, which eventually reviewed any commercial development above ten thousand square feet. Yet, issue still arise over who should have the ultimate say–the town or the region.

The key to any **Smart Growth** land use management plan appears to be its regional orientation. It may use the same tools as a **Balanced Growth** scheme, but it devises such a scheme on a regional basis, allowing for sprawl mitigation to be shared. In many respects, it has internal simplicity. It tends to convert "less land to urban uses, leaving more land in pristine, natural condition." (Audirac, et. al., 1990: 476). Frequently, the ballot box is used to assure democratic legitimacy (Caves, 1992). Again, the justification of a **Smart Growth** policy plan is associated with the need for local governments to play "catch-up" in public service provisions, making it less costly to the citizen taxpayer in the long run (Knapp and Nelson, 1992; Caves, 1992; Anderson, 1999). **Smart Growth** is a land use plan that needs a regional focus. It cannot succeed under local parochial terms. Otherwise, it simply shifts the development to another nearby community, creating a checkerboard sprawl.

Boulder, Colorado is praised as a successful implementation of the no-growth policy plan. In 1959, its citizens voted a city charter amendment that restricted water service and later sewer service above the elevation of 5,750 feet. In 1967, Boulder's citizens voted for a local option sales tax. The city earmarked this money to implement a plan for improving infrastructure and purchase open space. Within a green belt, urban growth boundary has been imposed. Again, development is tied to carrying capacity of municipal services (Lorentz and Shore, 2000; Kelly, 1993: 56-59). But, Boulder is not a true **Smart Growth** policy plan. Instead it is an **Urban Growth Boundary** strategy. It lacks a regional focus. Developers have simply leapfrogged beyond Boulder's jurisdictional borders. In six short years, between 1990 and 1996, nearby Superior's population has jumped from 255 to 3,377 persons. Superior simply took advantage of its opportunity to attract property tax revenue by supplying much needed lower-cost housing to those who wish to locate near Boulder. The Boulder example illustrates the need for a regional focus. Housing starts have simply leapfrogged to nearby towns, creating **"Checkerboard Sprawl."** This is the underlying weakness of many local land use management plans. Boulders' intentions are well meaning, but the plan fails to achieve its long term objectives. Without a regional focus, Boulder's land use plan has been criticized as being elitist, simply another "drawbridge" tool to keep out certain income groups from a community (Lorentz and Shaw, 2000; Kelly, 1993; Dowell, 1984).

Florida's Sprawl and Neo-Traditional Planning

Sprawl is defined by Florida's Department of Community Affairs to be: "scattered, untimely, poorly planned urban development that occurs in urban fringe and rural areas and frequently invades lands important for environmental and natural resource protection." Urban sprawl typically manifests itself in one or more of the following patterns: (1) leapfrog development; (2) ribbon or strip development; and (3) large expanse of low density, single dimensional development (Pelham, 1995: 106). Such sprawl is a complex phenomenon, often characterized by the loss of Florida farmland, escalating housing prices, and the degradation of the state's natural environment. Consequently, Florida's strategy has focused on the conservation of open space, prime agricultural lands and valuable natural resources. Such policy planning has a political perspective that makes it quite attractive to the planning profession; it requires government-sponsored intervention. At the same time, the implementation of such a policy plan requires some sort of technical planning skill (Leo, et. al. 1998: 181), implying that any policy planning scheme adopted by any level of government comprises of a collection of plans, programs and regulations which legitimize the role of the planning profession (Porter, 1996).

Growth management has been defined as a set of policy tools that will regulate the rate and timing of development within a community (Chinitz, 1990). Its purpose is to establish a set of rules for development "that is designed to preserve the livability, viability, and attractiveness" of an entire region. Such an endeavor is difficult, requiring "the achievement of a complex set of political trade-offs that, together, address[es] the conditions for the vitality and health" on a regional perspective. This implies an inherent willingness to cooperate among local communities (Leo, 1998). Politically, the operative phrases for most growth management proposals are localisms rather than regionalism.

The Florida **Growth Management Act of 1985** attempted to correct this weakness by providing a connective tissue that ties regionalism to local concerns. A key theme of the **Growth Management Act of 1985** is for local governments to assure their local comprehensive plans were "consistent" with county and adjoining jurisdictional plans [Section 163.3194, Fla. Stat.]. Moreover, each comprehensive plan would take into account the issues of compactness in their subdivision design standards so that local and regional "carrying capacities" for municipal services are not overburdened [Section 163.3177, Fla. Stat.].

The Neo-Traditional Planning, Sprawl and Small Towns

An underlying premise of Smart Growth is that our love affair with the automobile has discouraged the adoption of compact, pedestrian style communities. The new street layouts often cause shifts in existing travel patterns. For many small towns, their Main Streets, a key element for local social participation, have become threatened (Ch.6). By ignoring time honored pedestrian design standards, traffic engineers and planners began promoting disconnected communities, destroying a small town's social fabric. By repudiating the past, our networks of compact, agrarian towns have disintegrated in a few decades to sprawl (Kunstler,1996: 89). Porterfield and Hall (1995: 7-9) write that sprawl is a "random accumulation of parts or sections loosely tied together by roads and waterways." Towns within such a web are no longer independent economic units and are no longer able to stimulate civic engagement among its residents or able to provide "for their health, safety and comfort."

Successful suburbs and small towns require healthy, viable town centers (Moe and Wilkie, 1997). And, the bottom-line for town center vitality is the number people and the volume of pedestrian traffic it can attract. Or as Economic Geographer James Kenyon (1989: 13) claims, the more people who utilize a town center, the more interesting and significant a place it is. Generally, downtown viability derives "from an ability to attract people: the extent to which people are there partly because other people are there. A simple overall measure of a downtown's human measure is its pedestrian volume."

For the past three decades, the central city and the small town have both faced decline in patronage, jeopardizing their once preeminent position as principle shopping hubs. Prior to 1970, most isolated rural communities thought their respective Main Streets were immune to urban retail competition. The Interstate Highway System, with its high-speed, limited access highways, has altered this perception. Cutting travel time considerably, the Interstates Highway System, with its beltways, has dramatically shifted existing trade capture area boundaries, impacting on the very vitality of both the urban core cities and many smaller, rural towns (Mattson, 1996; Leistritz, et.al., 1989; Davidson, 1980). Indeed, most small town Main Streets emerged from a rural landscape, usually along historic transportation routes. The Interstates have skirted these old Main Streets, creating outlying shopping strips, known as **Interstate Villages**. Consequently, at these bypass interchanges, large threshold population dependent commercial businesses—fast food restaurants, gasoline stations and discount outlet stores—emerged to become direct competitors to the existing Main Street merchants, siphoning off potential retail dollars (Moe and Wilkie, 1997: Ch. 5; Francaviglia, 1996; Moon, 1989; Lamb, 1985).

Former President Jimmy Carter gives a perspective on the impact that the Interstate has had on a Southern small town. Recently, he wrote that Plains, Georgia might have had less than 600 folks, but it was a lively place in the late 1930s. Located in central Georgia, President Carter (2001: 130) notes that Plains' Main Street, with the exception of the bank building and his father's grocery store, comprised of "nine brick buildings, all with common walls, except for one narrow ally half-way down the row." Just across Hudson Street was the standard railroad depot, and nearby was a two-story drug store. On the west end of this angular Main Street, there were five wooden-framed structures that "housed a cafe, a barbershop, the post office, a grocery store, and a filling station." The railroad and paved Highway 280 were the only two transportation routes that connected Plains to the outside world. For the past century, with the exception of running water, electricity, and telephones, Plains' physical layout has not changed. Sadly, with the decline in rail traffic and the new Interstate, contemporary Plains is no longer the gathering place for farmers or town folk; no longer a place where both whites and blacks would shop or play. On a Saturday, the prime entertainment in such Georgia towns, according to Kenyon (1989: 12), is "watching the semi's roll through."

Cultural Historian Melton McLaurin (1987: Ch. 1) also comments on the loss of social activity in his boyhood Southern town due to technology and shifting trade patterns. He describes Wade, North Carolina as neither being "a pretty village, nor was it ugly." In 1953 the streets were unpaved and muddy after a summer's rain. Its physical appearance differed little "from that of 1933, or for that matter, except for the presence of automobiles and electricity, from Wade of 1893." Located in the heart of cotton and tobacco country, Wade's merchants and civic leaders were one generation removed from the farm. However, they still had deep love for the land and "retained their ties to it." Their politics and civic core values were rural, "clinging to the reassuring stability of family, church and community." The railroad not the highway was the town's only outside lifeline, playing a critical role in the town's economy. Into the 1960s, due to poor roads, townfolk and farmers shopped locally. The sawmill, the cotton gin and warehouses were located west of and adjacent to the railroad depot, employing a number of Wade's residents, black and white. For decades, farmers shipped cotton, watermelons and other crops from the railroad depot, "an elongated frame building with wooden loading docks, which received trainloads of fertilizer and agriculture implements from factories and warehouses in coastal cities." In the 1980s, the railroad spur to the cotton gin and sawmill was abandoned and fewer trains stopped in Wade, and far fewer people shopped. Indeed, the services and amenities that Wade lacks, the highway system made it easier to travel the twelve miles to the Fayetteville Mall.

Smart Growth has helped popularize the design merits of Neo Traditional Planning's compact, human scale development in the face of technological change (Ch. 12). The overriding goal Neo-Traditional Planning, according to Reid Ewing (1996: 17), is the restoration of a community's sense of place by mitigating the technological impacts of sprawl in "whatever form its takes place—whether scattered, strip or spread development...." For the Neo Traditional planner, high density, compact development does not necessarily mean congestion. Instead, it can be a manifestation of "finely integrated, walkable communities" that give us "convivial public places" (Calthorpe, 1993: 21). The ideal Neo-Traditional community provides for design standards that connect: (1) streets into a network so that "people can readily reach other sections" of their neighborhood or town; (2) customers to shops and services "by encouraging retail and institutional development" within walking distance"; (3) citizens to one another by insisting that "walkways be sociable"; and (4) age and income groups "by mixing" them together in houses and apartments "of assorted sizes and prices." By doing so, New Urbanism hopes to foster civic engagement among local residents (Langdon, 1994: 123). Or as Kemmis (1990) would claim, encourage "barn raising" by members of the community.

Neo-Traditional Planning and the Civil Community

The idyllic neo-Victorian eighty-acre beach town of Seaside is probably the most notable of all Neo-Traditional Planning prototype communities. Designed by Andres Duany and Elizabeth Plater-Zybeck, Seaside is located on Florida's "Redneck Riviera," just past the lazy little hamlet of Seagrove, Florida. Aimed at recapturing the kind of resort beach community that reached its zenith at about 1920, Seaside is a collection of wood framed, pitched roof cottages located on a network of sandy footpaths or very narrow, reddish brick streets. Each house has an old-fashioned looking "crimped metal roof" and a regulation size front porch, located behind a white picket fenced yard. The town center has several small retail shops, and a small, classically designed post office. The town is a delight to visit. For many, Seaside is an example of the basic design principles of Neo-Traditional planning. It has been a financial success, providing its architects an opportunity to expand their vision to larger projects, including Avalon Park in Orlando, Windsor resort village in Vero Beach, and the Wellington development west of West Palm Beach, Florida (Langdon, 1994: 107-119, 185-192; Audirac and Shermyen, 1994).

The Neo-Traditional communities are designed as islands of civic engagement within a sea of sprawl. But, these communities can be counterfeit communities, with most lacking the social institutional linkages that spawn civic engagement (Marshall, 2000: Ch. 1). Moreover, only a minority of Floridians is willing to make the trade-off between less private space for more communal space (*Florida Trend*, July, 1992: 32-36; Audirac and Smith, 1992; Audirac and Shermyen, 1994). Yet Calthorpe's Laguna Beach West and Duany/Plater-Zybeck's Kentlands have been successful, making money for the developers and providing an alternative quality of life within sprawling America. But, too often, New Urbanist communities are located on the suburban fringe, causing issues of in-filling and affordable housing to be questioned (Langdon, 1994; Fulton, 1996; Catlin, 1997; Shaw and Utt, 2000). Although they may be crime free, these Neo-Traditional towns are viewed to be exclusive. The design improvements do tend to minimize the negative social impacts of conventional suburban developments. Yet, there is a lack of the civic spontaneity that was found on yesteryear's Main Street or Town Square (Beatley and Manning, 1997: 43; Marshall, 2000: Ch. 1).

Chapter 3
ಐಂಧ
Florida's Economic Roots

Florida, with approximately 66 thousand square miles in area and about 8500 miles of tidal shoreline, is one of the largest states east of the Mississippi River (Figure 3.1). The fourth most populous state in the nation, it is assumed it would be highly liberal. Politically and socially, however, there is a strong conservative streak within Florida. To understand local policy planning choices and the county courthouse politics of small town Florida, it is beneficial to understand and appreciate its socio-economic history.

In 1763, at the end of the French and Indian War, Florida was ceded to England by Spain, who supported the French. But, British rule was short. It was returned to Spain in 1783, and remained in Spanish hands until 1821. After two and half centuries Spanish sovereignty, Spanish Florida was little more than three military garrisons at Saint Augustine, Saint Marks and Pensacola, whose authorities reached scarcely beyond their respective walls. Much of Florida was sparsely populated and comprised of a series of cattle ranches, sugar plantations, fishing villages, and Spanish missions along dusty trails within its piney-woods interior. Between 1810 and 1820, a series of regional clashes erupted between the land hungry Anglo-American pioneers and the Spanish authorities, resulting in the occupation of Pensacola and Fernandina Beach, and the burning of a Spanish trading-fort near Saint

Marks. These border clashes drove home to the Spanish authorities that its hold on Florida was tenuous. It became "a question of when, not whether, the United States seized Spanish Florida." (Mormino, 1993: 1060). After purchase from Spain in 1821, despite its hot, humid climate, the swamps, and the frequent outbreaks of yellow fever, land hungry rural Southerners began settling Florida's panhandle river valleys. Due to a protracted war with the Seminoles in southern Florida, the panhandle was the territory's primary population center, where cotton, tobacco, cattle, hogs, and turpentine became the principal exports.

Nearly fifty percent of Florida's territory was held in trust for the people as "sovereignty" land, which comprised of navigable lakes, swamps and tidal bottoms along its coastline. While the state could partially sell or permit alteration of these sovereignty lands, these parcels were expected to remain in the public domain. Without modern surveying aids, hundreds of lakes and millions of acres of tidal bottoms were lost forever to public ownership, when the boundary lines described in deeds were mistakenly drawn, allowing private ownership of much of these sovereignty lands (Catlin, 1997; Carter, 1974). In addition, Congress passed the **Swamp Lands Act (1850)** for the purpose of making marginal swampland agriculturally productive by drainage and the construction of levees. Consequently, the federal government transferred over 24 million acres of public lands for private development (Catlin, 1997: 19-20; Carter, 1974: 60-61).

Florida's Traditional-Individualism

Most towns south of the Mason Dixon line were located on rivers, bays or inlets that preceded any pre-plan town design. Moreover, the South was populated by men under different circumstances. Whereas in New England, the Puritan hierarchy offered a well-ordered, middle class society, the Southern colonies were filled with migrants from both the higher and lower strata of society, who were out to seek personal economic gain (Stiverson, 1977; Robinson, 1979; Fischer, 1989). The Southern colonies represented the opportunity for even the most lowly white male to gain wealth by exploiting the landscape. Further, despite the fact the planter gentry would dominate local politics, a poor man owed them no civic obligations (Stiverson, 1977).

Two strands of political culture emerged south of the Mason-Dixon line. The first form was a plantation society, populated by a small group of tough-minded landowners who resided throughout the southern coastal tidewater. As a group, they were to become the backbone of the "Traditionalistic" political culture (Fischer, 1989: 236-62; Robinson, 1979: 13-38; Stiverson, 1977: 85-113). The southern coastal shoreline allowed every land owner to be self-sufficient. There was little need for road improvements when each plantation constructed its own docks and warehouses along the rivers and inlets. Moreover, there was little need for towns, when most plantations function much like a town (Miller, 1966; Fischer, 1989). With few commercial centers, a dispersed settlement pattern emerged. Churches stood at the crossroads, with a lone tavern "that operated as a general store or, conversely, a general store that also provided 'spirits' by the drink" so that it might attract a predictable stream of customers (Wolf, 1993: 222). With the absence of a New England type town, the concept of place was tied to "kinship neighborhoods," where status rank was easily ascribed and marked "by deep and pervasive inequalities" that were tied to land ownership (Fischer, 1989: 235-46).

Southern civic participation was based on property and social status. Few white tenant farmers or townsmen met voting property qualifications. Besides, each white male was expected to openly voice his preference among the candidates. "Viva voce voting" was a 17th Century British institutional practice. It was assumed to be the "manly" way of declaring your political allegiance. "Swearing your vote" remained in place until the 1890s (Bourke and Debats, 1995: 8-9). County government was the principal form of local governance. Besides being a place for the storage of legal documents and for the place to settle commercial disputes, the county courthouse was the seat of political power (Robinson, 1977: 37-38). The county courthouse was a collection of taverns, mills and commercial stores. For the local planter elite, the county courthouse hamlet was the place that they could dominate local politics. Once a month, when court was in session, the county courthouse hamlet came alive. "Militia muster was held, peddlers offered their wares along the road, and great quantities of alcohol was consumed." Taking the trappings of an English country fair, neighbors mingled and all sorts of social opportunities took place (Wolf, 1993: 222).

The political destiny of the county was in the hands of the leading land owners. With wealth came the trappings of social status. The willingness to assume civic responsibilities, "with only scant remuneration, was "a defining mark" of a gentleman (Ellis, 1993: 99). Politics was regarded as "an obligation" and political office was regarded as "an expectation" for the wealthy (Miller, 1966: 111). A budding politician was usually a member of a prominent family, who felt that he had a right to govern very much in the "same way that he inherited land and slaves and social position." If political rivalries existed, it was usually between planter families who had a "falling out." (Syndor, 1965: 74). The concept of the "public interest" was narrowly defined, with the priorities of most public projects benefitting the county's first families (Syndor, 1965: 53-71).

By contrast, west of the Fall-line, which is the point where rivers were no longer navigable, an Individualistic political culture emerged. Characterized by weak social institutions, lawlessness and a high mobile population, settlements were small hamlets, usually consisting of a watermill, a tavern, a blacksmith shop and a trading post. With few finished products available, farming was the principle "concern of everyone," even the local minister farmed (Leyburn, 1962: 260). On the southern frontier, rivers were plentiful but often shallow. The road system was primitive. Prior to the railroad, the frontier was a subsistence economy. Corn became the staple crop, simply because it fed both man and beast. Besides, corn was easy to store, and with little rye or barley, it made a darn good whiskey. In 1794, when U.S. Treasury Secretary Alexander Hamilton decided to tax corn whiskey, the small scale farmers of southwestern Pennsylvania and northwestern Virginia nearly caused a frontier-wide rebellion, believing the federal whiskey tax was a threat to their very existence (Stock, 1996: 44-56).

The frontier communities always felt abandoned by their urban cousins. Given little protection or public services, frontier settlements were inhabited with mostly libertarian individuals. With a majority of settlers being of Scotch-Irish heritage, this libertarian strain can be traced back to the 13th Century when Scottish "burghs" populated by an "extended-clan" families were the principle form of governance (Leyburn, 1962). By 1750, a concept of **negative liberty** became entrenched in the southern back country. For most 19th Century frontier settlers, **negative liberty** meant the ability to make personal economic lifestyle choices. Yet **negative liberty** did not mean anarchy. For instance, if a new school or church needed to be built, all local residents were expected to turn out "with axes and adzes to buckle to the task" of completing the community project. If one failed to do so, he was "shunned" by his neighbors (Billington, 1974: 140-144).

Besides sanctity of private property, personal responsibility was the second cornerstone to **negative liberty**. Public order was in the hands of your neighbors. Moral freedom was defined by the community. There was no tolerance for Renegades who stole property and ignored local customs. This type of behavior imposed a threat to a family as well as the community. Borrowing an old Celtic folksaying, "honest men do not need a court to impose justice," each household was expected to uphold the custom and laws of the community. Vigilantism was common, swift and harsh. With circuit courts either being non-existent or days away by horse, troublemakers were beaten, tarred and feathered and even "lynched" by local regulators (Billington, 1974; Fischer, 1989; Stock, 1996: Ch. 2). Yet, social order was more fluid, and less rigid on the frontier, so long as the offender did not impose a threat to another person's family or property (Stock, 1996: 90-98; Fischer, 1989: 605-83). Governance fell on those who were truly charismatic, developing an "informal, but very real social class system" (Leyburn, 1962: 63). Frontier life encouraged a free-wheeling form of politics. For many generations, back country politics were mainly a collision of highly personal factions and followings, eventually blending into **Traditional-Individualism**. Until the 1950s, before television took hold, this style of county courthouse politics was quite prevalent in rural Florida.

Reconstruction and Its Aftermath

Outside of Austin, Texas, Tallahassee, Florida is the only other southern capital not to be occupied by a Yankee army. However, all its key ports were occupied by Yankee troops. Florida's road system, while hindering supplies of cattle and corn to southern armies, may have been a blessing in disguise because it essentially limited large-scale military operations by Union troops. Prior to the Civil War, most major towns were the state's river-seaports such as Apalachicola, Fenandina Beach, and Pensacola. In 1829, the first steamboat crossed the treacherous sandbar at the mouth of the St Johns River, making Jacksonville a important port of embarkation for the interior. By 1851 the steamboat Darlington had a thriving river trade business, transporting people and goods 200 miles up river beyond Palatka to Sanford (Waitley, 1997: 100). This same year, the state legislature established the **Internal Improvement Board**. The **Internal Improvement Board**, comprised of the governor, several state officials, and four private citizens, was entrusted with the responsibility to float bonds backed by state lands for the construction of railroads, wharfs and warehouses. For instance, the state built wharfs for the town of Apalachicola, establishing it as a seaport for the benefit of plantations within the interior of Alabama and Georgia. The board also funded the railroad lines that linked Fernandina Beach west to Tallahassee, and southwest to Cedar Key by way of Gainesville. At the same time, Saint Augustine, the old Spanish capital, declined because it was ignored by the state legislature, while Pensacola survived only because of the federal construction of a naval base (Tebeau, 1971; Catlin, 1997: 21). Bondholders were willing to make such investment because they would be paid by either revenues generated by fees collected from products shipped out from the state wharfs or from the sale of state-owned land. In many respects these were the first industrial revenue bonds. On the eve of the Civil War, there was 387 miles of track, linking many of Florida's river-seaports to the Alabama and Georgia interior within the Chattahoochee/Appalachicola watershed (Tebeau, 1971).

The hardships of the Reconstruction Era (1867–1877) shaped Florida's social and economic development politics for the next century. Prior to the Civil War, there were heated clashes in Florida between the Jacksonian-Democrats and Henry Clays's southern Whig Party over federal public improvement policies, forcing the state to devise private-public partnerships. Even after the demise of the Whigs in the 1850s, there was a strong pro-development faction among Florida's Constitutional Unionists, who, like the Whigs, found sentiment and support from Florida's urban centers (Tebeau, 1971: Ch. 13). After the Civil War, the northern radical Republicans asserted political rule. Congress appointed a former union general Harrison Reed as state governor. A political vacuum emerged that allowed for a coalition of former Yankee military officers (carpetbaggers), former southern Unionist-Whigs (scalawags), and former African-American slaves to dominate Florida politics. Instead of economic development by outside investment, this coalition focused on internal improvement through heavy state taxes. With the Tilden-Hayes Electoral Compromise (1876), federal troops were removed from the Florida, permitting Southern Traditional- Individualists to regain control of the state government.

The Bourbon Ascendency

Two tragedies are evident from the Reconstruction Era. The first is that U.S. Congressional policy failed to aggressively distribute land to former slaves and thereby provide a sound economic foundation to safeguard African-American civil and political liberties. In fact, "the idealism of the radicals exacerbated the South's fears, and southerners were determine to control the Negro when they returned to political power." (Billington,1971: 230). The second is a byproduct of the first. The price for Republican supremacy in the nation was Democratic hegemony in the South.

Nationally, the Gilded Age (1870–1900) was a time when the American way of life was being transformed from an agrarian to an urban-industrial society. It was a time when millions of farm laborers migrated to the cities and the railroads linked isolated towns to those cities. It was the beginning of corporate America. Moreover, it was a time when most wage owners, fearing a loss of income, adopted the nastiness of nativism and its hostile rhetoric towards foreign immigrants. In the South, this was the time of the "**Bourbon Ascendency**." The Bourbon Democrats promised to take back the county court houses and the state legislatures from the scalawags and the former slaves. They promoted state legislation that chipped away at African-American civil liberties. It was a time when limited government marched throughout the South, reversing Sherman's March to the Sea. The Bourbon Democrats were not the same men who dominated pre-Civil War politics. Although they appealed to the nostalgia of the Old South and identified with the Lost Cause, the Bourbons were a small coterie of younger planters, merchants, bankers and lawyers who sought to control the county court house and the state government for their own economic purposes (Billington, 1971; Rabinowitz, 1992).

Far from being democratic, the Bourbons remained in power by their willingness to suppress the political opposition. The Bourbon Democrats introduced a complex set of voting rules, all designed to discourage voter turnout. By dominating the county courthouse governmental apparatus, these courthouse rings (factions) established one-party rule in Florida allowing the Bourbon Democrats to rewrite the state constitution (1886). A "Traditional-Individualistic" philosophy with its emphasis on **plural executive governance** shortened the term of the governor and stripped him of many of his appointive powers. Moreover, many state offices were disbanded and their duties were delegated to quasi-legislative appointed commissions, establishing the foundation for Corporate City Planning (See Ch. 9). Thus, political power was dispersed at the state level so that the county courthouse rings of Jacksonville and Pensacola who allied themselves with rural counties such as Gulf or Putnam could dominate state politics.

Since the Republican Party was associated with Abolitionism, Reconstruction, and Lincoln, it was essentially weak, dominated by a small clique of former Yankees, who survived on federal patronage (Seagull,1975). Because of its extremes in geography, Florida state legislative politics was governance by factions. The term Democratic party had only limited applicability. It was far from being unified. Rather, it was a host of factional alliances. Its platform had no coherent ideological core, rather it was based on a candidate's personality. If there was a guiding ideology, it was low taxes, limited government, private enterprise, and white supremacy (Key,

1984). This factionalism had balkanized Florida politics, enhancing economic democratic elitism (Scher, 1992).

Throughout Florida, it was the local county courthouse rings, with its coterie of rotating officeholders, which ruled for themselves. Indeed, it was quite common for a petty officeholder to move regularly from one office to another. It was local party loyalty rather than ability which was the basis for one's position in the courthouse. If an individual was particularly ambitious, "with the blessing of party leaders he might move to a statewide post after serving his apprenticeship at the county level. In any case, no future existed for the political aspirant who did not reach an understanding with the courthouse ring." (Billington, 1984: 20).

Although the Democratic Party was dominant, its weakness was its factionalism. This became apparent with the Populist Revolt of the 1890s. In Florida, the Bourbon blueprint for economic development was quite simple. Keep the cost of government down, with no state debt. State policies were quite traditional-individualistic, emphasizing private sector investment. When a Congressional Southern Democratic-Northern Republican coalition repealed the Southern Homestead Act (1876), Florida obtained an additional 15 million acres of federal land. Rather than distributing this land to poor black and white farmers, the state legislature "lavishly conveyed this state-owned land" to Yankee investors (Hays, 1957: 122).

In 1880 the State of Florida was broke, facing a one million dollar bond default. Governor Bloxham found a solution by convincing Hamilton Disston, a wealthy Philadelphian manufacturer, to buy four million acres of state swampland for a million dollars. The **Internal Improvement Board** allowed him to drain the land. By doing so, Florida paid off its creditors, setting the stage for future land sales (Carter, 1974: 63-66). For instance, Henry Flagler, in 1884, bought the defunct Jacksonville-St. Augustine short line. He then secured land grants from the Board of Trustees of the Internal Improvement Fund, which replaced the defunct Internal Improvement Board. By 1896, Flagler had built a railroad from Jacksonville to the village of Miami, monopolizing most of the commercial trade along the coastal region. In 1888 a narrow gauge railroad known as the Orange Belt Railway connected Tarpon Springs to St. Petersburg. "Despite its inauspicious beginnings, a steady increase in rail traffic, its pleasant location on Tampa Bay, and the growing citrus market" made St. Petersburg a major destination point, with its population increasing from 273 residents in 1890 to 1,575 by the turn of the century (Stephenson, 1997: 16). Henry Plant, another Yankee industrialist, built the Waycross Railroad, connecting Jacksonville to Savannah, Georgia.

In another state "right-of-way" land deal, he then built the Jacksonville-Daytona Beach-Tampa line, with a luxury hotel at its Tampa terminus. At the time of his death, Henry Plant controlled a railroad system that connected west Florida to most southern cities as far north as Richmond, Virginia. By 1900, the improved rail road system brought winter tourists to Florida and shipped fresh, refrigerated tropical and citrus products out of Florida to northern markets, all with the help of the Internal Improvement Fund (Tebeau, 1971; Frazer and Guthrie, 1995).

Populism, Progressivism and Jim Crow

In the 1880s, the grandsons of Jacksonian Democrats began to resent state policies that appeared to favor the urban, Yankee commercial-industrial elites. The Panic of 1893 brought this resentment to a head, igniting the Populist Revolt. "Populism developed," according to Mc Math (1993: 17), "among people who were deeply rooted in the social and economic networks of rural communities, not, as some would have it, among the isolated and disoriented individuals." Railroad rates, the credit system and sharecropping were the root causes for the rise of Southern Populism. By 1892, with the growing belief that neither of the two major parties was sympathetic to the small farmer's plight, the Populist Party became a viable political force. From the onset, the southern wing of the Populist Party was at a disadvantage. Somehow, its national candidates had to convince their southern cousins to leave the Democratic Party, "the party that had overthrown the Republicans and had become the symbol of loyalty to the South." (Rabinowitz, 1992: 108).

The Panic of 1893 helped the **Populist Movement** by getting Populists elected in several southern states. Yet, the Presidential Election of 1896 became anti-climatic. Split over the national platform, its delegates supported William Jennings Bryan, the Democratic Party's nominee, weakening its identity. In Florida, William D. Bloxham soundly defeated both his Republican and Populist rivals, causing the movement's state demise (Tebeau, 1971; Cooper and Terrill, 1990; McMath, 1993). For the Bourbon Democrats, the Populist threat drove home the need to eliminate any future fusion coalitions between poor black and white voters. The Florida Democratic legislature passed laws to regulate the railroads, credit laws, and out-of-state corporations (Tebeau, 1971: Ch.19). After the Bryan debacle, the national Democratic party came to a "gentlemen's agreement" with its southern wing, allowing White southern Democrats to build a segregated society.

In Florida, the Democratic legislature systematically passed **Jim Crow** laws that deliberately clipped "the political wings" of blacks. Among the "ingenious contrivances to inconvenience the would-be black voter," the Florida Bourbon legislature introduced the dual-primary, the white primary, the poll tax, property qualifications, and a literacy test. "With the death of their party on the national scene," the southern white Populists dispiritedly returned to the Democratic Party, "which offered them more than the party of McKinley and Hanna" (Key, 1984: 8).

The **Progressive Era** (1901–1917) ushered in the next effort at state political reform. Composed mainly of urbanites, the Progressive Movement campaigned on public health, economic development and municipal public service improvements. These civic reformers believed that business-like management strategies would correct the social and economic ills caused by the dual beasts of industrialization and urbanization (Link and McCormick, 1983: Ch.2). The Progressive Movement's influence on social reform was mixed. In the South, the Progressive Movement was a bi- product of factional politics. Governor William Sherman Jennings, elected in 1900, sought to improved the state's public finances by selling 100,000 acres of state trust lands to pay state bond obligations. By the end of his term, Jennings had shifted state land disposition policy away from corporate giveaways to public sales to small landowners, establishing his Progressive roots (Tebeau, 1971).

Napoleon Bonaparte Broward, a Jacksonville politician, was Jennings successor. Known as the "fighter for the little man," Broward was a member of Jacksonville's Courthouse Ring. In 1905 he bullied the legislature to pass a drainage law that established the Board of Drainage Commissioners which was empowered to raise funds to construct canal systems and reclaim state swamp lands. Again, land sales became the means for state revenues. With improved drainage technology, a mini-land boom emerged in which 60 percent of the land was held in speculation (Tebeau, 1971). Yet, these "pet" policies were acceptable to only the young, progressive wing within Florida's Democratic party. State legislative policy conflict became more a generational dispute rather than an ideological one. On race, however, both rural Bourbons and the urban Progressives supported **Jim Crow** (Tebeau, 1971: 330-333). Broward's political position on Jim Crow was not unusual or contradictory as a Southern Progressive. After the defeat of Populism, southern white politicians of all stripes agreed that "blacks must never again hold the balance of power in the South" (Link and McCormick, 1983: 97). Southern Progressives were not social progressives. On the contrary, most believed that African-Americans "were innately inferior"; and, they had no intentions of overturning the existing social fabric (Billington, 1984: 49). This new breed of southern politician was quite "skilled at harking back to the demands of the Populists (without endorsing Populism's more radical proposals) and equally adept at issuing the extreme demands of white supremacy." (Link and McCormick, 1983: 97).

Southern Progressives were suspicious of the power and privileges of both "Big Government" and "Big Business." Accordingly, they did not wish to reject private enterprise; but rather, they wished to tame it so that the rules of capitalism for the white Southerner (Cooper and Terrill, 1990: Ch.22). Subsequently, urban white progressive politicians were equally committed, as were their rural counterparts to the maintenance of racial segregation. At the threshold of the Twentieth Century, Jim Crow was firmly established in Florida (Brownell, 1977: 145-150). By 1900, most Floridians lived in rural, small towns, with two-thirds concentrated in the northern part of the state. In 1930, Florida's population was still "overwhelmingly native born"(Arsenault and Mormino, 1989: 173). The Florida countryside was no longer composed of a collection of large self-sufficient plantations. Thanks to the railroads and Broward's land policies, it was dotted with a patchwork of small crossroad villages that soon became mini-trade centers. Since this hinterland population rarely had cash, these hamlets rarely mushroomed into urban centers. Instead, these hamlets were the agrarian small towns that Thomas Jefferson had visioned. Depicted in countless books and movies, these crossroad hamlets became the places where a new, small southern middle class emerged, selling the merchant goods, educating the young, and providing the services of lawyers, doctors and undertakers to the surrounding countryside (Ayers, 1992: 55-58).

In 1980, Florida became the place where everyone was from somewhere else. But, not in 1940, it was still the place where a majority of the population was native born, with about 36 percent being non-white, and very much a rural society (Dietrich, 1978: 11; Arsenault and Mormino, 1989: 170-173). Local parochialism was a fact of life. Reed (1986: 34-35) states that **local parochialism** means a "manifestation of geographical particularism—an appreciation of the qualities of one place as opposed to others." For southerners parochial localism meant the South's ruralness; and, until the 1960s, it was tied to its caste/class system of **Jim Crow**. By 1940 a wide assortment of laws had been adopted by the Florida legislature requiring the segregation of the races. Throughout the state, little signs reading "whites" or "colored" only "areas" for cafes, theaters, toilets, drinking fountains, courthouses, hospitals, and other public accommodations were commonplace. Indeed, **Jim Crow** replaced slavery as the social mechanism to keep African-Americans in their "place." **Jim Crow** shadowed the black man "throughout his life—from birth in a segregated hospital, to education in a segregated school, to residence in a segregated neighborhood and employment in a segregated job, to burial in a segregated graveyard" (Dye, 1971).

Jim Crow meant that blacks were at the town's bottom-rung, whether the African-American male was a college professor, a minister or a sharecropper, he was "equally likely to suffer from disenfranchisement, segregation and the threat of lynching." (Rabinowitz, 1992: 157). Jim Crow was a racial caste system. "Anyone—from a pale-skinned mulatto to the very dark-skinned—who had Negroid physical features was considered to be a Negro. Negroes were born into their caste and could not escape it by marriage or by personal achievement." (Cooper and Terrill, 1991: 545). Under these laws, social interaction was decidedly unequal. Southern whites determined the "laws, rules, attitudes and expectation." Blacks were placed in a position of complete dependency on "the white community for their survival, yet the most they could hope for was that the rules defining this dependence would be more paternalistic than draconian." (Scher, 1992: 64). And, **Jim Crow** was most strongly entrenched in the Panhandle towns such as Crestview, Gretna and Lake City. With comparatively large numbers of African-American residents, these towns were still very much like their Deep South neighbors in political and economic perspectives (Button, 1989: Ch.1).

The Great Depression and the New Deal

Both national political parties are composed of a collection of "unlike-minded men bearing the same party label" who come to Washington to hammer out public policies that will allow them reflect their respective regional differences (Brady, 1988: 8). Every generation or so, the national party coalition breaks down. Sometimes this breakdown means the demise of a party, such as the Whig Party. At other periods, a third party may threaten the stability between the two major parties, causing a rethinking of policy issues within and between the two major parties. The Populist Revolt was such an example. But it was during the Great Depression that a true political realignment took place. It was a time when an "intense, cross-cutting issue" emerged that dominated the national political scene, making members within each of the two major political parties rethink their allegiance (Flanigan and Zingale, 1998).

In the 1920s, the "Solid South" was a Democratic reality. Even by 1950, a southern Republican voter was a novelty, and a black voter was a rarity. On the eve of the Great Depression, The South was a region in which "no Republican had been elected to the U.S. Senate or to the governor's mansion" for decades (Bullock and Rozelle, 1998: 3). In the 1920s, except for the South, the country was solidly Republican (Brady, 1988: 92-94). In 1928, to be a Democrat was to be a member of a minority party. But, for southern Democrats, it meant domination within congressional committees as well as the national party convention. Until 1936, any Democratic presidential candidate needed two-thirds of the convention's delegates. Under the "gentlemen's agreement," the South voted in a bloc, assuring a veto over any national candidate. At the grassroots level, over four-fifths of the South's counties were qualified as Democratic, making the South the party's political base (Black and Black, 1992: 57-61). Even in defeat, Irish-Catholic Al Smith's campaign signaled the beginning of a new coalition.

Prior to Al Smith, the Republican Party 's grassroots base was outside the South. Because the North possessed three times as many electoral votes as the South, the Republicans had a decided advantage. However, Al Smith's campaign establish a strong, ethnic political base within the Midwest that chipped away at the Republican Party's strength. All that was needed was a "cross-cutting" issue which would allow for this Democratic coalition assume leadership. The Great Depression and the failure of the Republican's 'laissez-faire' doctrine would be that "cross-cutting" issue (Black and Black, 1992: 61-65). Like the 1980s, the farming regions, especially in the South, did not share in boom-boom prosperity of the 1920s. With plunging prices and trade embargos, southern farmers became heavily in debt. Falling farm prices were good news for the urban consumer, but bad news for the southern farmer (Smith, 1988; Schulman, 1991). Besides, mechanization was driving many tenant farmers off the land. Farm consolidation and declining labor demand meant many unskilled laborers sought work in the tight labor market of the cities (Wright, 1986). For black tenant farmers, falling agricultural prices and mechanization was especially disruptive. The northern migration for blacks had been on since the reconstruction, but exploded during The Great War. From 1914 to 1920, the South lost 550,000 blacks, with the Midwestern and Northeastern cities gaining much of this population (Marks, 1983: Ch. 4; Harrison, 1991).

Plunging commodity prices, chronic overproduction, floods, droughts and the boll weevil all added to the woes of black farmers, who had difficulty finding work in the mills, foundries and factories. Faced with no social services, no credit and potential poverty, more than 800,000 African-Americans of all social status picked-up and moved to the northern cities, where for the first time they could obtain work, decent housing and the vote (Harrison, 1991; Marks, 1989). The overall impact of this Great Migration on the southern black community was significant, causing much of southern black land ownership to be purchased by local whites. As a consequence, many of the rural black professional middle class also migrated North (Marks, 1983: 173).

The Great Depression simply worsened an already bad situation. At a time when America was mainly a nation of farmers, downturns in agriculture triggered a panic. On the other hand, the Great Depression was triggered by the 1929 Stock Market Crash which caused commodity prices to experience greater plunges. Overall, commodity prices declined by 40 percent (McElvain, 1984; Billes, 1994; Hughes, 1990). The urban worker was in no better shape. A post-Great War recession caused both ship yards in Tampa to close, and the Jacksonville yard to drastically reduce production. Cutbacks became routine. Even with reduced workweeks and wage cuts, paper mills, turpentine plants and ship foundries in Florida permanently locked their doors. By 1932, industrial employment rates had declined by 40 percent throughout Florida, Georgia and Alabama (Smith, 1988; Billington, 1984: 69-71). For county courthouse leaders, local initiatives simply were not enough. In Florida, only 17 of the 67 counties had some sort of relief program. Southern political officials, who helped elect Hoover, turned to Washington for help. The "Traditional-Individualistic" philosophy of the Hoover Administration was simply no match to rejuvenate an economy which had suffered a GNP 46 percent decline over the past four years (Billes, 1994; Hughes, 1990).

President Franklin D. Roosevelt set about to strengthen the alliance between the two Democratic wings. For decades, southerners "had resisted federal intervention, eschewing even the promise of economic development in order to maintain control over southern institutions and affairs (Schulman, 1991: 14). But the Great Depression forced a re-evaluation of the "state's rights" ideology. The collapse of the southern economy "proved a powerful antidote" to the rural South (Grantham, 1994: 118). Roosevelt's Administration changed their thinking. With promise to confine efforts to economics, the southern leadership accepted the Roosevelt initiatives (Brinkley, 1984).

For Floridians, the Great Depression began when the real estate bubble burst. In the 1920s, Florida real estate, banking, and contract laws encouraged land speculation. In the county courthouse system, title search and recording of deeds were not stringent. This laxity allowed for option buying in which a binder of five percent down held a piece of property for thirty days without any restrictions on the number of times it could be resold. Obviously, each land transaction of the parcel assured a tidy profit to the bank or the mortgage company as well as the investor (Frazer and Guthrie, 1995: 65-105). "Although little cash changed hands, such deals produced speculative profit that inflated land values far beyond what the market could actually bear." Inevitably, with most purchasers "not interested in improving the parcel, but in turning it over for a quick profit," the land bubble had to burst. It did so in 1926 (Stephenson, 1997: 82). Between 1926 and 1930, Florida suffered a series of bank failures, all tied to this real estate speculation. In 1928, there was an outbreak of a fruit fly infestation, causing the loss of eighty percent of the citrus crop. With its two principal economic sectors (real estate construction and agriculture) in trouble, there was a credit squeeze. The 1929 Stock Crash only added to the existing financial crisis. By 1933, 45 national and 171 state chartered banks had failed, contributing to the estimated 35 per cent unemployment rate, leaving one quarter of the state's population registered for emergency relief (Tebeau, 1971: Ch. 25: Frazer and Guthrie, 1995: Ch. 7).

The Great Depression became a political disaster for Florida Republicans. With the nation's per capita income falling 44 percent in four years, it should be no surprise that voters in all regions embraced Roosevelt who won by 57 percent of the vote, making the Democratic party the majority party in Congress. In the South, the Democrats retained 99 per cent of their grassroots base counties and even added many former competitive peripheral Republican counties (Black and Black, 1992). For Southern Democratic congressmen, the 1932 and 1936 elections were windfalls. The seniority system gave them positions of power and influence in Congress. Not wishing to antagonize the southern Congressional leadership, Roosevelt established close ties, especially on crucial New Deal policy issues. Thus, much of the early New Deal rural programs had a southern flavor. For instance, the Agricultural Adjustment Administration (1933) was a success because it won the support of the local rural power brokers. For most southern white landowners, this agency gave them price parity. It encouraged greater consolidation of farming, greater mechanization, and greater displacement of black tenant farmers, all to the benefit of the large white landowners (Schulman, 1991; Billes, 1994; Brinkely, 1984).

Florida's state fiscal policy had been to keep taxes low and to offset shortfalls with taxes imposed on land sales and tourism. But tourism hit rock bottom and there were few land sales. Moreover, a constitutional prohibition in 1926 on enacting a state income tax didn't help any. The state was simply broke. Roosevelt's New Deal programs came as a blessing. Most programs improved the quality of life for most Floridians. For instance, the Rural Electrification Administration (1935) provided low cost loans to local farm cooperatives to build electric lines in rural areas, bringing electric power to much of the northern Florida. The Federal Emergency Relief Administration (FERA) provided grants to the state, helping one third of rural and small town population in Florida. Both the Public Works Administration (PWA) and the Works Progress Administration (WPA) succeeded in switching the local rural population from direct relief rolls to work performance rolls, giving rural folk back their dignity and pride. In Florida alone, between 1933 and 1939, the WPA built 245 new schools, 601 municipal buildings, 27 water works, 6 municipal sewer systems, 1,237 bridges, 146 parks, 191 playgrounds and 6272 storm culverts with federal funds amounting to the sum of $51 million (Tebeau, 1971; Catlin, 1997: 34-36).

The Making of Modern Florida

A snapshot taken in 1940 of a Florida small town would simply be a "mirror-image" of a typical Bourbon-era town. Main Street would still have a hardware store, a drug store, a barber shop, and a local merchant's bank. The railroad would still be the dominant player in the town's economy, shipping out lumber and agricultural produce and bringing in mercantile goods. In most towns the Baptist Church would be the most prominent house of worship, with either a Methodist, Presbyterian or a Pentecostal church being a close second. African-Americans, of course, would have their own church within their segregated neighborhood. The town's hotel had not yet become an apartment complex for the elderly nor had the local café succumb to the Dairy Queen. And the local movie theater with a "colored" entrance had not given way to the mall cinema. The major technological change, besides electricity, was the automobile or pickup truck parked in front of the feed store.

World War II helped further diversify its economy. The New Deal, of course, left a legacy of acceptance of federal involvement; but, it was World War II that truly transformed Florida. The South received a disproportionate share of federal funds. Apparently, the weather, the availability of ideal sites, and congressional clout all played a part in attracting this federal investment. From 1941 to 1945 the federal government invested more than $7 billion in military installations alone in the South, with Florida obtaining $1.5 billion of these funds. Consequently, the US Government built 172 military installations, breathing new economic life into a somewhat moribund state economy (Tebeau, 1971: Ch. 26). Moreover, shipbuilding was revitalized, with more than $750 million going for the modernization of the shipyards in Tampa, Miami, Jacksonville and Panama City. In 1940, only six airfields could handle large four engine aircraft. By 1945, there were over 40 airfields. During this time frame, over 1600 miles of highway were either constructed or repaired in the state (Catlin, 1997: 35-36). The temporary disruption of the tourist trade was more than offset by the conversion of most tourist facilities into training schools and military housing. In the 1930s, Florida was the playground for the well-to-do. But, it was the families of ordinary servicemen who visited Florida that altered this playground. Many liked what they saw and remained, helping give Florida its forty-six percent population increase during the decade, with 81.5 percent of this migrating population locating to the peninsula (Tebeau, 1971: 417)

At the same time, many farm laborers left for the growing cities (Lee, 1992). In 1940, about ten per cent of the state's employment base were categorized as agrarian. By 1950, this category fell to 2.1 percent, indicating the continual shift of employment away from this sector (Dietrich, 1978: 25). In Pinellas County alone, between 1940 and 1960, the number of housing units increased by more than 400 percent, increasing from 40,525 units to 165,823. The county planning office noted that the manufacturing sector as a percentage of county employment rose from two percent in 1940 to fourteen percent by 1960, establishing a diverse and robust economic base (Stephenson, 1997: 118-119)

Between 1950 and 1980, the U.S. population had grown by nearly fifty percent. Among the four regions, the South in absolute numbers gained more people than any other region, with an increase by almost 27 million folks. By 1980, one out of every three Americans resided in the South (Weinstein, et. al. 1985: 3). With declining national birthrates, much of this population gain was tied to interregional migration. In one decade (1970–1980), four million souls, mainly from the Northeast and the Midwest, relocated to the South. Even within this region, population growth was not uniform, with much of the net in-migration occurring within the urban centers, where job opportunities were most likely (Weinstein, 1985: 9-14). Among smaller cities below 50,000, a U-shaped growth rate emerged, with high growth rates at the higher and lower population interval categories. Further scrutiny found that two factors attribute to the fast growing communities below 15,000 person category. These small towns grew because of an influx of retirees and the relocation of unskilled, labor-intensive industries (Wheat, 1978: 28).

Between 1950 and 1980, Florida's population tripled to 9.8 million residents. Throughout the 1980s, the state experienced a population explosion, with a steady population growth rate of 3.4 per cent per year or about 540 new residents per day. By 1990, six of the 22 fastest growing metropolitan areas in the nation were situated in the Sunshine State. By 2000, Florida became the fourth most populous state, with a recorded population of 15.8 souls (Dortch, 1995; *The New York Times*, December 29, 2000: 15A; *The Miami-Herald*, December 29, 2000). Much of this population growth had occurred along the southeastern and southwestern coast, as well as an urban corridor running along Interstate 4 from Tampa through Orlando to Daytona Beach (see Figure 3.1). The same region that experienced much of the federal government's initial investment and sprawl during this analysis. No longer is Main Street shaped like Apalachicola or Lake City. Florida's new Main Street had become a suburban strip mall, with its fast food taco stands, drive-in dry cleaners, Publix grocery stores. But, its civic culture has been shaped by its history, with its emphasis of private property ownership and state assistance to private investors. Its history has assured the blending of a Traditional-Individualistic model which stresses the importance of local parochial vested economic interests.

Florida's Economic Roots 43

Figure 3.1

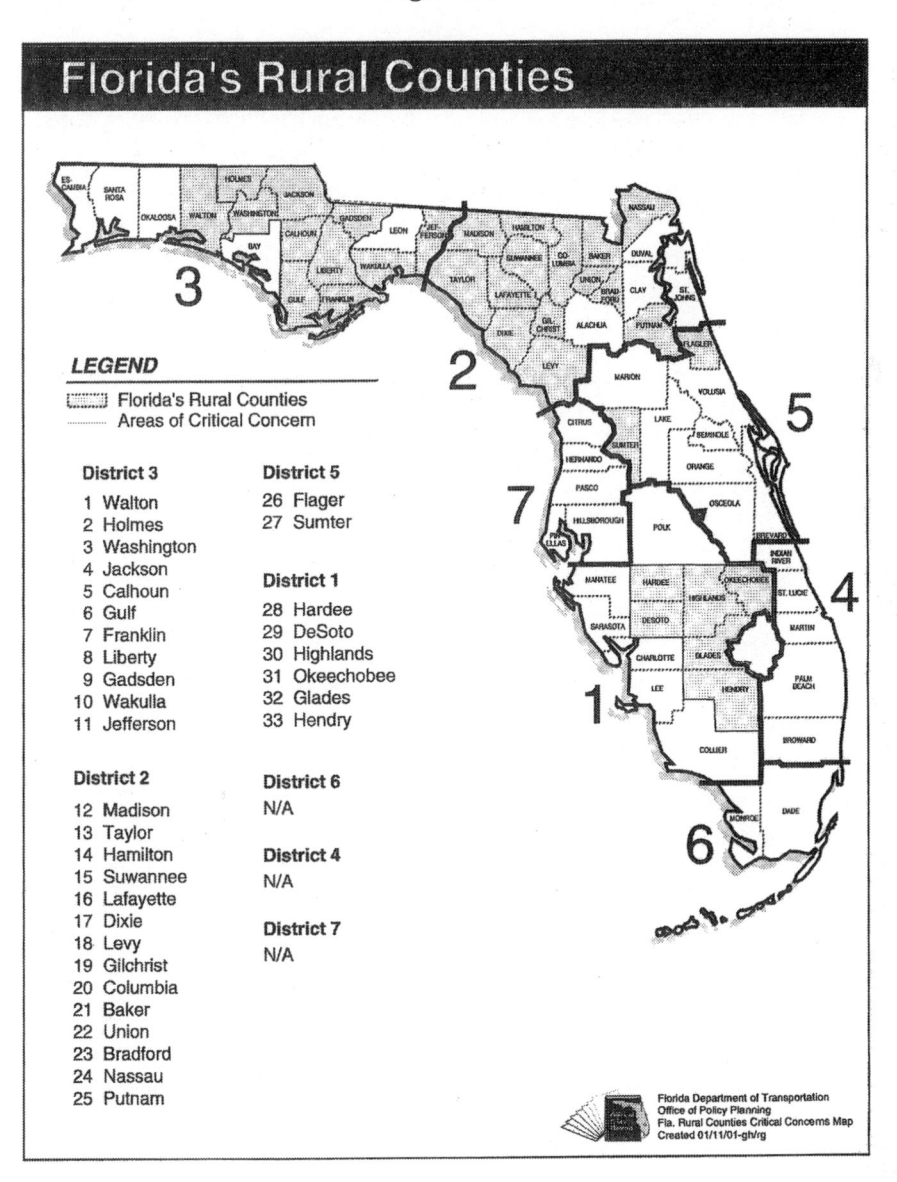

Florida's Rural Counties

LEGEND

Florida's Rural Counties
Areas of Critical Concern

District 3
1 Walton
2 Holmes
3 Washington
4 Jackson
5 Calhoun
6 Gulf
7 Franklin
8 Liberty
9 Gadsden
10 Wakulla
11 Jefferson

District 2
12 Madison
13 Taylor
14 Hamilton
15 Suwannee
16 Lafayette
17 Dixie
18 Levy
19 Gilchrist
20 Columbia
21 Baker
22 Union
23 Bradford
24 Nassau
25 Putnam

District 5
26 Flager
27 Sumter

District 1
28 Hardee
29 DeSoto
30 Highlands
31 Okeechobee
32 Glades
33 Hendry

District 6
N/A

District 4
N/A

District 7
N/A

Florida Department of Transportation
Office of Policy Planning
Fla. Rural Counties Critical Concerns Map
Created 01/11/01-gh/rg

Chapter 4
ஐCR
Florida's Changing Political Landscape

With the exception of Herbert Hoover, the Old Confederacy supported the Democratic presidential party for the first half of the Twentieth Century. Yet, with the Herbert Hoover-Al Smith 1928 contest, the South for the first time since Reconstruction temporarily moved towards and then away from the Republican Party. Even during the Dixiecrat Rebellion in1948, there were no Republican Florida legislators. It took former General fo the Army, Dwight David Eisenhower to make it respectable to vote Republican. It would be Arizona Senator Barry Goldwater that made it honorable to be a Republican in Florida (Tindall, 1972). Whereas Dwight Eisenhower sought to walk down a middle road, Barry Goldwater looked at the fork in the road. Then, he deliberately turned to the right. For many white, conservative southerners, Barry Goldwater was the Republican party's Al Smith. Almost two decades later, this alliance became the political base for Ronald Reagan's presidential victory.

The Solid South No More

In 1964, on the eve of the civil rights legislation, 73 per cent of all Florida voters were Democratic. Since then, the GOP has made steady gains, with the GOP obtaining parity in 1992. In fact, in ten of the last thirteen presidential contests, a majority of white Floridians have cast their vote for the

Republican Party's candidate (Black and Black, 1992; Glaser, 1996; Bullock and Rozell, 1998; *New York Times*, November 27, 2000). Like other Southern states, this shift in party affiliation has meant a competitive political climate at the state level, with Florida Republicans having been elected to the state's governorship three times (Claude Kirk, Bob Martinez and Jeb Bush) and to the U.S. Senate four times (Edward Gurney, Paula Hawkins, and Connie Mack). Moreover, the number of Republicans within the U.S. House delegation has consistently increased, beginning with the 1954 election of Republican William Cramer. By 1980, four of the 15 congressional House seats were held by Republicans. In one short decade, the Republican Party held a majority of the House seats; and by 1996, 15 of the 23 congressional House seats (Scicchitano and Scher, 1998; Lamis, 1988). Even with the razor thin win by Texas Governor George W. Bush, the Republican Party retained a majority of Florida's congressional delegation, with four delegates running unopposed, and holding onto all three open house seats vacated by Republicans (*USA Today*, November 9, 2000: 15A).

In 1950, there were no Republican state legislators. By 1970, 15 of the 48 state senators and 38 of the 119 house delegates were Republicans. In 1996, Florida became the first former Confederate state to have a Republican majority in both legislative houses. With six million state votes cast in the hotly contested Bush-Gore presidential election, both legislative houses remained Republican. Yet, like the national vote, Florida reflected the spatial cultural chasm that divides the nation, with Republicans deriving their strength from the large number of votes cast in rural northern and suburban central Florida (*New York Times*, November 27, 2000).

At the end of World War II, southern politics was characterized as a typical county courthouse system. State politics rather than national politics was key endeavor, with each county's courthouse elite distributing the benefits of federal goodies to some and denying them to others. It is a political axiom that political parties exist to recruit candidates for offices in order to win elections so that the party can control the "goodies." Although the "Old Confederacy" is linked by a common regional history, each state's political style is "as distinctive as those of 11 brothers and sisters from a single family." (Bass and DeVries, 1976: 3). Demographics have made Florida's political landscape different that its neighbors. With two-thirds of the state's population being nonsouthern, few post-War Floridians have any loyalty to "the Lost Cause" or the state's "Bourbon" past. This political rootlessness means that Florida newcomers lack the traditional political anchors—"lifelong church memberships, labor unions, long-established neighborhoods, family and friendship ties—that may have served as sources of political allegiance in their city or country of origin." (Dye, 1998: 5).

While many factors influence electoral participation (Verba, et. al. 1995), two socio-economic factors are especially germane to Florida politics. These two factors are: (1) the social transformation of Florida by the Civil Rights Movement; (2) and the state's rapid population growth. Both these factors have reshaped the state's policy choices as well as the prospects of Democratic one-party rule. Inevitably, both factors have caused tension among the county courthouses political clubs that once held Florida's Democratic Party together. The Bush-Gore cliff-hanger has thrust Florida's political landscape onto the national scene, spotlighting the cultural fault line between the two parties. For the most part, Florida Democrats have become the home of well-educated women, African-Americans, ethnic Jews, immigrants and unionized labor, while Florida Republicans are fast becoming the home for retirees, white males, religious moralists, gun owners and small town dwellers (*New York Times*, November 29, 2000: A19; November 27, 2000: A15).

Like the nation as a whole, Florida's suburban dwellers are the most divided. The Bush-Gore contest was a repeat of the 1996 presidential election, except there was no Ross Perot to be a spoiler (Abramson, et. al., 1998). The national vote tally indicated that Republicans won the West, the South and much of the Midwest, while Democrats won much of the Northeast, the West Coast and several Midwest industrial enclaves, giving Gore an edge in the popular vote. Exit polls further suggest a cultural divide. Texas Governor Bush's supporters were more likely to attend church, and think of national leadership in moral terms. (*New York Times*, November 9, 2000).

Florida has been described as politically conservative—"distrustful of government, concern about crime, opposed to higher taxes, yet unrealistic in its demands for more and better government services." (Dye, 1998: 33). It mirrors the prevailing political culture of The South. Rural southern voters, who overwhelmingly voted for Bush, are suspicious of big government, believing it is "stepping on their religious beliefs and out of step with their views on crime, abortion and guns." On the other hand, Gore supporters are fearful of Christian conservatives, expecting government to take care of people "like me" (*USA Today*, November 9, 2000: 19A). In the South, the central cities went for Gore by a three to one margin, but the small towns and the suburbs went for Bush (Sullivan, *New York Times Magazine*, November 26, 2000: 24; *The Des Moines Register*, November 8, 2000: 7). As

USA Today reporter Jill Lawrence (November 9, 2000: 19A) remarks, the Bush-Gore election illustrates that most urban dwellers are more socially liberal because the demographics of cities breed "a live-let-live mind-set that is a lure for young people, singles, minorities, gays, immigrants, and artists, most of whom supported Gore."

Secular Realignment and Wedge Issues

Partisanship represents a sympathy for and a loyalty to a specific political party. Once an attachment is made, normally derived from parents, it endures. However, partisanship can erode when changing economic circumstance or the party's basic ideological principles seem to change (Campbell, et. al. 1960). The term for this change is realignment. A **critical realignment** occurs whenever there is national crisis (Flanigan and Zingdale, 1998; Beck, 1997; Brady, 1988). In critical realignments the citizen-voter who is facing cross pressure will likely shift party loyalty and crossover to the other majority party, causing new voting patterns in succeeding elections. By contrast, a **secular realignment** is more subtle, with new voting patterns evolving slowly. Often, a third party such as George Wallace's American Independent Party acts as a "half-way house" for those who are unwilling to break with old partisan loyalties (Seagull, 1975: 17).

In the grand scheme, southern secular realignment took place during the last three decades of the Twentieth Century. A determining factor appears to be the role of the federal government and the region's racial divide. In the final analysis, whatever phase of southern political history one wishes to examine, sooner or later, the "trail of inquiry" always lead back to the African-American voter (Key, 1984: 5). Throughout the South the secular realignment began with the collapse of Jim Crow. Prior to the Civil Rights Movement, there were few ticket-splitters. Today this is no longer the case. In Florida, political fortunes are with the ticket splitters. Furthermore, it is the two other minority voting blocs (Latinos or Asian-Americans) that have become the most unpredictable blocs (Dye, 1998: Ch.1).

After the World War II, the Republicans sought to build a viable alternative to the Roosevelt-Truman. By abandoning isolationism, the Republican party adopted an aggressive free-market, anti-Communist, Cold War stance. By doing so, the GOP had altered its image, attracting support from both Old Guard social conservatives and young libertarian professionals (Harbour, 1982; Dunn and Woodard, 1991; Boaz, 1997). Even so, Democrats still have a slight edge in Florida. With voter turnout low, wedge issues are critical to winning state elections (Bullock and Rozell, 1998; Glaser, 1996: Ch.6; Black and Black, 1992; Scher, 1992). To say race is not a factor is to ignore reality. For Florida Democrats, black voter turnout is essential, especially within swing districts, as the Gore-Bush recount illustrates. In swing districts, black voters can give the Democrats a numerical advantage. Unless energized, the black voter fails to vote. For a Democratic candidate, he must devise a "winning coalition" that will successfully turnouts the African-American while not alienating independent white voters (Black and Black, 1992; Scher, 1992). On the other hand, Republicans must "tap into" the disenchanted suburban, white independents without appearing to be racist. For both southern parties, the politics of moralism (abortion, gay rights, drugs), affirmative action and economic development appear to be the contemporary "wedge" issues. Both parties, however, are faced with the same paradox. Neither party wishes to play the "race" card in a state that has purged itself of Jim Crow.

Civil Rights and the End of Jim Crow

Of all the regions, the South had been the region least sympathetic to socio-economic change, but has been the region to have changed the greatest. In 1960 there were two obstacles to two party politics in Florida: Jim Crow and courthouse politics. In one decade, one-party rule by rural factions was swept away. The Supreme Court's enunciation of **one person, one vote principle** was the wrecking ball that undermined the very pillars of "de facto" as well as "de jure" segregation in Florida.

Before voting rights, the county party organization was the key to Florida governance. The 1885 state constitution provided for **plural executive government** dominated by a rural legislature. Under the Redeemer Constitution (1885) many of the governor's duties were reassigned either to other independently elected cabinet members or to county officials (Tebeau,1971: 288-290; Williamson, 1976: Ch.7). With the Civil Rights Acts as well as three Supreme Court decisions—Baker vs. Carr (1962), Reynolds vs. Sims (1964) and Swann vs. Adams (1967)—all this was altered. No longer would rural stakeholders dominate legislative politics. That is, **one-person, one-vote principle** assured each citizen-voter would have equal representation (Urofsky, 1988: 830-836). After Swann vs. Adams (1967), the Florida legislature had reapportioned its legislative districts. In 1961, spatial size rather than population density of a district determined state legislative representation, allowing for 13 percent of the population to elect a majority of the legislators in both houses. After **one person-one vote**, three-quarters of the legislators came from districts representing Florida's ten metropolitan areas, making a more pluralistic legislature. In 1972 Florida's reform legislature, a group of young, urban legislators took power from the **Pork Chop Gang**. Known as the **Lamb Choppers**, these urban reformers modernized legislative procedures, making it possible to revamp the state's political agenda (Carter 1976; Dixon, 1973: 548-553). **One person-one vote** meant county courthouse politics would no longer be the same. It gave rise to a new breed of politician (Bob Graham, Rubin Askew, Lawton Chiles and Bob Martinez) who were able to convey a cosmopolitan outlook to state issues. Consequently, they began revamp county courthouse politics in the legislature (Lamis, 1988)

Civil Rights Meant Voting Rights

The 1948 Presidential Election was first crack in the Solid South. The Dixiecrats led by then South Carolina Governor Strom Thurmond established the State's Rights Party. As a protest to the Democratic Party's "Civil Rights" plank, these Dixiecrats sought to punish Harry Truman. However, Dixiecrats failed to cast a broad appeal in the urbanizing South, winning only 39 of the 127 southern electoral votes (Black and Black, 1992: 142-46). Although the South was divided over civil rights; there was no consensus "whether the South should abandon the [Democratic] party, turn Republican, or establish a third party" (Scher, 1992: 111).

In 1964, a majority of southern African-American voters were Republicans; by 1970, almost ninety percent were Democrats. In one bloody and difficult decade, the national Democratic Party's would shift its focus, with its southern conservative wing splitting off. The Civil Rights Movement politicized the African-American community, forcing Lyndon B. Johnson's administration to be the champion of civil liberties. In 1964, for many white Floridians, desegregating a lunch counter is one thing but giving blacks the vote was another. Voting rights threatened the soul of **Jim Crow** (Button, 1989; Fendich, 1993). Jim Crow had evolved into an intricate code of racial etiquette and white supremacy. Voting rights destroyed the myth of inequality, and white social advantages (Black and Black, 1992). Or as social historian David Goldfield (1990: 149) remarks,

> "Voting, like segregation, was a form of public behavior that reflected the status of both black and white. To admit blacks into the polling booth was to admit political equality, and the carefully tended myths of the

Reconstruction era had taught whites that electoral participation of blacks was an invitation to corruption, disorder and oppression. It meant that whites could find themselves on the other side of the color line.

The Eisenhower Administration's 1957 Civil Rights Act had no teeth. The law simply required any formal complaints to be made at the county courthouse. By contrast, The 1965 Voting Rights Act attacked the county courthouse power structure. In South Carolina vs. Katzenbach (1966), the U.S. Supreme Court upheld the 1965 Voting Rights Act, rendering the African-American as a potent political force (Urofsky, 1988: 791-797). Mississippi typified the political change in the Deep South. In Le Flore County, only 33 black voters were registered in April 1966. Within two months, after the arrival of a federal registrar, five thousand African-Americans were registered (Goldfield, 1987: 176). Overall, the 1965 voting rights law helped register 4.1 million Southern black voters (Grantham, 1994: 286-288). The voting rights law provided a similar change in Florida's political tapestry. In 1960, 39.4 percent of eligible blacks were registered, and by 1992 it was 54.7 (Beck, 1992). But, this percentage is very misleading. In 1960, black registration was proportionately higher in urban areas, where African-Americans did not constitute a political threat. By contrast, Florida's Panhandle where African-Americans were a majority, very few were registered. For instance, in 1960, the number was about three percent. After the passage of the 1965 Voting Rights Act, this percentage rose to fifty percent (Button, 1989). In rural Gulf County, two-thirds of registered voters were African-American in 1990 (Shermyen, 1991: Table 21: 30). In the Bush-Gore presidential contest, Gore took those counties where there was substantial black voter registration (*New York Times*, November 27, 2000: 15A).

The Voting Rights Act (1965) changed black leadership style. Under Jim Crow, black leaders didn't make "demands", rather they made "requests". As long as blacks behaved themselves, the "rule of the rustics" provided "token" public services (Dye, 1971: 154-156). Once blacks obtain political leverage, the county courthouse elite could no longer ignore their demands. If they did, blacks would rebuff them at election time (Button, 1989: Ch.4). In 1965, there were fewer than one hundred southern black officials. By 1990, there were more than five thousand (Grantham, 1994: 289; Goldfield, 1990: 174-177). In 1993, there were 136 black Floridian city and county officeholders. This is a far cry from 1965 when only three blacks held public office. Although small per cent of all offices, it does represent a significant change in the black political leadership (Shermyen, 1991: 537; Button, et.al., 1998).

Black office-holding has meant a policy shift. Prior to 1965, city and county government followed the **market equity** rules of public service delivery (Levy, et. al. 1974). Thus, Crestview, Florida, in 1966 indicated that 30 percent of the black neighborhood streets and 50 percent of the white neighborhood streets were paved and had proper drainage. Once elected, black officials negotiated a change in the allocation rules. By 1975 local and federal funds were targeted to both black and white poor neighborhoods so that all of Crestview's streets were paved and adequately drained (Button, 1989: 33-34). Both Gretna and Daytona, where whites felt the most threatened, experienced considerable political turmoil during the late 1960s. Once African-Americans began to vote, they gained better public services, with an emphasis on street lighting, street drainage and resurfacing. That is, the "nuts and bolts" public service (Button, 1989: Ch.5). The Voting Rights Act (1965) assured that a Black official was no longer just a symbol. Instead, a Black elected official made real allocation choices, substantially improving the quality of life for all town residents (Button, et. al., 1998).

Civic Stakeholders and Political Participation

Political efficacy is the belief that one's political obligations within the civic community will have some sort of impact on its civic governance (Abramson, et.al., 1998: 81-84). Political participation is at the heart of our democratic notion of local civic governance. It encourages active civic engagement. (Verba, et.al. 1995; Coulter, 1989; Helig and Mundt, 1984). Civic engagement is shaped by a variety of socializing agents—family, friends, and work peers—which in turn are shaped by the region's political culture. The influence of political participation lies "in its power to set reasonably fixed limits on political behavior" within a political community (Elazar, 1994: 3). A multiplicity of stakeholders can modify and revamp policy choices. In the politics of planning there are a variety of stakeholders. The most common are those who have a direct interest in the politics of sprawl, such as Realtors, home builders, neighborhood associations, and community planners. Much has been written in a micro-context describing the interrelationships of these formal policy actors on the issues of land use management and sprawl. But other citizen-taxpayers, who pay the property taxes, user fees and sales taxes, are equally important in the growth management game and should be considered.

The Yankee Newcomers

Today, less than half Florida's population can claim southern heritage (Bartley, 1995: 430). Post-War migration stream had principally located within a 19-county region that is shaped similar to a horseshoe (see Figure 3.1). This horseshoe stretches from Sarasota and the Gulf Coast counties extending northward through Tampa, and then northeast along the "I-4 corridor" linking Daytona Beach; and, then southward to Titusville along the Atlantic coast towards the Miami-Dade region. It is this area that has principally supported growth management initiatives at the state level. Three population cohorts principally entered this horseshoe migratory stream since the 1960s—the Cubans, the elderly Yankee newcomers and younger, upwardly mobile white professionals. With New Yorkers constituting the largest number of annual in-migrants, followed by suburbanites from New Jersey, Pennsylvania and Massachusetts. Overall, the GOP had benefitted from this in-migration.

In political surveys, Republicans were found to be Protestant, and residing on the suburban fringe, while Democrats are more likely to be Catholic and scattered throughout the region. Indicators of wealth and education have also provided differences. The Yankee Republican is better educated and more likely to hold a professional or managerial position than either h/her native, southern counterpart or h/her Yankee Democrat newcomer (Baker, 1990; Green and Gruth, 1990; McGlennon, 1998a; Steed, 1998). But, community ideology tends to differ between the two partisan groups. A Yankee Republican tends to rank h/herself socially conservative and less likely to support taxing and spending policies (Parker, 1988; Kelley, et.al. 1989; Carmines and Stanley, 1990; Steed, 1998). If there is any ideological factionalism among Florida Republicans, it is tied to Florida's fragile environment. Within Florida's horseshoe, Republican voters are more likely to support environmental issues (Kelley, et. al. 1989; Bowman, et. al. 1990; Steed, 1998; Brodsky and Cotter, 1998; McClennon, 1998a). Otherwise, Republicans are within the conservative mainstream on such issues as gun control, affirmative action, school prayer, the morality of marijuana, and business regulatory policy (Steed, 1998, 1988; Brodsky and Cotter, 1998; Carmines and Stanley, 1990; Kelley, 1989).

The Latino Stakeholders

Florida is a highly pluralistic state, with large concentration of both Cubans and African-Americans in such cities as Tampa, Miami and Jacksonville, with both ethnic groups competing for jobs, social services and political power. Hispanics have always been a part of Florida's cultural heritage, with Latinos comprising 15 percent of the population. Tampa's Ybor City has been the home of Cubans and other Carribean peoples for the past century (Mormino, 1983).

In the 1950s, air technology allowed many of the middle to upper-class Cubans to visit Miami as a vacation spot. The Communist insurgency under Castro gave impetus to Florida Cuban migration (Portes and Stipeck, 1993; Perez-Stable and Uriarte, 1993; Croucher, 1997: Ch. 4). In 2000, Florida's Latino population was still predominantly Cuban. Often middle-class, with strong family and religious ties, the Cubans have been more likely than other ethnic groups to identify with Republican positions on foreign policy and economic issues (DeSipio, 1996: 50-57; Moreno and Warren, 1996; *The New York Times*, March 13, 2001). With federal assistance of nearly a billion dollars, the Latinization of Miami has taken place with most Cubans holding managerial, technical and professional positions (Perez-Stable and Uriarte, 1993: 137-149). As Latino Republicans, Cubans are a political force in the GOP, helping to elect one of their own as governor—Bob Martinez, a Tampa businessman. Moreover, Miami Cubans have elected two members to the U.S. House delegation (Moreno and Warren, 1996: 172).

At the state legislative level, the Voting Rights Act has been especially beneficial to Cubans, assuring them 12 of the 25 house seats that lies in the Miami area, often bitterly contesting those seats from either ethnic Jewish or African-American Democratic politicians (Mohl, 1989; Porter and Stipeck, 1993: Ch.8; Moreno and Warren, 1993; Coucher, 1997: Ch.2). In recent years, other Hispanics have migrated to Florida, most notably Nicaraguans to Hialeah and Puerto Ricans to Orlando. Overall, Hialeah, Miami and Fort Lauderdale are the major cities with the highest concentration of Latinos. Hispanics generally share a conservative perspective. With 7.1 per cent of the statewide vote, Latinos are likely to become a major swing vote in the Twenty-First Century (DeSipio, 1996; Dye, 1998: 18-20).

The African-American Voter

African-American residential patterns are atypical of the South. In 1900, 44 percent of Florida's population was African-American and resided in rural areas. By 1970, this population cohort shrank to about 17 percent of the population. In 1900, Blacks began to settle in segregated communities along the Florida East Coast Railway from West Palm Beach to Miami. Mohl

(1995) found that Dade County Planning Board sought to control the expansion of Black settlement throughout this period. In a 1990 census tract analysis of Southeastern Florida, Lee (1992) notes that African-Americans resided basically in 97 tracts, suggesting that housing segregation still remains an issue. Although in the 1960s, Blacks districts did expand to absorb additional population, these tracts were located in the least desirable areas of the region, near light industrial or commercial development, often along natural features such as lakes or swamps or physical infrastructure features such as canals, railroads or highway. Rarely did Black districts abut white housing areas, and when it did occur, redlining became the tool of the 1970s (Mohl, 1995).

Even with the state's population explosion, Florida's African-American population has proportionately declined. In 1990, its population was approximately 13.6 percent of the state's population or about 1.76 million residents. By Fiscal Year 2000 the state's African-American population was 13 per cent. Located both within urban centers and rural areas, Florida's black population level appear to be far below its regional neighbors [21.8 per cent] as well as the national average [16.8 percent] (Dietrich, 1978: Table 3; Arsenault and Mormino, 1988: Table 9.6; Shermyen, 1991; *The Miami Herald*, December 29, 2000).

Well before the 24th Amendment, Florida's state legislature ended the poll tax (1937). Even with the end of Jim Crow, African-Americans did not enjoy instant political clout. By then Blacks in Tampa and Miami were being elbowed aside by newly arrived Cubans, continuing the sense of powerlessness among the black working class (Portes and Stipeck, 1993: Ch.8; Croucher, 1997: Ch.3). But slowly, African-Americans have begun to gain political power. As Button (1989: 212) comments:

> White politicians no longer dominated black political activity, and many blacks moved from a "subject" to more of a "participant" political status. Moreover, blacks began to utilize the political system and bargain effectively with whites in order to gain advantages for themselves. As a result, they not only achieved much greater control over their own destiny, but they also managed to modify, and perhaps change forever, white political dominance at the local level.

Although African-Americans have trailed whites in voter turnout, blacks do compose 11 percent of the state's electorate (Dye, 1998: 14). After the Thornburg v. Gingles (1986) decision, black leaders have gained favorably in redistricting. In 1976, there were only three African-Americans in the state legislature. By 1996, 14 state house seats and 5 state senate seats as well as three house congressional seat were held by African-Americans. Ms. Carrie Meek, the first African-American to be elected to the Florida senate, is now holds one of those congressional seats. Despite their loyalty to the Democratic party, few Blacks have gained entrance into upper echelons of Democratic leadership circles. Less than 10 percent of the party's precinct positions were held by African-Americans (Bowman, et. al, 1990: 58: Scicchitano and Scher, 1998).

Black precinct activists have a strong, moral-religious compass, attending church more often than their white, Democratic counterparts. Moreover, those in leadership positions tend to be solidly middle-class (Bowman, et.al. 1990; Steed, 1990; Hadley and Stanley, 1998; Button, et.al., 1998). A study of second generation Black-elected officials found that their political agenda has changed beyond traditional civil liberties issues. They have moved on to moral as well as socio-economic concerns such as health care, the environment, housing quality, and employment needs. This not surprising. With the exception of certain social "wedge" issues—the morality of abortion, homosexual lifestyle and school prayer—African-American rank-and-file members are said to be the "liberal-communal" anchor in the Southern Democratic Party (Hadley and Stanley, 1998; Steed, 1998; Prestage,1991; Moreland, 1990; Clawson and Clark, 1988).

Gender and Generational Stakeholders

The elderly, which is defined as the population cohort of 65 years and above, has been only 15 percent of the migratory stream in the 1990s. Instead, it is the young adult cohort, known as **Generation X**, which are those residents between the ages of 20 and 34, that have had the greatest migratory stream numbers, comprising about 23 percent (Dortch, 1995: 4). Still, the elderly voter plays a crucial role in the political landscape. Unlike young adults, most elderly purchase real estate, pay property taxes and have high voter turnouts. Consequently, it is feared that the elderly will use "their considerable voting strength to promote governmental services " important to them while "vigorously opposing increased spending programs and new taxes to underwrite essential public services" (Button and Rosenbaum, 1986: 179). As stakeholders, the elderly have been socially conservative on most taxing and spending issues, supporting this belief (Rasmussen, 1989; Simmons, 1990; Benton and Daly, 1992; MacManus, 1992, 1995; Mullins and Rosentraub, 1992). In 1996 Clinton was able to make "wedge" issues pertaining to medicare and social security. With 50 percent of Florida's elderly voting for Clinton, Florida had shifted into the Democratic Presidential column (*New York Times*, November 7, 1996). Indeed, Bob Dole had captured most of the heartland and the Southeast. But Florida had eluded him (*New York Times*, November 18, 1996). Election returns for the Bush-Gore election suggest older residents tended to support George W. Bush.

In 1990, 2.33 million or about 18.3 percent of the state's population was within the elderly cohort, exceeding the national norm of 12.2 percent (Shermyen, 1991; Pardum, 1989; Arsenault and Mormino, 1988; Dietrich, 1978). Recent census information indicates that the elderly population has increased to 2.9 million, or about 21 percent of the state's population, with most of the cohort residing on the suburban-rural fringe (Dortch, 1995: 6; *The Miami-Herald*, December 29, 2000: 18A). With voting turnouts at about 75 per cent in local elections, they consistently support policies that increase spending on crime fighting, keep spending on education at a minimum and resist any other taxing policies that do not sustain immediate benefits to them (Dye, 1998: Ch 3; Button and Rosenbaum, 1986).

In the 1990s, **baby boomers** accounted for about 19 percent of the state's population. Baby boomers, who are the population cohort born between 1945 and 1964, increased to 3.7 million residents in 2000. Most Florida baby boomers are Republicans and are less likely to be southernly born. They are the newcomers, who have resided less than ten years within the community. As better educated than the state's mean, these Republicans have been able to penetrate the party's leadership. By contrast, Democratic boomers are slightly older and are more likely to be public or blue collar employees. Both cohorts have mixed opinions on land use and environmental management, expressing highly localized concerns (McGlennon, 1998a; Brodsky and Cotter, 1998; Bowman, et. al, 1990).

Women in precinct leadership categories have been found to be college educated. But the similarity ends between the two parties. Republican women describe themselves as "home-makers," with young school-age children. On taxing and spending, social welfare, school prayer and the morality of marijuana, these Republican precinct women are consistently more conservative than their Democratic counterparts. On the issues of ERA, abortion, gun control, home schooling and the environment, there is a bipolar split, with just as many Republican females taking a liberal as well as a conservative stance (Fowlkes, et.al. 1980; Kelley, et.al, 1989).

Prior to 1960, very few women were active in Florida politics. Since the 1970s recruitment in the Republican party has been by the party's leadership. On the other hand, Democratic women candidates have independently sought office (Black and Black, 1987: Ch. 8). Even so, this does not imply that there are greater opportunities for leadership among women precinct workers. In fact, Clawson and Clark (1988) found little opportunity for either African-Americans or white women activists to move into the upper echelons of the party leadership.

Distance from Jim Crow and the Bourbon philosophy has change recruitment patterns among the young. Consequently, the GOP has become the net gainer (Prysby, 1998; Green and Guth, 1990). A generational schism has emerged. Bread and Butter issues such as social welfare, quotas, and tax credits has attracted many younger white voters to the Republican cause. If there is a split among the young, it is over certain social issues—gay rights, gun control, abortion, and the morality of marijuana—with younger Democrats taking the party's liberal position (Steed and Bowman, 1988; Green and Gruth, 1990; Carmines and Stanley, 1990; Moreland, 1990; McGlennon, 1998a; Clark and Lockerbie, 1998; Brodsky and Cotter, 1998).

Overall, **Generation X** has supported Republican fiscal policies. This loss of younger, white voters means that the New Deal-Great Society coalition has little relevance for them. Indeed, for many young voters of both genders, Big Government has become "wedge" issues. Thus, many younger, white Floridians are just as likely to reject these issues as elderly Floridians are likely to embrace them.

Churches and Civic Participation

The South looks upon itself as a society of small town values. This is a paradox, since "two out of every three southerners today are urban folk...." (Reed, 1991: 25). In Florida, the Orangebelt has given way to the Sunbelt. Despite this economic change, religion is still one of its pockets of southern distinctiveness. Native Southerners are still likely to be a socially active within a church (Reed, 1986: Ch.6). While the North moved towards religious pluralism during the Progressive Era, the South remained the land of Protestant fundamentalism and tent revivals.

In the era of "joiners," the most influential social organization that reflected and reinforced the prevailing ideals of community life are the churches (McLauren, 1978). The town steeple or small, white framed buildings on a crossroad marked not only the moral compass for southern towns but also a town's sense of place. Although there are doctrinal differences, collectively the various sects reflect the mores within the civic culture. Each encourages traditional gender roles and sexual morality. A majority frowned on the pleasures alcohol, tobacco or gambling. More importantly, the various sects offered the basic doctrine of traditional- individualism—the equality of individuals, the importance of self-sacrifice, and the assumption of responsibility for one's own actions.

There were and are class distinctions in attendance, with the town's business elite being members of mainstream Protestant churches, while the factory worker, the store clerk or the farmer more likely being a member of a Pentecostal church (Ayer, 1992; Cooper and Terrill, 1991: 629-639). Preston (1991: 200) notes, "Southerners are the most church going people in the nation, and from camp meeting through riverside baptism to huge urban congregations, the tone and temper of Southern Protestantism is evangelical." In a region where its cotton fields and orange groves are being transformed to industrial parks, the "old time" religion can be a safe anchorage not only to those "who resisted becoming part of the new society, but also for those swept along by its currents...." (Goldfield, 1987: 220).

Redemption is both biblical and personal for many small town residents. It is understandable that religion has spilled over into the political arena. For many, the nation's salvation is tied to such social issues as abortion, gun control, feminism and evolution (Grantham, 1994; Cooper and Merrill, 1991; Preston, 1991). Morality is often defined in both public and private terms. "Whatever behavior may actually be, the approved morality in the South is an austere one, with peculiar regional emphasis," (Reed, 1986: 69). Southern churches have always had a great deal to say about the human condition. And, on any Sunday, one can hear the small town preacher give a sermon on how Washington's bureaucrats are endangering the nation's spiritual soul (Kosmin and Lachman, 1993; Prysby, 1990, 1998).

Evidence indicates that conversions to the GOP are tied to the compatibility of the core values of Traditional-Individualism. As a political culture model, it looks to our small town past—a past of strong social and family bonds. While socio-economic change has been moving the Democratic Party into the urban civic culture, the GOP is gaining political strength by absorbing these small town social conservatives (Prysby, 1998; Clark and Lockerbie, 1998; Green and Guth, 1990; Carmines and Stanley, 1990). Small town Republicans are definitely socially conservative. This implies that these converts are tied to social and moral issues. As Carmines and Stanley (1990: 32) report, this conversion "does not mean that white Southerners have become more conservative (and hence, more Republican) in recent years." No such thing has occurred. Instead, southern conservatives simply felt "out of tune with the Democratic party...." Consequently, small town residents have reassessed which party represents their political preferences.

Due to the population dynamics, at least in urban Florida, fundamentalism has given way to Roman Catholicism and mainline Protestantism. Even so, Florida is still very much a Traditional-Individualistic, socially conservative state (Morgan and Watson, 1991; Dye, 1998).

Policy Implications

Over the half past century Florida politics has been transformed. African-Americans are solidly Democratic, while whites and Latinos are becoming Republican. At the grassroots level, the Yankee baby boomers, Cubans and the elderly are actively engaged in county courthouse politics. But, the wild card is the young, adult cohort, known as Generation X, who are more likely to see themselves as independents.

Florida gained four new House seats from the 1990 census. Recent census data supports two additional House seats. No doubt, one of these additional seats will be in the Miami-Ft Lauderdale area, forging new tensions between the Latino and African-American populations. Even with federal court mandated redistricting, Republicans are likely to maintain a comfortable edge in U.S. House seats and in the state legislature. However, Republicans are still a minority with 41 per cent of the registration with the issue of environmentalism splitting by gender and region. The nonpartisan voter is the swing vote who is tied to environmentalism. Yet, Baby Boomers and Generation Xers appear to be fiscally conservative, making future races to be quite interesting if not frustrating for both political parties.

Chapter 5
The Politics of Florida's Growth Management

Besides the 10 states that have initiated some sort of state comprehensive planning program to tackle sprawl, in November 2000, there were 23 growth management initiatives on state and local ballots. A crucial policy debate issue faced by each individual initiative is how the respective land use management plan assures tighter land use regulatory control guidelines without jeopardizing a locality's unique economic, environmental or quality of life attributes. In an effort to gain political acceptance by local citizens and officials, no growth management plan can meet everyone's expectations. Indeed, modification seems to be the norm and not the exception among the states.

Sprawl and the Dynamics of Multi-Cultural Parochialism

In 1940, with 1.89 million people, Florida ranked 27th, trailing behind Iowa and Nebraska. Forty-five per cent of its population was still rural, with highly dense urban population concentrations within Miami-Dade, Tampa Bay and Jacksonville areas. In six decades, Florida ranked fourth in population. Like the country as a whole, Florida has become suburbanized. Between

1950 and 1980, land development became a principal state policy for its economic post-War boom, causing Florida's population to triple to 9.8 million residents. Throughout the 1980s, the state experienced a population growth rate of 3.4 per cent a year or about 540 new residents per day. As Kolankweicz and Beck (2001) writ, the flood of sprawl had surged upward, moving its boundaries steadily up the state's Peninsula. From 1970 to 1990, the per capita land consumption among the state's 20 urbanized areas had consistently outpaced the population ratios, raising questions pertaining to the efficient use of land development practices. Between 1990 and 2000 the state's population rose from 11.2 million to 15.98 million, with almost half the state's residents were scattered outside the formal municipal boundaries. In every one of Florida's 20 urbanized areas, state and local government has failed to contain the population within existing urban boundaries. Since 1970, Florida's urban density ratio levels have fallen, from 2283 persons per/sq. mile to 1,215 persons per/sq. mile (Ewing, 1999:5).

No longer is Florida the postwar state comprising sleepy, self-contained southern hamlets surrounded by citrus groves, vegetable fields or pine trees. No longer is the typical Main Street shaped like Gretna or Milton. Before1960, like other Sunbelt states, Florida had a clear delineation between its cities and the countryside, with county courthouse politics mirroring this delineation. The sprawl machine has worked too well. As a motorist travels northward on US 41, US 27 or US 441 up from Southeast Florida h/she finds far fewer Palm trees and far fewer grinning lifeguards, but still will pass by the now familiar strip shopping centers. Most inland towns' economic bases have become more diversified, and are not typical of the tourist/ retirement communities that hug the coast. Of course, each inland town will have its little antique-tourist district. But, these towns are beginning to replicate the wealthier, self-contained homogeneous seaside towns, with their isolated, gated housing communities. These inland communities' Main Streets and neighborhoods are increasingly looking like any Californian community, with suburban strip malls, fast food places, drive-in cleaners and Big-box stores.

As Kolankweicz and Beck (2001) have noted, Florida's sprawl is a consequence of population growth, land consumption and infrastructure subsidies. In Florida, the following land use pattern has emerged since 1970. The dynamics of population growth and changing demographics has meant that the additional population requires either extra rural land for its urban needs, or these newcomers facilitate a leapfrog movement by the existing residents to more rural land. In either case, more rural land is converted to urban uses, thinning out existing population densities. Sprawl has three principal culprits according to the New Urbanism literature. These culprits are modern technology, developers who manipulate an antiquated locally-based civic culture of land use management and an infrastructure subsidy system (Ch. 1). Overall modern technology in the form of communication and automobile related technology help make modern Florida possible, and with air conditioning tolerably. Sprawl in the form of leapfrog development would have taken sufficient hold unless local governmental land use decision-making did not occur. Indeed, better road and better communication systems do play a critical role in Florida's population sprawl. Local homes rule and fragmented land use regulatory policy had assured its early success. Cornell University Professor Rolf Rendell ("New Research on Population, Suburban Sprawl and Smart Growth," Sierra Club White Paper, November 2002) found in his analysis of one thousand jurisdictions, sprawl was driven by myopic public policymaking, population growth, local civic norms and irresponsible private practices.

As pointed out by Tiebout (Ch. 1; Ch. 10), local land use regulatory policymaking and the public service subsidies are two key ingredients for the leapfrog development process. Sprawl, when defined in terms of land use consumption patterns, population density levels, and municipal service delivery networks, becomes quite understandable. Since 1950, outlying communities have actively competed for households and firms with the locally dominant central core city. By doing so, each community hopes to maximize its own tax base. Known as fiscal zoning, this local policymaking activity has had its implications—leapfrog development, isolation of housing and workforce, and costly infrastructure subsidies. Without public subsidies of local municipal infrastructures it is less likely that fiscal zoning would have been successful. Or as the Sierra Club's Cost of Sprawl Report (2000:2-8) notes, national suburban sprawl, though aided by federal spending, is really a by-product of state and local land development subsidy decisions. "We've subsidized sprawl at such a basic level for so long, that many people believe the status quo is actually fair and neutral." Sadly, studies on sprawl have intimated that there is no guarantee that fiscal zoning over the long run will dramatically improve the town's fiscal base, at least where low density, residential development occurs. In fact, such residential development appears to cost in terms of public service delivery. That is, taxes derived from residential homeowners are less than the public service costs, especially for the placement of certain types of infrastructures (See Ch. 12). Yet, politically it is difficult for a local jurisdiction to drop a subsidy policy and/or adopt stringent development codes to contain infrastructure costs. To do so, a developer can simply **leapfrog** beyond the town's boundaries.

Much of the current growth management and Smart Growth policy debate is focused on the validity fiscal zoning goals, and on the issue of **which** governmental entity will be responsible for local land use management (Innes,1992). We will define growth management as a set of policy tools that will regulate and restrict the rate, the pace and the extent of land use development (Dowell, 1984; Bollens, 1990; Anglin, 1990; Leo, et. al. 1998; Diaz and Green, 2001). Smart Growth rests on the assumptions that we can curb sprawl by building better kinds of communities by in-filling and revitalizing existing communities or by establishing the elements of town centers, mix-land use and greenbelts in new ones (Gilliam, 2002; Duany, et.al. 2000; Langdon, 1994; Calthorpe, 1993). 1986, 1981).

Florida's Entry into Growth Management

The Florida Legislature's initial entry into growth management was a top-down, regional growth management strategy. The 1972 Florida legislature expanded state statutory authority over local land use planning, forcing cities and counties to become more accountable to state delegated agencies (DeGrove and Turner, 1991:213). Overall, the legislature's policy planning strategy was to assure that: (1) the state's unique natural environment was protected; (2) the cost of spiraling municipal services was contained for local municipalities; and (3) the state's overall economic vitality was not threatened.

Like the other top-down growth management states (Oregon, Vermont and Hawaii), the Florida legislature soon recognized land use implementation required a coordinating state agency. This agency would have to impose sanctions, if necessary, on those municipalities and counties which fail to submit "a plan that meets established state standards, or in other ways choose not to comply with program requirements" (Gale, 1992:435). Compliance to state goals at the local level would be the keys to successful implementation. Furthermore, like any other state-sponsored growth management program, Florida's plan was not without its critics. With a strong heritage of Traditional-Individualism, few towns were willing risk their local autonomy. Local land use management has many symbolic meanings (Rudel, 1989; Innes, 1992).

For many of Florida's local officials, the state's mandated growth policy plan has been perceived as a threat to their very political existence (Catlin,

1997:Ch.7). Since the municipalities or counties are the only two governmental entities directly responsible for regulating and implementing the state plan, these local officials must bear the brunt of criticism "for everything that occurs" within their jurisdictional boundaries (*Florida Planning*, August, 1992:19). Besides, land development is the biggest business activity in a county or a municipality, frequently providing enormous profits for the well-connected citizens (Mills and Davis, 1962; Gottdiener, 1977; Rudel, 1989; Vogel and Swanson, 1989; Greenberg, 1996). Furthermore, local land development rule-making allows any property owner to exercise political influence. It is Jacksonian democracy at work, assuring that any property owner will have a say as to how other property owners are utilizing their respective plots of land (Tarrant, 1976; Rudel, 1989).

Environmentalism and Local Parochialism

The issue of "carrying capacity" of Florida's fragile environment became the political issue that modified Traditional-Individualistic administrative land use rule-making within the Sunshine State (Seimon, 1989). **Carrying capacity** is ecologically defined as the ability of the "ecological system—availability of water and mineral resources as well as its fertility of soils—to assimilate refuse generated from land use intensity associated with population growth." The carrying capacity of a biological system decreases as the population density increases because "greater demands are placed on the environment as a source [supply or resource of land and water] and as a sink [a waste disposal to the air, water and land surface]" (Veri, et. al. 1975:67). As a concept, it undergirds much of the increasing skepticism voiced by environmentalists toward the assumptions that "growth is good." In Florida, however, carrying capacity has a broader definition, including the adverse impacts imposed on public facilities by unbridled development (Ch. 163.3177).

The environmental movement gained political strength when residents realized those local capital facilities could not stem the continual degradation of the state's air, water and land resources (Dewey, 1999). "Even pro-growth advocates," according to DeGrove (1984:3), "began to be swayed by the argument that environmental degradation from unwise development was a threat to the economic vitality of their community and state." Earth Day saw Floridians throughout the political spectrum rally on Tallahassee's capital steps. After Earth Day, the environmental movement could no longer be dismissed as a small group of "weirdos" or "tree huggers."

Although Earth Day did manifest that environmentalism had widespread support, public opinion has not been always uniform. In general, national polls indicated that Southerners were unlikely to support state or federal intervention. For the most part, Southerners perceived their towns and cities through the lens of the countryside. For them, only the industrialized North actually faced pollution problems (Dunlap, 1991:70). Of course, in Florida, traffic jams were becoming "prodigious, pollution getting worse, and occasionally a note of irritability [crept] into the otherwise sweet music of Southern conversation." But, as one Floridian noted, 'It beats the hell out of pellagra'" (Goldfield and Terrill, 1991: 135).

For most Floridians, environmental issues are backyard issues. Global warming or oil spills off the Norway coast means very little to the average Joe Six-pack. Specific environmental issues spoken in the abstract rarely gain his support. But an oil spill off Clearwater which prevents him from an afternoon swim or a fish kill in Okeechobee Lake will catch Joe Sixpack's attention. In the South, a politically viable environmental issue must be "close to home" (deHaven-Smith, 1987: 30-35; Dewey, 1999; Arp and Boeckelman, 1994). Apparently, in Florida, the proximity of pollution has been the **policy trigger issue,** making the intensity of support tied to local conditions. In a 1984 poll, the northern and central regions of Florida, "where environmental problems have been relatively isolated and disconnected," were more "fragmented" and "disjointed" when asked to support a state mandated policy. Indeed, environmental policy preferences among residents were shaped "to the configuration of environmental problems in the geographic area in question" (deHaven-Smith, 1987:33). Furthermore, the willingness to support state activism is tied to the degree of local impact . A 1990 survey comparing city and county attitudes conducted by FAU/FIU Joint Center for Environmental and Urban Problems found that counties were twice as likely to perceive environmental protection as a problem issue. Although both entities saw water quality protection to be an issue, counties saw threats to the natural environment—a wetland aquifer recharge area—as a greater problem issue. This divergence of concern between city and county is not surprising "when one considers that such threats are often the results of sprawling, low density development patterns that are occurring" in Florida's suburban and unincorporated areas (*Florida Planning*, March, 1992:10). Giventer and Neeley (1984) report that both Georgia and Florida county commissioners gave high priority to water pollution, drainage, solid waste and sewage treatment. They saw each of these infrastructure problems as aspects of their jurisdictional responsibilities because they tended to be in their backyard. On the other hand, planning and zoning issues were viewed as "city" problems, and best left in the hands of the municipalities.

Political party affiliation has played a mixed role in environmental policy preferences among Floridians. Again, proximity to the issue is a critical determinant. In the heavily populated Tampa Bay-Miami Beach corridor, both Republicans and Democrat voters are likely to support environmentally sensitive issues, with the high affluent residents more likely to support environmental protection policies that pertain to land use management and the state's ground water aquifer (Dewey, 1999; Stephenson, 1997; Catlin, 1997; deHaven-Smith, 1987). By contrast, the sparsely populated and less affluent Panhandle communities are more likely to sacrifice environmental safeguards and other planning related issues (deHaven-Smith, 1987; Parker, 1990: 12-22). A Florida State University Policy Science Program poll (Parker, 1990, Dye, 1998) discovered that taxing and spending issues on economic development concerns were more critical for Florida county residents. On the other hand, the ongoing water shortage and the continual problems associated with sprawl have kept both planning/ environmental issues alive.

A Florida League of Cities' Quality of Life Survey conducted in 1991 found similar results. When tied to a geographic region, a majority of Panhandle voters [58%] would not support higher taxes to support state expenditures to pay for water quality and solid waste disposal improvements. Interestingly, this poll consistently found that a majority of the voters throughout the state felt that local governments, when compared to the state, were better managers of "quality of life" initiatives. Again, differences by region and income base, proximity to the issue was a factor. Overall, the fewer economically stagnant small towns are found to be more willing to maintain local control over their destiny. Furthermore, poorer towns were more willing to get on the "growth is good" bandwagon. From their perspective, it is to their self-interest to climb aboard. Besides, such opportunities for development can be quite seductive, especially for those communities which have not yet experienced the deleterious effects of unbridled growth.

By the 1990s, toxic spills, air and groundwater pollution, and overflowing landfills had caught up with Southerners. In a nationwide survey, 78 percent of all Southerners favored some sort of environmental protection. Moreover, a majority of Southerners ranked toxic wastes and the threat of air and water pollution as the "most important" and "second most important" issue facing their region (NBC News and Wall Street Journal Poll, Survey Number 6, 1990). In Florida, several environmentally related issues—the Cross-State Barge Canal, the Big Cypress Swamp Controversy, the Boca Ciega Bay Development Proposal, and ITT Palm Coast Development—were the **land trigger issues** that placed Florida in the forefront of Southern environmentalism (Healy and Rosenberg, 1979; DeGrove, 1984; Stephenson, 1997). The **flash point** for each of these projects was the threat to the state's water supply. Indeed, urban Floridians are especially sensitive to the problem of water pollution and water quality. As **1000 Friends of Florida** activist Nathaniel Reed has remarked (Diamond and Noonan, 1996:150), "Water will control land use. Water will control our economy."

Ninety percent of Florida's water supply is derived from a limestone aquifer, located just below its surface along the state's spine. It is highly vulnerable. For decades, developers have drained the state's wetlands and filled in its tidal estuaries. Sporadic threats in the 1950s to the state's water supply were less severe and largely ignored. Inevitably, the 1971 drought cycle exposed the precarious nature of the state's water supply. The drought saw water levels of the Everglades and Lake Okeechobee fall to historic lows, threatening wildlife and residents alike (Carter, 1974; Veri, et. al., 1975; Dzurik, 1984). In Pinellas County alone, 700,000 residents had to obtain potable water from fields beyond the peninsula (Stephenson, 1997:144). The point was driven home to Floridians "as never before that indiscriminate drainage and headlong growth in South Florida had combined to produce an environmental crisis of truly major proportions." (DeGrove, 1984:106).

Phase One—All Thumbs and No Fingers

State senator Rubin Askew, a native Floridian, was elected governor on a campaign against the prevailing "growth is good" philosophy. In August 1971, Governor Askew appointed a Task Force on Resource Management to devise a plan to protect the state's drinking water. This Task Force drafted a series of recommendations calling for a state-sponsored land and water use plan. Under the strong leadership of Governor Askew, the reapportioned 1972 state legislature passed four environmentally oriented pieces of legislation. These laws included the Environmental Land and Water Management Act (Chapter 380), the Water Resources Act (Chapter 373), the State Comprehensive Planning Act (Chapter 23), and the Land Conservation Act (Chapter 259). In addition, the succeeding legislature passed a companion law, known as the Local Government Comprehensive Planning Act (Chapter 163), required all local governments to prepare and adopt a comprehensive land use plan. "Almost overnight Florida changed from a typical southern state devoted to boosterism and unfettered development into a national leader in growth management" (Stephenson, 1997:147).

Florida's hostility toward central authority dates back to the Reconstruction. In 1885, Florida drew up a state constitution that severely limited the governor's powers. Among other things, it forced the governor to submit key policy decisions to an executive cabinet who for the most part are directly elected by the voters. With the administrative power shared, a **plural executive style** of governance emerged which was not changed by the 1968 state constitution. The governor must therefore compete with other elected cabinet officials for administrative control over state agencies, often resulting in turf wars (Pelham, 1993; DeGrove and Turner, 1991; Catlin, 1997:53-69). Accordingly, there was a lack of clear lines of implementation authority which had allowed Florida's first venture into growth management [1972–1984] to evolve into "strong thumbs and weak fingers" style of policy planning, a system "capable of squashing or redirecting selected types of land uses" but not a system able to guide development in a coordinated or desired direction (deHaven-Smith, 1991:323).

Under the statutory authority of the **Environmental Land and Water Management Act of 1972 (ELWMA)**, Florida's state planning bureaucrats became involved in the land use regulation of large scale commercial and residential projects. The **ELWMA** was established to deal directly with the water crisis by creating five watershed management districts within the state, with each district initiating a land use conservation plan that would assure the adequacy of water supply within their respective district. In addition, under the ELWM Act, each district office was responsible for coordinating and evaluating on large development projects that may have an adverse impact of the watershed's water supply. If necessary, the watershed district management office was authorized to initiate, upon the recommendations of the Florida Cabinet, a moratorium on the proposed project if it is deemed to have an adverse impact on the region's aquifer-recharged areas.

Indirectly, the watershed district planning offices assumed responsibility for regional environmental and land use management, often coming into conflict with the Governor's Department of Community Affairs or the local municipalities. At best, both the **developments of regional impact (DRIs)** and **areas of critical state concern (ACSC)** were "interim measures to give the state time to put in place a more comprehensive approach to growth management" (Pelham, 1993:97). Yet, both provisions could have teeth. **DRI's** did give oversight responsibility to the 11 regional planning councils for any proposed development project that is likely to have significant adverse effect on the citizens of more than one county within their jurisdiction (Ch. 380.05[2], F.S.), while the **ACSC** provision was design to protect those areas "containing, or having significant impact upon, environmental, historical, natural or archaeological resources of regional or statewide importance" (Ch. 380, F.S.). These two provisions, and the accompanied law, known as the **Local Government Comprehensive Planning Act (1975)** (Ch. 163), were considered at the time as "far-reaching, progressive, even radical" pieces of legislation in trying "to address the issue of balancing of the environment with the needs to accommodate growth in a responsible way" (DeGrove and Miness, 1992:9).

The **Local Government Comprehensive Planning Act of 1975 (LGCPA),** as the second piece of planning legislation, was designed to foster regional planning cooperation. In 1972 the legislature set up a study group, known as the Environmental Land Management Study **[ELMS1]** Committee, to mitigate local land use problems created by the DRIs. In 1974 only half of the counties and less than a dozen cities had development regulations or comprehensive plans. Whereas earlier legislation **permitted** counties or local governments to prepare comprehensive plans, the **ELMS1** drafted a bill that would **require** counties and cities to adopt one and, "once doing so, no zoning ordinance could be in conflict with the plan and no development that was in conflict with the plan could be approved, *even if it met other Development of Regional Impact criteria*." In addition, there were provisions requiring that development would pay its own way and that such developmental projects could not outpace or exceed the "carrying capacity" of the natural environment (Catlin, 1997:58). This piece of legislation had hoped to "radically" reorder the partnership between the state and its local governments by requiring local governments to prepare and submit "procedural [not substantive] standards" to the state and regional planning bodies for review (DeGrove and Turner, 1991:227).

From its inception, local parochialism caused flaws within the legislation: **First,** there were no funds provided by the legislature, creating a financial burden for small towns. Obviously rural towns met this mandate with little enthusiasm. **Second,** the legislature failed to give specific guidelines for the state comprehensive plan. The document became a compilation of broadly defined goals, objectives and policies, which the state legislature was "simply unable or unwilling" to evaluate. Instead of approving the plan as official state policy, as provided by the original state statute, the legislature amended the statute, making the plan an "advisory" document, thereby substantially "weakening" its effect (Pelham, 1979:156). **Third,** the legislation had no state regulatory teeth. The state agency could not enforce its powers to assure local compliance. Whenever a local plan came into conflict, the local government either ignored the state's advice or amended its own comprehensive plan to fit its local developmental needs (deHaven-Smith, 1991:324). It was planning by default.

The regional planning bodies and the Florida DCA used the "backdoor" approach to regulate land use. That is, Florida DCA tried to exert control by the **permitting process.** This caused greater tensions between the regional planning agencies and the local political leaders, who felt a lack of local policy control. Moreover, most development permits contained conditional uses that were not appropriate to local circumstances within rural areas, causing greater anxiety at the local level (DeGrove, 1984:131-153; Pelham, 1979: Ch.5).

Phase Two—Strong Thumbs and Strong Fingers

In 1982, Rubin Askew's successor, Governor Bob Graham attempted to exert greater executive leadership over the state's growth management policy scheme. He called for a second Environmental Land Management Study [ELMS 2] committee to review the Environmental Land and Water Management Act (Ch. 380, F.S.) and all related growth management programs. The **ELMS 2** committee findings were mixed. For developers, there was fear that all economic growth would come to a screeching halt were unfounded. Anti sprawl advocates who expected new laws "to solve every aspect of Florida's environmental and growth problems" were equally disappointed (DeGrove, 1984:121). Rather the ELMS2 report found that this early initiative lacked funding, coordination, and consistent standards to accomplish specific state goals and objectives. The ELMS2 group urged the adoption of a new law, known as *The County and Municipal and Land Development Regulation Act of 1985*, often referred to as *The 1985 Growth Management Act* **(GMA).**

As a "top-down" policy management approach, **The 1985 Growth Management Act** provided additional authority to Florida's DCA and the Regional Planning Councils (RPCs). More important, it stressed the willingness of a state legislature to intervene into local planning matters. The state comprehensive planning activities (Chapter 187), as an integrated part of the local planning process, were placed principally in the hands of the governor's Department of Community Affairs, violating a century-old custom of shared executive power. This Act required all 67 counties and their municipalities to prepare "functional" land management plans in specific areas ranging from health to transportation that are consistent with the state plan's goals and policies.

Unlike the 1970s series of policy plans, this time the legislature appropriated funds to assist local governments in their comprehensive planning endeavors. A three-prong growth management approach is at the heart of this new growth management system. Firstly, **The State Comprehensive Planning Act (1985)** requires all state agencies to develop a set of *Functional Policy Plans* which distinguishes the infrastructure needs for that particular agency. Next, under the *consistency clause*, the state's **Growth Management Act (1985)** required all 392 municipalities and 67 counties to submit a comprehensive plan to the Department of Community Affairs [DCA] which would review their local land use plans to see that they are consistent with state's comprehensive plan. Further, each local municipality must indicate how its respective land use development activity corresponds to the development objectives of each of their respective neighbors within the region. Therefore, the **consistency** requirement meant that a city's local plan must devise design standards that are "compatible with those of neighboring governments (horizontal consistency) and with regional and state plan goals and policies (vertical consistency)." (DeGrove and Turner, 1991:228).

On the other hand, the **concurrency** requirement is the more demanding aspect of the new law. **Rule 9J5** called for government to establish adequate levels of public service delivery in six specific areas. No longer would growth be by installment. Deficit spending for public services would not be tolerated at the local level. Instead, DCA's administrative **Rule 9J5** meant that each county and city was expected to come to terms with how it would pay for its public services. Indirectly, **Rule 9J5** was another "backdoor" approach to regional planning. It required all cities to take capital facilities planning seriously. No longer could a city simply draw-up a **wish list of projects** to meet development needs. Now a city must specify "the timing and resources needed to assure that programmed facilities were activated" (DeGrove and Turner, 1991:229). Finally, under this new system, each county and city must submit a *Fiscal Policy Plan* to comply with **Rule 9J5** to the Florida Department of Community Affairs (DCA). This fiscal policy plan would give details as to how the community was going to pay for existing and future infrastructure development (DeGrove and Metzger, 1993).

If a municipality approved a development project but lacked adequate thresholds levels for public services (i.e. road network, fire or police protection, recreational space and activities, utilities, schools, etc.), the Florida Department of Community Affairs could impose a development moratorium on the community. In many respects, **The Growth Management Act (1985)** has become known as the *Pay As You Go Act* because of this fiscal policy provision. It was designed to give both the state and localities viable planning options. In many respects, the state legislature formulated a middle ground compromise between the two political camps—the 'no growth' versus the 'unbridled growth'—within the state. Many local officials perceive the **1985 Act** be a direct attack on the sacred cow of home rule. Or, as William Fulton writes, "in a nation where land use decisions form the basis for home rule, the top-down orientation of Florida's law constitutes nothing less than revolution" (*Governing*, 1990: 70).

Phase Three—Weak Thumbs and Strong Fingers

On February 17, 1992, Governor Lawton Chiles sent a letter to the Senate President and the House Speaker urging them to reject any efforts to "undermine the integrity" of Florida's growth management program. He hoped that they would not "back off" the state's commitment to protect Florida's "precious natural resources" and her "taxpayers from the costly financial burdens of unbridled growth." He then invited them to participate in a third Environmental Land Management Study [ELMS3] group (*Florida Planning*, March, 1992:1).

By 1992, Florida, which depended for more than 50 percent of its state revenues on consumption taxes, faced an economic recession and budgetary shortfalls at the state level. Governor Chiles, finding his state facing the same economic problems as other Sunbelt states, had hoped to defuse growing efforts to dismantle the state's growth management policy plan. By September 1992, all but three of Florida's local governments had submitted plans. Among the 455 submitted plans, two comprehensive plans were still under review and 184 were found in compliance. Of the remaining 269 plans not initially found in compliance, 136 were brought in compliance through negotiated settlement and 65 other communities would be in compliance under a mutual compliance agreement. Of the remaining 68 local governments, under the Florida Administrative Procedure Act (FS 163.3213), each could have requested an adjudication hearing (Pelham, 1993: 109). Overall, most noncompliance issues had been tied to Chapter 9J-5 F.A.C. standards, causing considerable tension between DCA and the local entities. Although early state adjudicatory hearings upheld the DCA's role in the growth management planning process, there had been limitations placed on its authority. With economic downturns looming, pro-growth special interest saw DCA's vulnerability and pushed for reforms.

ELMS3 had a decidedly pro-development focus, with only two professional planners—V. Gail Easley and Richard C. Bernhardt—were members. Even with Dr. John DeGrove and the Executive Director of the 1000 Friends of Florida as stakeholder members, the majority of 174 recommendations were essentially a blueprint for economic development. The main thrust of the study was phasing out DRIs, downgrading the role of the regional planning councils, and returning planning back to the county courthouse (Catlin, 1997:223-225). The state legislature quickly adopted these provisions into **The Planning and Growth Management Act (1993),** and thereby, changing the landscape of public planning, weakening state and regional planning efforts. It was essentially a return to local parochial planning.

New Laws, New Guidelines

The new law required the phasing out of the DRI process and the installation of additional requirements under the Intergovernmental Coordination Element (ICE). In March 1994, the Florida legislature stipulated that local governments must submit under broad guidelines on a rolling schedule any project that has adverse impact on surrounding jurisdictions to the Department of Community Affairs. Under the guidelines, each local government must identify large-scale projects within their respective jurisdictions and must determine whether such a project is incompatible with the policies and objectives of their comprehensive plan. In addition, The State Comprehensive Plan will be considered the minimum threshold criteria of acceptability for a particular development project. Under the guidelines, there are several apparent weaknesses. **Firstly**, communities had a deadline of FY 1999 for compliance. **Secondly,** the local government is not required to initiate inter-jurisdictional coordination to mitigate potential impacts. **Thirdly**, since it is the responsibility of the local government to initiate the review process, the regional planning bodies and Florida DCA have advisory roles at best. **Fourthly**, the performance impact standards tend to vary widely, with each local jurisdiction devising decision rules to determine if the development proposal would have significant impact of resources, facilities, or other community characteristics identified within the ICEs, suggesting a return to local parochial planning. In many respects, the DRI process originally initiated in the early 1970s has been eviscerated.

This chapter has illustrated the seesaw relationship that exists in attempting to balance the needs for environmental protection with the needs for local economic development. The 1993 legislation represented a retreat from the "top-down" style of planning. The return of "Traditional-Individualism" into the planning process meant a retreat from Smart Growth. The legislative presumption is that local county and city government has matured and no longer needs state oversight. With the "phasing out" of DRI's, even the somewhat independent Watershed Districts no longer have say in the overall impact that a particularly large development may have within a county.

Under the 1993 state guidelines, both the state and the regional planning councils became advisory agencies. Concurrency under **Rule 9J5** remained, but with local governments establishing service-level standards. This weakening of **Rule 9J5** oversight meant a return to **local parochial planning.** There are no guidelines for design standards. Instead, each community can interpret its own standards, **ignoring consistency design standards, a linchpin of Smart Growth.** As former Lee County Growth Management Director Bill Spikowski remarks, "If such evasion of concurrency were permitted, of course the purpose of concurrency would be defeated." Yet, so long as concurrency is seen as a punishment, Spikowski believes that local official resistance is inevitable. Too many towns are "not willing to damage their economies by stopping development in response to facility deficiencies" (*Florida Planning*, August, 1992:4). The 1995 amendment modified the administrative land use rule making allowing local governments to determine the peak load transportation requirements within built-up areas (Ewing, 1999).

The Locational Lottery into the New Millennium

In 1985 the bipartisan legislature and Democratic Governor Chiles had high hopes that top-down planning would tame Florida's sprawl. In 15 years the demographics of sprawl appeared to have tamed the growth management program, with the latest census detailing the fact that 6.8 million Floridians, or half the state's population resided beyond the boundaries of the local municipalities. The changing demographics and population dispersal are continually redefining the stakeholders on Main Street and at the county courthouse. For instance, Latinos now comprise 17% of the state's population, overtaking the African-American community (15%) as the largest minority population cohort. Of all the regions, Southeast Florida is the most multi-cultural. Just a jet flight away from most Latin American and Caribbean nations, it has long been the state's immigrant haven, with its tourist industry attracting entry-level employment. According to Thomas Boswell, a University of Miami demographer, South Florida grew by 23 per cent or one million folks. A majority of these newcomers were either Latinos or Caribbean Blacks, fleeing the economic and political instability of their own nations. Today, Miami-Dade politics is no longer the politics of Cubans, African-Americans and ethnic Jews. It is quite diverse. In Fact, non-Cuban has reached parity in numbers with Cubans, with even Little Havana no longer a Cuban political stronghold. Or as Jose Largos, a Honduran-American political activist has proudly remarked, "you find us [Hondurans] living in Little Havana, or opening businesses on Biscayne Boulevard in downtown Miami. You find us picking tomatoes in Homestead and doing construction in Fort Lauderdale ("How we've changed," *The Miami Herald*, March 28, 2001; "Many lands give Florida its Latin Flavor," *The Miami Herald*, July 25, 2001). Fom Key West to the Georgia Border, Latinos are spreading beyond the familiar barrios of Jacksonville, Miami and Tampa. Since 1990, the Latino population has grown by 70 percent, and with this population growth the Latino community has gained political clout (Ch. 4; "Hispanics fuel state growth," *The Miami Herald*, March 28, 2001).

With cultural diversity minority home ownership has increased. Statewide, 70 percent of Florida home owners live in homes they own. Typically ownership rates among non-Hispanic white householders have been higher than for minorities. The 2000 Census has noted that sprawl has benefitted minority families, who have obtained homes in many of the formerly aging, white inner-suburban communities of Tampa, Jacksonville and South Florida. Statewide, 50 percent of African-Americans reside in homes they own, as compared to 60 percent of Asian and 56 percent of Latinos ("In past decade, more of us owned homes," *The St Peterburg Times*, July 25, 2001; "More Blacks, Hispanics opt to own their own bode," *The Miami Herald*, July 25, 2001; "First Coast family incomes boom," *The Florida Times-Union*, May 24, 2002). Home ownership tends to vary among counties, principally correlated to population growth rates and income levels. In most cases, minority homeowners share a few common attributes. Many are first time home buyers, who are two-income families, and were able to finance their homes through federally-sponsored home subsidy programs. Partly due to "aging in place" of existing white non-Hispanic population, minority home owners have been taking advantage of adequate, above standard housing upon the death of a non-Hispanic white homeowner within these inner-suburban ring communities. Or as South Florida regional planner Dick Ogburn claims, Latino and Black middle-class families are simply replacing non-Hispanic white households, and getting good buys in good neighborhoods ("Loss of White households a stark contrast to South Florida's growth," *The Miami Herald*, March 29, 2001; Bricknell area bursting at the seams," *The Miami Herald*, April 25, 2001; "Citrus ownership stays high," *The St. Peterburg Times*, July 25, 2001). As an indicator of community stability and commitment, middle-class Latinos and African-Americans home ownership does imply a possible policy shift. No doubt, like white home owners, minority home owners are concern with similar issues— property taxes, public service levels and other quality of life issues, making it difficult for Tallahassee lawmakers to neatly package all minority concerns into one basket.

Sprawl has turned Floridians' strangers, with one's lifestyle centered on the automobile—living in one place, commuting to another, and shopping at a third place. Overall Florida has benefitted by the new technology, with the state's personal per capita income at $27,836 for FY 2000, ranking 21st nationally (*Governing Sourcebook*, 2002). However, this can be quite misleading because there are disparities of wealth present from town to town, county to county, with a community's diversity index tied to race, income and home ownership. Sprawl can partially explain for this disparity. Palm Beach County, with a median family household income of $45,062, is a case in point. The Glades, a set of farming communities located on the shores of Lake Okeechobee, has one in four family households residing in poverty, or 37.9 per cent of the population in the towns of Belle Glades, South Bay and Pahokee. By contrast, the towns of Manalapan, Gulf Stream and Palm Beach, along the Atlantic Coast, are the state's third-, sixth-, and seventh-richest communities, with one of every 20 local homeowners being millionaires ("Gap widens between the haves and have-nots," *The Palm Beach Post*, June 4, 2002). Bonita Springs is another example of the blessing of leapfrog development. Located about 30 minutes south of Fort Myers near I-75, it was an unincorporated agricultural, fishing village. In the 1980s, long time resident Ben Nelson describes Bonita Springs as a place with a few unremarkable restaurants and stores. He states, "When you said you were from Bonita Springs, they thought you were barefoot and had a piece of hay in your mouth and you smelled like fish." When the Dairy Queen was built, we thought "we were blessed." Today at the Mediterra, a gated community, you can purchase your 3500 square foot villa from $700,000 to $1.5 million, and pay $7,900 annual green fees at the development's golf course. Or, you can eat at Roy Yamaguchi's signature restaurant, located in the Promenade shopping plaza, where a meal entre begins at $25 and a salad at $9.50, with free hot dogs for your kids. Bonita Springs has not done much for the 17 percent of its Hispanic residents, who remained after the tomato fields were converted into upscale housing and shopping centers. Most cut the lawns, tend the golf courses, wash the dishes in the restaurants or stock the shelves at the local Publix or Albertson grocery store. Adequate housing is an issue, with most Latinos consigned to the older parts of the city, crowded into "30-year-old homes with as many as 10 to 15 people" to a dwelling unit or is squeezed into "old recreation vehicles with little more space than a walk-in closet at Mediterra." And, for many of Bonita Spring's original white homeowners, taxes and house prices simply forced them to move beyond Bonita Springs, commuting to their places of business (T.C. Tobin, "Liven' Large," *The St. Peterburg Times*, June 2, 2002).

For most newcomers urban Florida is no longer attractive. Most indicate sprawl to be the issue. As noted (Ch. 3; Ch. 4), a majority of non-Hispanic white households hail from the Midwest or the Northeast, with most fleeing the auto-dependent congestion of both areas. Less likely to be tied down by a job or a young child, they may have second thoughts about residing in a highly congested urban area. Or, as someone hits the 50-year-old mark, he or she may have second thoughts of remaining in the congested areas of Tampa Bay, South Florida, Jacksonville or Orlando. For an older person, "the density and intensity" of local traffic presents a lot of challenges, making such urban areas less inviting to remain. No wonder, former retirement hot-spots like Hollywood have fallen in disfavor by the 65-74 age cohort, while young families see them as good buys, with paid up schools and urban services ("Retirees less common in long time havens," *The Miami Herald*, May 23, 2001). Nationally, the average middle-class commuter spends 500 hours per year in h/her automobile, or equivalent of 12 work weeks (Duany, et. al. 2000:124). In Florida, in the past decade, the average commute has risen for its metro areas from 41.8 minutes per day to 43.6 minutes. USF's Center for urban Transportation Research Director Steve Polzin claims that this is a very drastic jump, because most people are basically "intolerant of spending more than twenty minutes traveling" each way to work ("Getting to work takes much longer," *The St. Petersburg Times*, August 6, 2001). Yet, congestion is not simply tied to commuter-work traffic. In fact, 80 percent of traffic is generated by social or shopping trips (Ewing, 1996; 1999). No doubt, if given the opportunity, the homeowner will vote with his or her feet. Or as regional planner Dick Ogburn explains, the home owner with few ties may simply say, "I had it. I'm going to Lee County. I'm going to Fort Myers or Naples." Or, even out of the state, as one Miami-Dade resident had voiced ("Loss of Whites a stark contrast to South Florida's growth," *The Miami Herald*, March 29, 2001).

Throughout Florida's landscape there are similar scenes of former sleepy towns being inundated by well-to-do Yankees, seeking housing to escape the congestion of Florida's urban areas. Even Clearwater which has boasted for the last three decades as Florida's chief retirement haven, has become a bit younger because many transplanted retirees have relocated. Many "second-move" retirees, who are defined for being already retired to Florida, no longer wish to "age-in-place" in places like Fort Lauderdale, Clearwater or St. Petersburg. Now they are simply seeking smaller communities, as places that are free from the "traffic and crowds, and get more for their money." With relatively low interest rates, such places as unincorporated East Lake, Pinellas County or Crystal River, Citrus County or Spring Hill, Hernando County are fast becoming Tampa Bay's new middle-class retirement enclaves ("Way of life in Citrus a matter of opinion," *The St. Peterburg Times*, April 23, 2000; "Citrus ownership high," *The St. Petersburg Times*, July 25, 2001; "Census shows a wealthier north county," *The St Petersburg Times*, June 2, 2002; "Home buyer in Hernando has it best," *The St. Petersburg Times*, June 3, 2002). In every corner of Florida, with low interest rates, baby boomers are taking advantage of housing choices. You can drive through any Pinellas beach community and see late 1970's three bedroom houses, which cost about $80,000 newly built, priced at $400,000. In Tierra Verde, an unincorporated beach community near St. Petersburg, nearly 20 per cent of the households earn $150,000 and up, and can easily afford such prices ("Tierra Verde has the highest percentage of wealthy folks," *The St. Petersburg Times*, June 2, 2002). Nor is the First Coast immune from leapfrog development. Homeowners in Palm Valley and Pointe Vedra Beach, a stone's throw from the City of Jacksonville, typically earn almost $88,000, helping to drive St. Johns County incomes up 73 percent over the past decade. A nationally ranked golf course, the Mayo Clinic and nearby state and federal wildlife management areas that stretches the length of State Highway A1A to St. Augustine has made the area quite attractive, with nearly 8000 local families earning above $150,000. A former Pointe Vedra Lakes duplex, near the intra coastal waterway, that sold for the high-eighties in 1987, now goes for $250,00 to $300,000. St. Johns County is ranked the highest median family household income in the state at $50,099 ("Gap between haves and have-not widens," *The Palm Beach Post*, June 4, 2002; "First Coast family incomes boom," *The Florida Times Union*, May 22, 2002). Leapfrog development and inflationary housing has nothing to do with a town's economic opportunities or the overall quality of its homes, rather it has to do with the home's location.

Sprawl has its benefits. It does maximize the choice for the home buyer by creating competition in the marketplace. The free market allows for leapfrogging, which assures a greater range of housing prices for different locations and different housing types. At the same time, it allows the land owner to make a profit from the sale of potential developmental value (Utt and Shaw, 2000). The problem of sprawl is how these land use choices are made, which are often in isolation by individuals and local governments on a case by case basis, without having a complete understanding or accounting of the fiscal and social implications of such land use decisions.

Jeb Bush and the New Millennium

At the end of the 20th Century the Republicans controlled the governorship and the legislature. The Wise Use Movement was making its way East from the Sagebrush Rebellion West. In 2000, the state's population had grown to nearly 16 million, a 41 per cent jump since the adoption of the 1985 Growth Management Act. With term limits forcing 62 lawmakers out of office, many legislators were quite willing to take on the controversial issue of growth management. In the final weeks of the session, the 1985 Growth Management Act and other environmental initiatives came under assault. Developers, business lobbyists and private property rights groups, who all had substantially contributed to GOP legislators, saw an opportunity to dismantle the state growth management process (J. Saunders, "Growth debate has lawmakers pressured," *The Florida Times Union*, April 20, 2000).

One of their key targets was the Florida DCA, which they felt often acted heavy handed with its **One Twenty Rule**. In 1989, the Florida DCA issued a technical memo outlining indicators for sprawl. This technical memo was considered by many simply to be a strategy to shift the comprehensive planning process from a bottom-up (local) initiative to that of a top-down (state) one. Within a year, the Florida DCA signaled an unwritten decision rule that was known among planning circles as the **One Twenty Rule**. This rule implied that any local comprehensive plan that established land use development activities which accommodated more than 120 per cent of the projected population for the jurisdiction, the comprehensive plan would be held in a moratorium. Although the rule was perceived to be a rational response by some (environmentalists, preservationists and regional planners), it was considered to be an unjust and unreasonable response by others (developers and land owners). Moreover, for local government officials, this rule was looked upon as an indirect assault on home rule and the spirit of "localized" planning within the 1985 Growth Management Act, making the Florida DCA the principal target.

Governor Jeb Bush, as a former land developer, saw an opportunity intervene and put his own stamp on growth management. He proposed the creation of a Blue Ribbon Panel to study sprawl (Executive Order 2000-16), and named Mel Martinez, who was then Orange County Commissioner, as its Chairman. The Growth Management Study Commission was a mixture of state and local governmental officials, developers, lawyers, citizen planners and one environmentalist. Jacksonville City councilwoman Alberta Hipps set the tone of the commission' s inquiry by declaring that the study commission's mission would not merely rehash the traditional sprawl battle between environmentalists and developers. Instead, it would be devising a workable solution by placing sprawl in its context for the next century. Chairman Martinez, who is now the U.S. Secretary of Housing and Urban Development, warned the public that, "if we weren't careful enough, no one will want to live here." ("State growth plan needs attention, official says," *The Florida Times Union*, August 10, 2000). The Commission held 9 regional meetings and conducted citizen surveys for the next six months. The product was a report to the 2001 state legislature entitled *A Liveable Florida for Today and Tomorrow*, giving Governor Bush and the legislature 89 recommendations that ought to tame sprawl.

Although aspects of the study are reported in Chapter 12, the politics of growth management and property ownership were key concerns within the study. For instance, the report noted that the 1985 Growth Management Act had succeeded in getting all 472 local governments to adopt a comprehensive plan. But the state's approach was often heavy handed, relying on threats of "litigation" when confronted by property rights disputes. As a consequence of these disputes, there were feelings of state encroachment on private property, often creating deficiencies in the management of comprehensive planning. The most glaring was a neglect by most county and local governments to establish a "good linkage" strategy between future infrastructure planning and the local budgeting process, causing the present infrastructure backlog (*A Liveable Florida for Today and Tomorrow*, February 2001). To alleviate future conflicts and deficiencies within the comprehensive planning process, the Growth Management Study Commission recommended a streamlining of the process, with less attention given to regulation of impacts for land development activities and more attention given to the analysis of the costs of such land project activities. For a majority of commission members, the best strategy was a modification and revamping of the roles of both Florida DCA and the 11 Regional Planning. First, the Bush study commission called for the Florida DCA to stop acting like a policeman and become a technical advisor. Second, the Bush study commission urged that the regional planning councils be given a greater role in the realms of local technical assistance, coordination and dispute resolution (pp. 31-39). By doing so, the Growth Management Study Commission felt that fewer project disputes will arise and a seamless planning management process will emerge between the state and it localities. Of course, the most controversial set of recommendation was tied to the concept of "full a cost accounting" of public services, which requires local governments to undertake fiscal impact analysis as a means of denying a proposed land development (pp. 20-21), with critics claiming that this was a shifting of responsibility onto local government from the developer. Like all blue ribbon commissions, a majority of these recommendations are a compromise, reflecting the political landscape of Florida. Critics felt that the study commission intention was to dismantle the top-down Planning style by greater limiting the role of Florida's DCA. On the other hand, the proponents of Growth Management Study Commission claim that the recommendations recognized the important role being played the 11 regional planning councils and local governments. In fact, critics believe that most recommendations will place land use planning back in its proper perspective, recognizing the importance of home rule in the realm of land development and infrastructure planning.

Concluding Remarks

Overall, the Jeb Bush growth management study suggested that planning authority should be shifted back to the localities, believing that after 15 years of top-down growth management local jurisdictions have the planning management capabilities. Our research would question this assumption. Cablin (1997) in his analysis of the status of Florida's comprehensive planning tends to agree. Indeed, he found that there is no indication that the comprehensive planning process will be consistent among local communities, especially among rural communities. But, the mood of local officials is the belief that local parochialism can do a better job. Many taxpayers tend to agree. The Florida DCA growth management poll discovered that 90 per cent of Floridians residing in or near a city are not happy with sprawl related issues. Although few felt that any level of government was overly effective in dealing with sprawl, at least at the local level, a majority felt their opinions on sprawl are heard and respected (www. dca.state.fla.us/fdcp/DCP.). This poll, although skewed to those who are financially better off and likely to be newcomers, does suggest that there is a shifting mood among Florida's residents. If this poll is any indication, the mood seems to favor the Traditional-Individualistic perspective in combating sprawl, namely from the bottom-up. How well local governments can resist the pressures of local developers' remains to be seen. If the proposals of the Jeb Bush growth management commission are adopted, Florida's grand experiment will likely see another contentious phase in the land development process. This time the debate will be over not who will pay for growth, but how it is to be paid.

Chapter 6
ಸಂಖ್ಯೆ
Civic Engagement and Governance

Even with the persistence of poverty, most people see rural, small town America as part of the American Dream the place they would like to reside. A key attraction for this American Dream sentiment is its spirit of place. It is the reminder of a simpler time; a place where everyone has an equal opportunity to succeed and to have a voice on how public policy is made. It is a place where Jeffersonian democracy works best.

Civic Commitment and Postwar Sprawl

From New York to California and from Maine to Florida, small towns on the urban-rural fringe are being redefined. In 1950 these towns were out of the daily reach of most Americans, accessible only by railroad or bus. Main Street was very much a lively documentation of America's past cultural life. A place of icons and sacred symbols of prefreeway American life—the corner drug store, the church steeple, the town hall, the village movie marque, the bakery, and the local bank—reminding us that Main Street represented a spirit of commitment and attachment (Kenyon, 1989; Hester, 1990; Brooks and Searcy, 1995). Main Street was always recognizable by the buildings that line it; where most were "rather elaborately detailed and formed, distinctive enough in style to command our attention and interest" (Francaviglia, 1996: 2).

Main Street's tenants were the civic volunteers who guided the town's civic institutions. Even into the mid-1960s, "hanging out" meant, to most teens, the town square, the drug store or the cafe. Main Street was still the linchpin that facilitated local attachment, connecting the town's citizens to the community's social and economic civic leadership. By the 1970s, the new superhighways with their bypass commercial shopping strips began to siphon the vitality of Main Street. By then, "hanging out" meant a climate controlled strip mall, where impersonal, non-connected chain stores undercut Main Street's merchants (Lamb, 1985; Moon, 1989; Moe and Wilkie, 1997). Slowly small town residents began to disconnect from their Main Street, their merchants and their social institutions (Davidson, 1980; Kenyon, 1989; Powers, 1991; Brooks and Searcy, 1995).

Building a Civil Community

Modern technology (transportation and communication) has altered the psyche of the small town resident. The automobile, the interstate and the computer all have encouraged professionals to flee the crime and grime of the "big city" and to resettle in small town America. As "newcomers," they rarely have an emotional attachment to the churches, social clubs and business establishments that make up the basic social fabric of any community. Too often they relocate on the town's fringes, in newly formed, detached suburban developments or on scattered, two acre-hobby farms. Loyalty remains with the nearby city, where they commute to work and tend to play. The town's Main Street theater, clothing store or café is quaint, but cannot compete with the bistros, shops and theaters of the regional mall. Fewer than half attend church, political participate or join a social club within the community (Ladd, 1995; Verba. et. al.at, 1995; Lowry, 1964). Or, as Peter Drucker (1994) claims, "The old communities—family, village, parish and so on—have all but disappeared...." Instead, these "newcomers" see the community in a "non-territorial" perspective; it is a disconnected community based of a "community of common interest" (Freie, 1998; Fowler, 1991; Wilkinson, 1991). Simply put, the new comers are not joiners of the local community.

For many scholars, a disconnected community is bothersome. Without spatial boundaries that define a sense of place, citizens are likely to ignore their civic responsibilities, making small towns nothing more than any contemporary housing tract. A social connectedness is critical to inner workings of local democracy. As David Easton (1965: 185) wrote, the "we-feeling" or "sense of community" indicates "political cohesion of a group of persons, regardless of the kind of regime they have or may develop...." A sense of "belonging together as a group" means not only they share a common political structure, but more important, they share a common "political fate." Or as Bert Swanson (1970: 93-98) aptly points out, no community remains "viable for long without certain levels of political support and participation...." Our emphasis on personal career advancement and our "ingrained preference for a private life" allows "little patience, time or attention" to become involved and be "instrumental in community affairs, certainly as they involve the larger metropolitan region."

Spatially defined places provide the conditions for the "locus of opportunities" to assure civil society. The term civil society connotes "the idea of localism, both in reference to community and small-scale local associations." In such a civil community the bonds of personal attachment are likely to be fostered, assuring the willingness to sacrifice some of one's private interests on behalf of others (Eberly, 2000: 8). Time and again, scholars suggest that a spatial place emotionally bind citizens together and encourages a willingness to be civically engaged (Freie, 1998; Goodwin, 1995; Fowler, 1991; Wilkinson, 1991; Kemmis, 1990). One of those design elements that give individuals a sense of community is a **sacred symbol**. A sacred symbol such as an old woolen mill, the old post office, the former town library or the local swimming hole gives the town a civic cultural reference point. They provide the community with "symbolic spatial" reference points (Hester, 1990). By having a "symbolic" spatial map, a citizen is more likely to reconnect with h/her civic obligations and devise community boundaries, especially in times of social conflict or disruption. (Fitchen, 1991). The Founding Fathers understood this. When grappling with governance, the importance of "politics of local engagement" is critical in defining the town's spirit of place (Garnham, 1990). Or as Goodwin (1995: 71-89) reminds us, the cornerstone of civic engagement is the collective expression of "community sentiment". And, without the preservation of sacred symbols, it is difficult to have a rally point for acknowledging the local boundaries of a civil community. One hundred and seventy years ago, Alexis de Tocqueville (1945: Vol 1,p. 63) made a similar observation when he wrote: "A nation may establish a free government, but without municipal institutions it cannot have the spirit of liberty."

Small Towns, Political Culture and Civic Core Values

Political culture has been defined as a pattern of beliefs, attitudes and values manifested within a community's policy setting. It has been suggested that our political culture not only defines who we are but also who we were (Elazar, 1972; 1994; Kelley, 1979: 265-281). It provides us with a guidebook that articulates the parameters pertaining to how civic participation ought to operate within our American creed or American ethos (McClosky and Zaller, 1984; Verba, et. al. 1995).

A political culture should not be confused with political ideology which is designed to help simplify, organize and give meaning to an otherwise confusing policy environment. Ideology is very helpful within a society undergoing social change because it helps maintain a political community's self image (Lutz, 1992). Ideology is far from being a coherent and comprehensive set of beliefs. But, it does give a reference point for citizens for guidance within a changing society (Ball and Dagger, 1995). Three political functions of governance are performed by ideology. **First**, ideology provides a political community a set of beliefs, sentiments and preferences about how to govern. By doing so, a political ideology generates an ideal vision of the conditions under which human beings can truly fulfill themselves (Ingersoll and Mathews, 1986). **Second**, a political ideology will either support or oppose the existing political institutions of governance, placing social change in context. And **thirdly**, a political ideology justifies a course of action by its followers (Ingersoll and Mathews, 1986; Dolbeare and Medcalf, 1988; Ball and Dagger, 1995). From these three functional tasks, a worthy political ideology will establish some sort of framework to assure legitimacy for the community's sub-political culture (Lutz, 1992: 12). In short, ideology refers to a belief system that will "defend and justify one's present position" within a political community (Lowi, 1995: 20). To most students, ideology is associated with the "isms," such as Marxism, socialism, or conservatism. Rarely do ideologies have a consistent set of internal assumptions. As Ingersoll and Matthews (1986: 9) remark, "it can be argued that for purposes of attracting dedicated followers, inconsistency is desirable...."

Besides ideology, myth-making is equally important for shaping a community's civil core values. Myth-making gives a "philosophic meaning" to everyday life (Lutz, 1991: 154). Myths often evoke shared emotions, establish social cohesion and stimulate social consciousness. A myth does not argue its ideology; myth's exemplifies it. Myths provide an example of a heroic or virtuous situation to support an ideology. Yet, myths seem to work best "with sweeping generalizations encapsulated in slogans; or, in vivid legends which incorporate but rarely explicate" the reality of the situation (Roelofs, 1976: 42). No wonder the characters of legends or storylines, whether they are symbolic composite of stylized character attributes (John

Henry or Paul Bunyun) or of actual historic personages (George Washington or Harriet Taubman), seem to be larger than life (Smith, 1978; Nash, 1967; Moore, 1957). Thus, the purpose of myths is to represent a self-justifying civic core value system. Although myths may tend to idealize a society, they do not tell us how to get things done politically. This functional role is left to our political culture (Roelofs, 1976: 40).

Traditional-Individualism and the Civil Community

Unlike Europe, America was a vast wilderness. From the beginning, we saw ourselves as a very special kind of people, who resided in small towns, villages and hamlets. An ideological myth of the small town populated with rugged individualists was perpetuated and became part of our national political psyche. Indeed, it was Thomas Jefferson who claimed that the New England small town was the wisest invention perfected by man for the exercise of self-governance. Countless books, plays and movies have inculcated a set of civic core values that are closely associated to the pastoral identity of small town Traditional-Individualism.

Small town political culture is peculiarly American. Left on our own for most of our colonial history, small town politics is a practical political theory. That is, it is tied to aspects of the American Creed that espouses the beliefs of popular sovereignty, the sanctity of private ownership and equal economic opportunity (Kammen, 1986). With hundreds of years of self-governance, most small town Americans are suspicious of a centralized authority, and above all else, they desired "to be left alone in their relative equality, with the means to prosper and the right to shape their own moral and political worlds." (Shalhope, 1990: 46).

The American Creed has maintained its roots in **Jeffersonian Agrarianism**, under the guise of Traditional-Individualism. Based on our agrarian roots, Traditional-Individualism has three basic components—democracy among equals, local autonomy and the sanctity of private ownership. That is, each citizen is equal before the law and there is no inherited class privilege. Civil liberty means equal liberty; equal liberty means that everyone could aspire to any socioeconomic status. After the American Revolution a new level of optimism swept the nation. The everyday person—the seaman, the artisan or the laborer—had an equal opportunity to participate in the political process and to seek his own fortune.

Under Traditional-Individualism, the role of government was quite limited. Government's chief function was to assure that individual citizens can pursue their own economic interests with minimal government constraint and political participate if he chose to do so (Bowie and Simon, 1977; Stone, 1988). Known as the doctrine of **negative liberty** or **negative freedom**, this sentiment found wide acceptance. As Clinton Rossiter (1956: 113) declares:

> "In an age when breadwinning consumed all a man's time and energy, when travel was difficult and political parties non-existent, when government was severely limited in scope and touched many man not all, and when the pace of life was slower, political indifference—to elections, to office-holding and to issues—was well-nigh inevitable."

Negative freedom in this context puts forth "the proposition that human beings are free only when they are left alone to pursue whatever personal goals they wish irrespective of what that pursuit might imply for others" (Greenberg,1996: 3). And, this political perspective is very much alive in contemporary small town America (Lowry, 1964; Ladd, 1972; Bryan, 1981; Young, 1999).

Traditional-Individualism has nicely dovetailed with the social contract theories of Locke and Hobbes. Yet, Traditional-Individualism with its beliefs in self-reliance and self responsibility has allowed us to devise a uniquely American approach to British-Scottish Enlightenment governance, nurtured by our frontier experience (Potter, 1992; Turner, 1994). Dolbeare and Medcalf (1993: 13) write, "Probably no country in the world has had a deeper cultural commitment to individualism as the United States." The citizen by implication is completely responsible for h/her socio-economic standing. Apparently, one's "prestige and property" reflects one's "personal effort, character and achievement" (Dolbeare and Medcalf, 1993: 14). Obviously, this imposes a psychological burden upon every citizen, especially when a society makes "life a race" and tags contestants either winners or losers (Wilkinson, 1988: 77).

The Dimensions of Personal Freedom

The American style of individualism is a two-edged sword. We are in constant turmoil over the yearning to be part of a social community, and a desire to make commitments outside one's own family. But by doing so, we become equally fearful that we will sacrifice our personal identity and our personal freedom (Freie, 1988; Fowler, 1991). Rupert Wilkinson (1988) claims that this is the manifestation of the "fear of being owned." It is a fear of the "loss of our autonomous self" to the greater society. How does one reconcile the conflict between his own interests and the common good of the greater community? Apparently, the answer is to define personal liberty within the context of civic community.

Personal freedom or personal liberty rests upon four dimensions. The first dimension is the notion that each individual is intrinsically equal under God. As individuals, a crucial aspect of the social compact is that government has a political and moral obligation to protect the ideals of civil community and safeguard the natural liberties of human dignity (Harbour, 1982: Ch.4). The freedom to civically participate is the second dimension. Civic engagement allows each citizen an equal say in how h/she is to be govern (Eberly, 2000). Again, this second dimension implies that "all people possess equal worth and have the right to share in their own governance— to rule themselves either directly or through leaders of their own choosing. The ruled, in short, must consent to their rulers, who are in turn accountable to the govern." (McClosky and Zaller, 1984: 2). Tied to this idea of civic obligation is the notion that each individual should have the opportunity for self inquiry [freedom of thought] and self-expression [freedom of speech]. Each of us should have the opportunity to think and express our views without fear of retribution (Stone, 1988; Lutz, 1992; Boaz, 1997). Finally, personal freedom means that an individual can seek self-fulfillment, both materially as well as spiritually. Often referred to as the pursuit of happiness, this final dimension of personal liberty is undergirded by private property ownership and equality of opportunity. Interestingly, for planners this desire of freedom to pursue happiness tends to be the most controversial.

Sanctity of Property

Locke wrote that one of the chief aims of government is to assure the preservation of property. As Kammen (1986: 5) explains, liberty and property went hand and hand, "[to] deprive or deny one, and the other is instantly in jeopardy." For this reason, the federal Constitution contains certain institutional and procedural safeguards for private property. For the Framers, private property protection provided a bulwark for political independence. As noted, civic virtue will prevail only as long as the individual citizen feels secure that his participation will not invite retribution. Otherwise, loyalty can vanish. For this reason, the Founders set ground rules for governance under the rubric of common core values. One such core value is the sanctity of property. Private property ownership permits "a citizen to participate responsibly in the political process," for it allows him "to pursue spontaneously the common or the public good, rather than the narrow interest of the men or the government" upon whom he is obligated for his livelihood (McCoy, 1980: 68). Or as one social commentator has written, "Property rights are the border guards around an individual 's life that deter political invasions." (Bovard, 2000: 10). Yet, there is no inherent right to property; only the right to remove barriers that obstruct one's opportunity to seek and acquire property (West, 1997; Matthews, 1995).

For Traditional-Individualism private ownership is the cornerstone for political autonomy. James Madison noted that political factions often arise within the political community over the desire to acquire such property (Matthews, 1995: Ch.5). "Those who hold and those who are without property have ever formed distinct interests in society." (Federalist Papers, Number 10). For this reason, The Framers sought to remove the barriers to the acquisition and retention of private property by rejecting the feudal concepts of primogeniture, entail, and hereditary privileges. Moreover, The Framers sought to place a protective wall around the individual's personal property by limiting the scope and power of government confiscation (Ely, 1991). Overall, The Framers hoped to establish a socio-economic system that will permit everyone "to buy, sell and use his property without asking leave of government, a system that does away with legally mandated special privileges that have no reference to individual achievement." (West, 1997: 47). Our Democracy is based on a system of private property ownership. It reflects the rights and freedoms of individuals "to produce and to consume, to enter into contractual relations, to buy and sell through the market economy, to satisfy their wants in their own way, and to dispose of their own property and labor as they decide." (Macridis, 1989: 23).

Economic Opportunity, Pursuit of Happiness and Political Culture

Tocqueville wrote that Americans had a "passion for equality." Most Americans believe that each individual should have political equality and the opportunity to succeed according to his or her skills and talents, without regards to social rank or governmental intrusion (McClosky and Zaller, 1984). Freedom and equality became the twin pillars within the American social order. Unfortunately, it appears that these two civic core values are often in direct conflict, "so that one or the other must give priority. In other words, the more of one, the less of the other" (Dolbeare and Medcalf, 1993: 18).

For a majority of Americans, we accept the American Creed's beliefs in "equality before the law" or the "equality for economic opportunity" . However, most Americans are largely uninterested in promoting economic "equality of results." When defining economic opportunity, a substantial majority of Americans see it in terms of Traditional-Individualism. The pursuit of happiness simply means the ability to achieve success by limiting the constraints placed upon an individual's actions [negative liberty]. More specifically, it means "freedom from government's interference in one's personal liberty or economic activities" (Dolbeare and Medcalf, 1993: 19). It implies a wall between the actions of government and the actions of private citizens so that the national government will not become the tool of the well-connected, or the rich, who then can use their political influence "to gain special privileges for themselves and to mulct the less fortunate...." (McClosky and Zaller, 1984: 86).

The Micropolitan Policy Community

According to Tweeten and Brinkman (1976), a free standing micropolitan community is defined as a municipality that has specific trade area boundaries located outside the Metropolitan Statistical Area (MSA). Considered a "mini-urban node," such an town is often referred as a "free standing" city. Thus, a micropolitan community constitutes a spatially fixed socioeconomic unit that operates as a separate distinct trade area within the urban to rural continuum (Mayer and Hayes, 1983: 79). Located on the economic periphery, many of these non-metropolitan towns are struggling to avoid becoming ghost towns (Lyson and Falk, 1993).

The micropolitan community represents the collective behavior of personal liberty within the context of the Traditional-Individualism. As a political cultural model, Traditional-Individualistic community's political life is based on a "system of mutual obligations rooted in personal relationships" that places a premium "on limiting community intervention—whether governmental or non-governmental—into private activities" (Elazar, 1970: 260). This model does not oppose to policy innovation so long as such innovative policymaking does not disrupt the existing social order. At the local level, public officials are normally expected to play a custodial role in city hall by taking a back seat to informal policy plan making. Consequently, small towns tend to exhibit an informal and less bureaucratic form of governance (Hahn, 1970; Wolensky and Groves, 1977; Keller and Wamsley, 1978; Exoo, 1984; Kanervo, 1994; Young, 1999).

The notion of public policy-making as a pattern of governmental activity designed to accomplish specific community goals is a useful reference point. It suggests that public policy choices just do not happen. Instead, a deliberate course of action is undertaken. Policy choices become the consequences of purposive, goal oriented behavior (Anderson, et.al., 1984). Or, as Buchholz (1988: 5) claims, public policy making refers "to what governments actually do, not what they say they will do or intend to do with respect to some public problem." In this context, small town governance and policymaking does take place. But, political alignments are often tied to socioeconomic interests (Mills and Davis, 1963; Gamberg, 1968; Hahn, 1970). What constitutes legitimate government action reflects the underlying political culture within each civil community (Elazar, 1970: Ch. 7). Thus, a community's population size, diversity and density influence policy choices within the political cultural setting. Horizontal and vertical linkages, for instance, will serve as linkages that influence how well a community will respond, initiate and adopt innovative policy making (Young, 1999; Baker, 1994; McGuire, et. al. 1994; Kanervo, 1994; Perry and Kramer, 1979; Buck and Rath, 1970). The narrower the population base, the fewer the horizontal and vertical linkages are for a small town's policy domain, making it less likely there will be imaginative policy choices. Thus, a small town's population scale (demographic size and composition) is a limiting factor for innovative public policymaking.

Small town governments are "rickety structures" that tend to be cautious, parsimonious and fearful of internal social conflict (Lingeman, 1980; Hatch, 1979). Because of community scale [population density and composition], small towns lack partisan elections, actively diverse citizen participation groups and professionally trained staff, all necessary for innovative policy plan making. Moreover, in such a policy setting, civic engagement is informal and highly personalized. With few "goodies" and a limited "scope of authority," small town have difficulty in attracting a large, talented pool of office seekers. Those who do seek office, are either well meaning "civic minded" amateurs or individuals with self-serving ambitions. In either case, most local officials have other full time occupations (Wikstrom, 1993; Tauxe, 1993; Baker, 1994). With few rewards and little prestige, most small town politicians are elected on their personalities rather than on specific policy issues. Since local policy disagreements can linger for years, there is a strong desire to avoid controversy and social conflict within the community. Thus, small town public policy making tends to be by default (Mills and Davis, 1963; Gamberg, 1968; Hahn, 1970; Buck and Rath, 1970; Tauxe, 1993).

Policy Implications

A community's political culture not only defines the vision of the community but also places that vision within a socio-political context. It provides a guidebook that gives the planner explicit instructions pertaining to what policy choices are likely to be implemented. A distinct political culture is deeply ingrained into the ethos of every community; it is expressed in the daily thinking and activity of the community's civic life. In effect, a community's civic cultural system is a framework for governance. It establishes the parameters by which local officials decide "who gets what in the way of protection of life, rights and property" and it influences how citizens organize themselves to obtain these goodies (Elazar, 1970: 257). In short, a community's political culture defines "what politics is and what we expect from government" (Elazar, 1972: 112).

The Traditional-Individualistic political cultural tendencies of small towns are derived from our frontier, Jeffersonian agrarian experience. It not only holds certain civic core values sacred: sanctity of property, negative liberty, economic opportunity and civic responsibility. Moreover, Traditional-Individualism plays a role in local policy adoption and implementation. Equally important, Traditional-Individualism is spatially grounded to non-pluralistic communities, suggesting that its civic core sentiment is critical component to a small town's land use management policies (See Ch. 7).

Chapter 7
Small Town Planning in Florida

Since the development of growth management strategies, the functional roles of community planning have been in transition. Planners are no longer simply viewed as technical problem-solvers who prepare long-range, single purpose master plans (Vasu, 1979; Alexander, 1992). Instead, Florida's growth management policies have carved a broader role which requires the possession of skills and competencies that are beyond those of a zoning "arbitrator" or subdivision "map maker." At the community level, where most planning decisions are made, policy-making is a matter of persuasion and influence. It is said to be a process for the translation of public needs and desires into public policy. In this chapter we will look at small town planning in rural Florida and how traditional-individualism hinders the planning innovation that is expected by the "top-down" approach of the state's growth management initiative.

Three Tasks of Small Town Planning

Politics plays a prominent role in contemporary planning. Few contemporary planners deny that most planning is local and quite political (Vasu, 1979; Catanese, 1974, 1984; Lucy, 1988; Benveniste, 1989; Forester, 1989). Politics is nothing more than "who gets what, when and how." However, Easton (1965: 21) provides a more encompassing definition by claiming that politics is "those interactions through which values are authoritatively allocated for society; this is what distinguishes a political system from other systems that may be interpreted as lying in its environment." Accordingly, politics is the byproduct of competing demands within the local policy environment; and, as part of that struggle, politics legitimizes the "authoritative allocation of values". Planning becomes political because of its outputs. Outputs (budget allocations, zoning changes or park site selections) are considered rewards given out for the purpose of resolving the conflicting demands among the competing "game players." Or as the Wheaton's (1970: 155) have observed, "Politics as the means for identification and allocation of the non-measurable, non-marketable goods has always been an acute concern of planners."

Within urban policy settings there are a variety of stakes and rewards that give incentives for policy participation. The local plan-making process attracts a multitude of "game players" who wish to participate in determining the "authoritative allocation of values" and scarce resources (Johnson, 1989). In contrast, in small towns, many stakes and rewards are held by the planner, who is the principal allocator for the distribution of the few "goodies" (Rabinovitz, 1969; Catanese, 1974; Rondinelli, 1975; Rudel, 1989). By virtue of his professional skills and credentials the small town planner is a principal game player. He is not only expected to formulate and recommend policy plans, but also is expected to establish the decision rules by which the goals and objectives of the policy plan are achieved (Lucy, 1988; Klosterman, 1980; Catanese, 1974). Unlike the rational economic man, the community planner must be normative, willing to adjust decisional policies to a changing political environment. Since any policy plan involves the allocation of scarce resources, the planner becomes the designated resource allocator, whether it is the location of a water and sewer line extension or the approval of the construction of a shopping center.

Although most public agencies' scope and power are limited by law, a planner is cognizant that a planning agency's prestige and power are dependent upon its ability to complete the tasks assigned by the community. The planner, like the town engineer or the town attorney, is assigned tasks that tend to be unique and exclusive. However, it is the community that ranks, evaluates, and rewards the planner's performance. If the planner performs his tasks well, he will achieve greater prestige, authority, and influence; but, if he fails in his delegated tasks, then his power and prestige will most likely diminish in the court of public opinion (Smith, 1991; Forester, 1989; Catanese, 1974; Ranney, 1969).

Planners as Administrative Rule-Makers

Similar to other public bureaucrats, beyond statutory legitimacy, planners have at least two other sources of political influence at his or her disposal. Formal authority based on a state statute does not ensure effective policy implementation. A small town planning agency is a publicly funded organization, with an administrative structure that allows its staff to adopt administrative rule making. Administrative rule making (decision-rules) is the second source of formal power a town planner possesses. Decision rules are a manifestation of administrative routine tasks and/or procedures which allow a public agency "to codify the repetitive decisions" as a means of dealing with recurring situations encountered by the agency (Jones, et.al., 1980; Sharp, 1986). The underlying normative assumption is that decision rules help the public agency perform its resource allocation tasks in a fair, predictable and just manner. There are essentially two types of decision rules.

Program task rules and/or **demand processing rules** comprise the first categorical type of decision rule making. These are internal administrative procedures to promote administrative efficiency by providing low level staff with a consistent set of standard operating procedures, known as SOPs. Within planning agencies, the enforcement of zoning standards or building codes would fall under this category. Program task rules are important because they aid the agency in establishing a consistent set of implementation procedures and standards when responding to citizen needs. Demand processing rules are designed to structure the flow of information within an organization and to maintain organizational boundaries (Mattson, et. al. 1993). Combined, both sets of rules should assure that administrative rule-making is carried out in a non-biased manner.

Policy performance rules are the second category of administrative decision rules. These rules are designed to establish equity and program performance standards for the purpose of measuring the actual delivery of such public services. Policy performance rules help standardize budgetary allocations based on the goals and objectives. Such rules are devised to assure the program objectives are being achieved as intended (Jones, et.al. 1980; Lineberry,1977). Policy performance rules are a special interest to planners and other public managers because much of their professional legitimacy is based on the premise that the adoption of decisional rules will promote equitable redistribution of public goods and services (Mattson, et. al. 1993: 60). Policy performance rules require the professional planner to look at the long term distributional outcomes of project planning, while the program performance task or the demand processing rule assists the planning agency in its day-to-day operations.

Both program task and policy performance rules are devised to evaluate whether an agency is accomplishing its specified mission. The underlying assumption is that, as rational implementors, public planners ought to carry out policies in a technically neutral manner. Decision rules are expected to reduce uncertainty, and ensure goal compliance. Administrative rule making has equity consequences. For instance, spatially fixed facilities (parks, libraries, police stations) have "lumpy" benefits, meaning their location distributes benefits disproportionately within the community (Lucy, 1988; Jones, et.al., 1980). Public agencies are frequently motivated to devise rules that support their own agency's survival maintenance objectives (Jones, et. al. 1980; Anagnoson, 1983; Mattson, et. al. 1993). Or, as Lineberry (1977: 154) comments, "There are two remarkable things about decision rules in bureaucratic allocation of public services. The first is how low in the bureaucratic hierarchy decision rules are formulated and implemented. The second is how insulated the rule makers are from external constraints." Thus, administrative rule-making by planners can either enhance or inhibit equity outcomes (Mattson, et. al. 1993, 1986).

Planners as Resource Allocators

Besides decision rule authority, another source of policy power is the claim of expertise in resource allocation. According to the planning profession, expertise is derived from synoptic comprehensive planning. Proponents of the comprehensive planning process declare that it allows the policy planner to make intelligent choices according to certain standards of internal consistency and logic (Branch, 1981). According to Alexander (1992: 47), rational comprehensiveness involves a "deliberate selection among possible courses of action by evaluating these options in terms of the goals they are design to achieve." Also known as rational problem solving, it prescribes four step "rational" procedure that emphasizes: (1) the scientific predictability of goal setting; (2) the identification of policy alternatives; (3) the evaluation of means against ends of the policy alternatives; and, (4) the selection and implementation of the one specific course of action or policy alternative (Alexander, 1992: Ch.3; Johnson, 1989: 101-132; Faludi,1987). Rational comprehensive planning presumes that the following two attributes are part of the community policy setting. First, each of the participants within the planning process represents a specialized self-interest. Second, each participant is a utility-maximizer who can compete as an equal on the same "playing field."

The beauty of the comprehensive planning process is the simplicity of its internal logic. Ford (1990: 13) writes it is a three-step process.

> First, a town adopts a plan showing how land *should* be used; second, local leaders carry out this plan by legislating how land *can* be used; and, third, as development occurs, land *is* used according to the plan's designations.

This comprehensive planning process is said to be an objectively derived technical process (Levy,1994: Ch.8; Faludi, 1987; Branch, 1981). Former City of Albuquerque planning director Hebert H. Smith (1991: 211) disputes this belief. "As someone with years of experience in community planning, I have long known that we have not provided a strong, commonly accepted base of understanding of the planning process and its importance." Indeed, too often we focus on the process and ignore the product. Or as Lucy (1988: 224) contends, the product is not a "fixed sequence" of decisional steps with its end-product "being a bound report." Instead, the product should and ought to be the achievement of **social equity through resource allocation.**

For decades, the planning profession has been confronted by the issue why bother to plan. Or as Smith (1991: 2) declares, "Planning is a the most difficult concept yet conceived by humankind to sell to the public." The authors of *The Small Town Handbook* (Daniels, et. al. 1995: 5) claim that planning is the "mark of good community sense and intelligent thought." By doing so, the small towner can "anticipate change" so that h/she can "take action to solve problems before they become worse."

If small town planning entails **the authoritative allocation of values and scarce resources,** a guiding premise for comprehensive planning has been the "task of creating and maintaining agreements between groups and leaders who have good reason to disagree but also stand to gain from cooperation." (Johnson, 1989: 207). In reality, however, the scarcity of stakes and rewards prevents cooperation. Too often the rural property owners see comprehensive planning as an impediment on their liberty to use their property as they see fit. Planning is viewed as regulation by decisional allocation rules. It can limit profits from property use.

Local government has for decades been entrusted with the power to regulate private property. Our courts have acknowledged that the **nuisance doctrine,** as developed by the English courts, is a reasonable use of local police powers. A landowner does not have the right to use his land in way that may harm others. Government can impose limitations that will mitigate public nuisances. Over time, community land use planning has evolved to mean that the community, under certain procedural conditions tied to the comprehensive planning process may restrict private property rights to assure the public's health, safety and welfare.

Comprehensive planning is both a process as well as a product. It is not only a process by which a consensus is derived for defining community goals, but also a strategy for implementing an agreed-upon goal for the protection of public health, safety and welfare. **Comprehensive planning** is defined here as a *policy planning activity* which is a *future oriented, anticipatory decision-making activity*, requiring a consensus between individuals and groups pertaining to possible alternative program policies that can help us *clarify and promote intentional change*. Or as Britton Harris (1972: 10) claims, comprehensive planning is a "well known paradigm" that is "conducted by groups in a social setting" which allows for "anticipatory decision-making". Although critical as a means for accomplishing certain objectives, it is not an end in itself. Instead, it is a means for determining policy strategies within a community.

All policy planning strategies must deal with uncertain contingencies. Comprehensive planning facilitates the establishment of "decision-making parameters" (Lassey, 1977: 5). By doing so, all the "game players" derive a common language for legitimizing a course of action for the distributional consequences of a particular policy strategy (Ranney, 1969: 139-145; Branch, 1981; Faludi, 1987; Alexander, 1993: Ch 3).

Planners as Guardians of the Community's Public Interest

Among all the design professions, the planning profession is delegated the responsibility of being **the guardian of the public's interest or the common good**. As the guardian of the public interest, the community planner is expected to allocate scarce resources in an impartial manner. It is in this task that planners frequently encounter political conflict (Hoch, 1995; Forester, 1989; Mayo, 1984). This conflict is not tied to "whether planning will reflect politics, but whose politics it will reflect" (Long, 1959: 169). In small towns, individuals and groups come into conflict whenever they believe that policies over public health, safety, or welfare threaten their personal interests (Hicks, 1946; Mills and Davis, 1962; Connery, 1972; Hatch, 1979; Kemmis, 1990; Tauxe, 1993). Planning generates conflict because changes in the rules of the allocation game will often alter and affect the numerous and diverse stakeholders for extended time periods (Dalton, 1989).

Planners see their special knowledge as a means for protecting the public interest. Indeed, much of a planner's professional legitimacy is based on the premise that his technical expertise allows him to devise such allocation rules (Rosener, 1982; Klosterman, 1980; Howe, 1994; Hoch, 1995). Yet, some scholars question the zealousness of such an assertion. Or as Judd and Mendelson (1973: 177) comment,

> Imbued historically with a missionary fervor, planners have rarely doubted the moral superiority of their own cause. The tendency to equate their own roles, aims, and objectives with righteousness and virtue has had a profound impact upon their professional life. It has made their attachment to certain values virtually unshakable, and has also nurtured a self-image which dominates practically all standards and definitions of their professional life.

For many town folk, a planner's expertise is h/her personal vision of how to protect the community's health, safety and welfare. Disputes arise because small town dwellers are fearful that planners will act similar to "big city" bureaucrat. The planner will not act as the implementor of policy choices derived from their guidance (Gamberg, 1968; Hahn, 1970).

While the concept "guardian of the public interest" is a key descriptor of the planner's role (Wheaton and Wheaton, 1970), how the planner defines it within the civil community will determine how the planner will "guard it" (Howe, 1994: 60). The origin of the "public interest criterion" can be traced back to the progressive reform movement, when thousands of European immigrants and displaced farm workers from the countryside were invading the cities. Unfortunately, lacking an adequate network of public services, these nineteenth-century cities became overcrowded and congested with vast slums, which were characterized by poor housing and sanitation and rising crime rates (Marcus, 1991; Boyer, 1983; Leavitt, 1982). Confronted with the growing importance of city functions, civic minded reformers sought to restore the civic order by empowering public agencies with the authority to prepare coordinated plans for improving traffic circulation, open space and housing (Boyer, 1983). Planners began to institute "some of the first steps to restrict the use of private property and thereby avoid the ills of overcrowding and congestion produced by growth (Zovanyi, 1998: 63).

Civic Culture and the Growth Machine

Our understanding of small town political culture is that it implies a synthesis of traditional and individualistic civic core values, with the latter being dominant. Although given the individualistic underpinnings, governance is controlled by a recognized elite. Policy choices are made out of self-interest within the marketplace of competing interests (Elazar, 1971: 12). The civic community's political life is tied to an intricate system of informal mutual obligations (Elazar, 1994: 230-247).The civic institutions of governance tended to serve the participants' personal interests even to the exclusion of others. Within a small town setting, Traditional-Individualism does not concern itself "with the question of the 'good society' except insofar as it may be used to advance some common conception of the good society formulated outside the political arena..." (Elazar, 1971: 12-13). A 'good government' is one that maintains the existing social patterns, "and, if necessary, their adjustment with the least possible upset" (Elazar, 1970: 265).

Traditional-Individualism differs from the Communal orientation of the urban planning process, in which consensus for shared goals is essential in a pluralistic setting. In a communal setting (Elazar,1994: 233), the role of politics and policy planning is "to intervene in the sphere of private activities when it is considered necessary to do so for the public good or the well being of the community." By contrast, within Traditional-Individualism, local officials are expected to give "the public what they want" and rarely initiate "new programs or open up new areas of government activity on their own recognizance" for the common good of the collective community (Elazar, 1971: 15). Instead, policy choices are likely to favor those who can exercise political clout, which are normally the economic elite within the community, violating an underlying premise of the comprehensive planning process that all parties are on an equal footing (Alexander, 1992; Kemmis, 1991; Branch, 1981; Catanese, 1974 ; Hahn, 1970; Gamberg, 1968).

Lacking the independent authority "to commit public funds, to enact laws, to enter contracts or to exercise the power of eminent domain" (Levy, 1988: 79) the planner's ability to decide how community programs and/or projects will be implemented is limited by h/her ability to persuade the community to adopt proactive activities within a traditional-individualistic policy setting. In many small towns, the successful planner is the "**technocratic-entrepreneur planner**" (Gamberg, 1968; Hahn, 1970; Catanese, 1974, 1984; Wolensky and Groves, 1978; Nellis, 1980). This planning style nicely dovetails with the prevailing Traditional-Individualistic political culture, because as a philosophy it emphasizes the importance of being an apolitical technician who provides his clientele with a "bag of empirical tools" for enhancing the community economic position within the region (Rabinovitz, 1969: 80-90; Vasu 1979; Baum 1983; Howe,1980).

The **Technocratic-Entrepreneur planner** has a narrow view of the town's constituency. The planner sees his functional role as that of a **community developer** (Baer, 1977; Howe, 1995). He puts together the funds, the administration and the political support for planning projects (McClendon and Quay, 1988). Thereby concentrating his efforts on buildings, land use practices, traffic corridors and physical features of the environment rather than on problems and deficiencies within the economic system or the community's social structure (Getzel and Thurow, 1979; Blakely, 1989; Ford, 1990). The **Technocratic-Entrepreneur** relies on the design perspective, presuming that many of the social ills of the community can be corrected by altering the physical landscape. Therefore, he or she is more comfortable on the "aesthetics and efficiency in locating parks, designing civic centers, and rationalizing land use or protecting property values through zoning" (Baer, 1977: 62). The dominant thrust is to avoid normative allocation issues that can engender community conflict between the haves and the have nots (Raymond, 1978). The physical order of a community thereby equals the social order.

The small town "game-players" are likely to be proponents of the growth machine thesis. It is a theory of community decision making that stresses the importance of "pro-growth" coalitions within local governance (Molotch, 1976; Rudel, 1989; Vogel and Swanson, 1989). Or as Vogel (1992: 13) explains:

> In a sense, growth machine theory is an important modification of elite theory, in that it does not require an elite to dominate or always win on all issues. It also provides a window for government officials to be parties to the coalition without being subordinate to it.

Politics of Small Town Planning

Small town planning is frequently characterized as a tool that protects property ownership and other vested rights (Tarrant, 1976; Powers, 1991; Kemmis, 1991: Ch. 7; Greenberg, 1994: Ch.5). Traditionally, small town residents exert control over the character of the community by simply utilizing an informal planning management style that I call **pre-emptive negotiation**. As Mills and Davis (1962: 17) point out, "politicians will prefer a resolution of a conflict to a compromise and a compromise to a clear-cut choice among contestants." Rudel (1989: 21-24) suggests that this form of community planning is also known as **bi-lateral relational control**. Its justification is that, by planning informally, the town's economic image is protected and community conflict is avoided. Besides, the legalism of formal public hearings can invite restrictions on policy options for local policy elites. **Pre-emptive negotiation**, as an informal planning style, allows the local leadership to avoid hair-splitting the minutiae of zoning or subdivision reviews on a weekly basis. While public review of zoning and subdivision plat reviews makes for effective administrative oversight, it leaves little or no "wiggle" room for flexible policy initiatives or interpretations on behalf of economic development (Greenberg, 1994; Johnson, 1989; Mills and Davis, 1963)

The small town is the ideological heir of Jeffersonian Agrarianism view of policymaking. Any planning issue will invite controversy over private property rights versus community rights (Powers, 1991: Kemmis, 1990; Rawson, 1989; Tarrant, 1976). As Kristina Ford (1990: 119) has observed, planning issues often ignite community antagonism because all policy choices tend to be framed in a "zero-sum" game, where one segment of the community wins over another segment of the community or one group win over the individual. In such a policy setting, rarely does a "win-win" situation emerge.

Until 1975, small towns within Florida had the authority to adopt whatever plans they thought necessary to carry out their responsibilities. Governor Askew and the state legislature altered this policy style. The passage of the **Local Government Comprehensive Planning Act (1975)** was a modified "Top-Down" growth management initiative. It was a landmark piece of legislation for two reasons. First, it evolved from a number of earlier failed attempts to influence development in Florida by encouraging local governments to be more responsible in their own planning and growth management. This was to be accomplished by preparing, adopting and implementing a municipal comprehensive plan with eight mandatory elements (Starnes, 1986). Second, the law radically "reordered" the relationship between the state and local governments by deepening state involvement in local land use planning (DeGrove and Turner, 1991: 227).

The one of the most controversial issues to emerge from Florida's growth legislation has been who would be responsible for the preservation of community's character. Any community plan ought to encompass some sort of vision plan defining the town's "sense of place" (Mattson, 1996). But, as Daniels (1999: 51) notes, "it is difficult to form a vision for a community or identify a planning area when commercial highway strips and scattered houses in the countryside are pulling economic and social vitality away from cities, towns and villages." The town's planning and zoning commission is often called upon to interpret such a vision plan. As the ultimate arbitrator, this quasi-legal board is expected to restrict specific kinds of people and economic activity that is presumed will ruin the community's image while improving the town's economic/tax base, normally defined in the context of some sort of land use improvement.

Composed by civic minded volunteers who wish to do the right thing (Powers, 1991; Slater, 1984: Ch. 6; Tarrant, 1976), a town's planning and zoning commission finds itself passing judgement on neighbors, fellow lodge members, or relatives. Lacking professional expertise, these civic minded citizens have a strong desire to defuse potential controversy and community conflict. Indeed, they are often reluctant to ask the hard questions. From 1985 to 1995, Florida's small towns had to be "in compliance" with "the state comprehensive plan, the appropriate regional policy plan," and must be "consistent" with these plans (Ch. 163.3184(4)(b),F.S.). Under this **top-down, communal policy planning model**, state and regional planners had the sole authority to decide how local jurisdictions will cope with local land and social policy issues.

Policy Implications

As Linowes and Allensworth (1973: 23) claim, it is easier for individuals to accept the "generalities of planning than it is to reach agreement on specifics." As we will see, the history of Florida's growth management initiative has often been shaded in such generalities. Planning choices are usually tied to specifics such as the favorable routing of traffic flows, zoning changes, or the construction of sewer and water systems (Mills and Davis, 1963; Catanese, 1974; Ford, et. al., 1990: 4-52). Since any one of these planning issues can engender a debate over the future character of the community, planning board members like to conduct broker-type agreements that ignore the finer technical points of a town's comprehensive plan. The small town planner is expected to walk "a fine line between strong American attachment and the rights of property ownership and the community's collective concern" (Nellis, 1980: 68). Under Florida's growth management laws the fine line has become blurred. In the next few chapters, we will investigate how aspects of Florida's growth management had been implemented under the conditions of the 1985 Growth Management Act.

Chapter 8

ಐಐಅ

Decision Rules and Community Development: The Florida Grant-Getting Experience

During the Great Society legislative period, state and local officials witnessed the proliferation of categorical grants. This shift from a Dual Functional "layer-cake" to a Creative Federal "marble cake" model was viewed as an improper intrusion by the states and their localities. By 1970, critics of the Great Society advocated the adoption of the "block grant" system as an alternative funding system by claiming it would allow for implementation of specific national objectives without infringing on the delicate balance agreed upon by the Founders. One of the earliest block grant programs to be authorized by Congress was Title I of the Housing and Community Development Act of 1974. Popularly known as the Community Development Block Grant (CDBG) program, for the past three decades, this single-purpose grant has delegated program priority authority to local officials.

Within policy implementation doctrine, the CDBG model reflects a conservative shift in intergovernmental relations by allowing for the decentralization of power to local implementors. For this reason, many liberal Congressmen believe that social goals of the Great Society are in jeopardy, especially those that emphasized "people" oriented programs. On the other hand, advocates of the CDBG program argue that the administrative decision rules for task objectives can assure that the continuation of Congressional intent for the Great Society legislation. The focus of this chapter is to examine this controversy under the pressure of growth management.

Administrative Rules and Federal Block Grants

Block grants are bold attempts to redefine and strengthen the role of state and local governments. Before the Great Depression, Congress made funds available to states for specific national economic objectives, such as road construction and water retention dams. During the New Deal, a variety of socially oriented grant programs were added with policy discretion remaining in the hands of state officials. It was The Johnson Administration's Great Society system that assured all three levels of government would share functional responsibilities (Zimmerman, 1992: 112-126; Peterson, 1995: Ch. 3.).

One approach for understanding the implications of grant policy intent is to investi-gate the rational criteria for decision rule-making (Anagnoson, 1983; Arnold, 1980; Goggin, et. al., 1990; Johnson, 1992). The normative assumption of administrative rule-making is the belief that such decision rules will help perform tasks in a fair, consistent, and equitable manner (Jones, et. al., 1980; Mattson et. al. 1993). Yet decision rules are not an "either/or thing that one has or doesn't have, but is a matter of degree, depending on how binding administrative directives are on an employee's actions." If they choose, a public manager can "deviate from prescribed agency policies" (Gummer, 1990: 104). Decision rules are of a special interest because much of small town planner's legitimacy is based on the premise that the adoption of decisional allocation rules will promote impartial policies (Mattson, et al. 1993; Jennings, et.al. 1986; Mattson and Solano, 1986).

The CDBG Program

Federalism is both an idea and a structure. For the Founders, federalism was based on the premise that the social compact existed not only between the states and the national government, but also between the people and the national government. Politically, Federalism distributes power in a manner so that all parties involved are protected; that is, the national government, the states and their localities as well as the individual citizen (Beer, 1993; Zimmerman, 1992, 1991). Political power was deliberately diffused so that "it cannot be legitimately centralized or decentralized without breaking the spirit of the Constitution." (Elazar, 1984: 2). Or, put differently, each level of government "insists upon its right to act directly upon the people. Each is protected constitutionally from encroachment and destruction by the other" (Leach, 1970: 1).

By the time of the New Deal, a modified form of governance was devised. It allowed for both "centralized and decentralized forms of government to function simultaneously", with each level of government not having to assume "all the functions of the public sector." Instead, each level of government performs those functions that it can do best (Oates, 1972: 14). Grants funds were passed down from the federal to the state and from the state to the city as if each entity was part of a **layer cake**. Experience has shown that no one level can function without the cooperation of the other two levels. The use of this **layer cake** model became the mechanism to bind the nation's diverse regions. From Roosevelt's New Deal to Johnson's Great Society, however, critics claimed that this layer cake model was incapable of adopting the innovative policy planning. A principal reason was that there was a tendency to be dominated by **functional specialists** who operated grant allocation similar to a **picket fence, with each state tied to specific political ideology** (Peterson, 1995; Zimmerman, 1991, 1992). In contrast, the **marble cake** form would allow for federal intervention at the local level, causing criticism that **marble cake** federalism meant an unwelcome intrusion or preemption by federal officials (Reagan and Sanzone, 1982; Howitt, 1984: 7-34; Zimmerman, 1991, 1992).

In the Federal policy implementation game, innovative grant getting requires at least three prerequisites to be in place. **Firstly**, the policy goals as intended by the funding legislature (Congress) must be clearly stated, understood and accepted by the lead agency. **Secondly**, there must be adequate resources (funds and staffing) to properly accomplish the policy goals. **Finally**, most importantly, all policy actors (local publicly elected officials, grant implementors and citizen groups) must be willing to cooperate in an honest effort to carry out the program's objectives (Van Horn, 1979; Goggin, et. al. 1990; Johnson,1992). Under The "New Federalism" strategy, local governance would re-emerge with little federal oversight. At the same time, an "equality of condition" among communities of similar size and circumstance would be accomplished by CDBG funding (Hall, 1983; Ervin, 1985; Fox and Reid, 1987; Fossett, 1987; 1989; Watson, 1992).

Overall, the Community Development Block Grant program with its discretionary latitude should have silenced criticism. However, this has not been the case. Instead, supporters of the Great Society's **marble cake** model claimed that CDBG's social policies were vulnerable. Critics argued that the conservative, small town elite oriented political leadership were likely to ignore social equity initiatives (Rainey and Kline, 1979; Gabris and Reed, 1978; Krane, 1987; Fox and Reid, 1987; Watson, 1992). Obviously, if this were the case, it raises doubts as to whether the CDBG program would succeed in rural communities without strong federal oversight.

Grant Getting and Small Towns

The passage of the Omnibus Budget Reconciliation Act of 1981 by the Reagan Administration made it apparent that the elimination of strong federal oversight was to become a reality. For the Reagan Administration, block grant devolution meant the Republican Party could keep its campaign promise to return to **layer cake** grant activity. Secondly, the CDBG grant devolution would allow the state governors to decide projects priorities, giving them political clout. Finally, the Reagan Administration could target funds without having to assume responsibility if there was an abuse or misuse by the states (Morgan and England, 1984; Jennings et. al., 1986; Fossett, 1987; Pelissero and Granato, 1989; McKenna, 1990; Watson, 1982).

Even with the possibilities of criticism, state governors were keenly interested in obtaining direct responsibility over the federal funds. In one year, thirty-six states took control of the small city's program (Morgan and England, 1984: 477; Howitt, 1984). Early analysis discovered that the overall number of rural communities awarded CDBG grants tended to increase. However, actual dollars to each awarded community tended to decrease. An allocation decision rule known as **grant spreading** emerged from the takeover. By **grant spreading**, state bureaucrats make a conscious effort to fund a large number of smaller projects to gain "networking" support (Jennings, et al, 1986). This "political networking" or "spreading" policy style may help mend political fences, but as critics have noted, such grant policy behavior does not assure that congressional guidelines are being accomplished (Anagnoson, 1983; Mattson and Solano, 1986; Mattson, et. al., 1993).

At the same time, critics claimed that state functional specialists with narrow political loyalties would begin to make allocation decisions. Moreover, with limited federal oversight, small towns would be squeezed out of the "grant getting game" by this revival of **picket fence federalism**. Even if the smaller cities were funded, these functional specialists had a tendency to seek out local elites. Early research tentatively implied that the CDBG's national objectives were being subverted by the political concerns of the small town elites (Ervin, 1985; Morgan and England, 1984; Fosset, 1987; McKenna, 1990). Given this inconclusive evidence, did the Reagan/Bush Administration's policy changes discourage the poorer rural towns from participating? And, if so, are the projects funded still having income redistribution overtones?

The Policy Research Design

During President Carter's Administration, access to CDBG process was simplified so that small towns, especially those with greater social need, could easily seek a CDBG award. Moreover, federal oversight was strengthened. After the Reagan landslide, the CDBG formula funding was modified, giving critics an opportunity to suggest that a "picket-fence" federalism had returned. This analysis investigates the criticisms of the small town CDBG program performance experience in Florida between fiscal years 1983 to 1992 by evaluating a selected sets of attributes involving small town policy planning behavior. A **Logistic Regression Analysis (Logit)** was utilized.

As a quasi-experimental research design, Logistic Regression tends to utilize comparison groups that are similar on most every account. Therefore, the logistic regression analysis rather than ordinary least squares is appropriate. Logistic regression measures discrete outcomes or events. That is, the dependent variable captures the binary choice, and there is a probability of one of two events taking place, given the influence of the independent variables. Logistic Regression is especially appropriate when explanatory variables are both continuous and categorical. compared to ordinary least squares (OLS), logistic regression is more precise when the coefficients are significant in a predicted direction. In an logistic analysis, a coefficient actually measures the extent to which one unit of difference in an independent variable is the log of the odds of the dependent variable (Haushek and Jackson, 1977: 190-203; Affi and Clark, 1984; Freund and Wilson, 1997: Ch.11). Finally, logistic regression is for discrete categorical variables, the higher the parameter estimate, the greater the proportion of variance, making it possible to measure both the direction as well as the probability of whether or not a community obtains a CDBG grant.

The program evaluation was conducted by data derived from the Florida Department of Community Affair Files, FY 1983-1992. These annual reports indicate which Florida communities obtained CDBG funds, as well as project type. Additional information on the communities themselves comes from the following sources: *Florida Statistical Abstract (1991)*, the Florida Advisory Council on Intergovernmental Relations files (1983-1991), the *U.S. Census Summary of Social, Economic and Housing Characteristics: Florida (1990).* and *U.S. Department of Commerce: County and City Data Book,(1994).* Specifically, the focus of our investigation was the policy grant behavior among the smaller communities under 50,000 person that were eligible for a CDBG discretionary funds.

Florida DCA and Small Towns

Back in 1950, Florida's economy could be characterized as a three-legged stool, consisting of agriculture, real estate and tourism. As earlier noted (Chapter 3), Florida has become somewhat more diversified, with the introduction of high tech manufacturing and international banking. The transformation came about by a coalition of legislative leaders, large land owners, and local chambers of commerce who established a business-friendly image. Given the state's natural beauty and reputation for low taxes, this public policy strategy achieved results beyond the dreams of the progrowth alliance. By 1990, of the 22 fastest growing metro areas, six were located in Florida, with a large proportion of the state's elderly population located within these and the adjoining 9 counties.

Planners are resources allocators and protectors of the public interest. The policy plan-making process involves citizens and special interest groups placing demands on planners, frequently asking for a program that will solve perceived public problems. Florida's Growth Management Act (1985) was based on a "Top-Down, Communal" policy planning model that required, under the concept of compact urban development, a land use/capital facility plan for each of the 362 municipalities and 67 counties that detailed how their growth objectives are consistent with the state's land use policy plan, as well as the development goals of their sub-state regional neighbors. These plans are reviewed by the Florida Department of Community Affairs. However, the Florida DCA does not have the final say for environmental or land use regulatory matters. Instead, this authority is in the hands of The Florida Administration Commission, which consists of the governor and the six elected statewide cabinet members.

The Florida DCA did have multiple planning responsibilities under the 1985 Growth Management Act. It coordinated the state comprehensive plan's elements submitted by the various departments. Moreover, it reviewed regional planning councils and county plans for consistency with the state plan. Further, its responsibilities to local government were extensive. First, the Florida DCA reviewed a city's comprehensive plan to determine its compliance. If a local city failed to comply, the Florida DCA could issue a moratorium against that city. Second, the Florida DCA was and is responsible for providing technical assistance to local communities in the form of either grant money or technical planning advice.

Florida's cities are legally restricted as to how they are able to raise revenues to pay for the cost of growth. Consequently, there are few fiscal policy planning options for rectifying infrastructure deficiencies. As DeGrove and Metzger (1992: 7) observed, "No other state says flatly that, after a local government has adopted its comprehensive plan and land development regulations, no new development may be permitted unless the concurrency requirement has been met." "At best," according to Stein (1992: 220), "concurrency has placed considerable financial stress on Florida's communities, and, at worse, has brought development to a virtual standstill." Therefore, the challenge to most municipalities is to meet public service expenditure levels. For towns with a limited fiscal capacity, the grant getting game was one of the few policy planning options available.

Factors for Grant Getting

This CDBG program performance analysis will cover a funding period during the Reagan-Bush Administration (FY 1983–1992). During this period, 362 communities under 50,000 persons were eligible, with an average of $36.7 million set aside for these towns annually. The Florida DCA files indicate 104 towns received grants, with 72 of the mayor council and 32 of council manager cities obtaining at least one CDBG grant while operating under the restrictions of growth management.

Our analysis will contain two contextual variables partially derived from data files. Besides the city variable, we will contrast the state's 31 micropolitan and 36 urban counties. As **Table 8.1** indicates, we will examine independent variables such as wealth, percentage of non-white residents, percentage of elderly and area attributes. An urban county is operationally defined as being located within the Metropolitan Statistical Area (MSA), while a rural county or community is defined as being located outside Florida's metropolitan areas. During this time period, 46 counties had communities that fell within this category.

For analyzing CDBG program performance, **Table 8.2** (CDBG policy choices) contrasts several independent variables that play a role in grant planning performance. For instance, scale of a city is by population size **(POP)**. We believe that the larger the city, the more pluralistic. Such cities spawn multi-culturally oriented demand for the CDBG program. Wealth is another indicator. Wealthier towns have greater resource capacity. For our purposes, Median Family Income **(MFI)** acts as a surrogate variable for wealth. As an ordinal measure, we divide the communities into three different classifications: low income, middle income and high income. The low income range includes those towns with a median family income level one standard deviation below the mean, which in this study period is calculated to be $19,436. Likewise the high income range is one standard deviation above the mean, or above $44,990. Of course, dummy variables were used in the logistic regression and the of Palm Beach, Florida was removed.

We have two city forms. Commission-Manager **(CM=1)** cities are more likely to have professional management capabilities and more likely to seek and obtain economic enhancement type CDBG grants. By contrast, Mayor-Commission **(MC=0)** tend to be more income diverse, with strong independently elected mayors (Vogel and Swanson, 1989; Dye, 1998: 157). Prone to conflict, Mayor-Commission type cities tend to seek socially oriented grants as a means to mitigating political conflict. Besides government form, a second independent variable to measure political/administrative capacity is planning expertise **(PLNG)**. Under growth management, each municipality is expected to demonstrate planning capabilities by devising infrastructure plans that assure carrying capacity. Moreover, the professional norms of planners require its practitioners to assure the common good. Towns with planning expertise are more likely have a comparative advantage in the grant getting game. This variable is a dichotomous, nominal surrogate variable that allows us to separate communities into those with or without in-house professional planning staff. The Florida Department of Community Affairs' (DCA) 1990/91 directory was used to code this variable.

The location of a community **(DIST.)** is another important variable. Urbanizing towns **(DIST=1)** are more likely to be motivated to seek CDBG funds. Furthermore, under growth management guidelines these towns are more likely to utilize CDBG funds for development type activities, shifting the cost of state-mandated infrastructure onto federal funding rather than their own source revenue base. Two additional political variables will be investigated—the per cent of minority **(MIN)** and the per cent of elderly

Decision Rules and Community Development 117

(ELD). Both demographic factors influence public policy choices. Moreover, towns funded by Florida DCA with high percentage for both groups will comply to federal guidelines. We know that the elderly tend to vote in high proportions and tend to actively campaign to minimize local tax impact (Dye, 1998; MacManus, 1992). Therefore, cities with high concentration of elderly are likely to seek infrastructure type projects. In contrast, minority populations (MIN) are equally resistant to developmental or distributive type grants, especially when the state is cutting back on social welfare programs (Dye, 1998: Ch.11). With scarce public dollars, towns with large minority populations are likely to substitute CDBG funds for own source revenues in such policy areas as housing, parks and neighborhood facilities (Swain, 1983; Button, 1989).

Table 8.1 gives a code summary for each independent variable. In addition, it provides a performance measure for two dependent variables—**Grant Award and Grant Type**. **Grant Award** is a dichotomous variable that indicates those community factors that influence whether a town obtains a CDBG grant. **Grant Type** tells the reader whether a town received a socially oriented grant or an economic development economic grant. It is also dichotomous, indicating the type of (redistributive or social policy =1, or distributive or brick and mortar policy=0) CDBG funded grant. **Table 8.2** interprets grants' policy behavior. **Equation 1 or Grant Award (AWARD)** gives us the city characteristics that are most likely to enhance grant getting. **Equation 2 or Grant Type (TYPE)** tells the reader what type of grant was obtained by a town. That is, the likelihood of obtaining an social policy or brick and mortar grant.

CDBG Policy Allocations

During the Carter Administration CDBG grant getting was simplified, especially for those towns in greater social need. However, some scholars suggest that under Republican Reagan/Bush Administration, grant participation was altered to reflect local political bias and local management capabilities. That is, in heavily urbanizing Florida, the better off and more conservative towns will dominate the CDBG grant getting process.

In a case of social service planning, David Swain (1983) discovered that in the City of Jacksonville was heavily dependent upon intergovernmental funds to sustain social services. As a Traditional-Individualistic City, the local officials sought federal funds to pay for social services in an effort to free-up own source tax dollars for brick and mortar type projects. How-

Table 8.1 Florida Program Variables

	Dependent Variables
Grant Award	Eligible cities that did or did not receive an award. (received=1, did not receive=0)
Grant Type	Types of CDBG grants awarded to cities which applied. (Redistributive=1, distributive=0)
TIF	Tax Increment Finance Participant
PRIV	Privatization Participant

	Independent Variables
SCALE	Ordinal categories of a city's population.
MFI	Ordinal categories of low, middle, and high income based on the median family income of the community
FORM	Type of governmental structure. (city manager=1, mayor/council=0)
PLNG	Access to a professional planning staff. (yes=1, no=0)
DISTrict	Location of the city in the state. (urban area=1, micropolitan=0)
BOND Rating	Ordinal categories of Bond Ratings (A= High, B = Medium, C= Low or Poor)
MINority	The percentage of non-white persons within a country. (> state average=1, < state average=0)
ELDerly	The percentage of elderly persons within a county (> state average=1, < state average=0)
LN Pop	Log of Population Change of City
CHMBER	Chamber of Commerce (1= Yes, 0=No)

Source: UNF Center for Local Government Update Survey (1992).

ever, whenever there is a choice between the two types of federal grants. The economic enhancement grant was likely to be sought. At best, local political priorities influenced grant application and implementation.

Catlin's (1981) analysis of nine Florida cities noted a targeting policy behavior that was quite similar. Of these nine Peninsula cities, all except Hollywood which had African-American populations located within distinct neighborhoods, the local public officials were likely to spread the benefits to both the needy and not so needy neighborhoods. Local officials utilized a "probability of success" criterion, targeting most dollars to public works projects. In Catlin's opinion, this was a retreat from the program original intent. For the low income Black citizen-taxpayer, DCA allocations in the 1970s meant that the politically weak African-American districts were "most adversely affected" by the targeting rules.

Button's (1989: 169) analysis of six smaller Florida communities—Crestview, Gretna, Titusville, Daytona Beach, Riviera Beach and Lake City—discovered that Florida's DCA used the former urban renewal program for much of the late 1970s and early 1980s. Again, town officials simply substituted federal dollars for local tax dollars for public works projects. However, they did spruce up black neighborhoods and downtown commercial areas. "No doubt the deplorable conditions of housing and public services in black neighborhoods enhanced the eligibility for such projects." Overall, public work's projects are politically acceptable by most residents in small towns because everyone seems to benefit from drainage, paved streets or curbs, when scale precludes sharp and distinct neighborhood income cleavages (Mattson and Solano, 1986).

Who Participates?

Table 8.2, Equation 1 gives the reader some insight into this policy behavior. To minimize for distortion, we removed Palm Beach, Florida from our analysis. This equation explains 19.8 per cent of the grant awarding policy behavior. This table notes that 232 CDBG grants were awarded during this time period by the Florida DCA. The positive intercept tells us that rural communities on the urban-rural fringe were more likely to obtain the grant. A check of files indicates that proportionately there was a near even distribution of grant applications by district. But, then location variable (**DIST**) suggest that these urbanizing counties were obtaining the CDBG grants. Morever, this equation indicates that city form, planning professionalism, the per cent of elderly or minority were not factors during this time period. Overall, a Florida city that was most likely to have the following traits. It was small (POP) and wealthier (MFI) city on the urban/rural fringe (DIST). The Florida DCA was politically adept by utilizing **grant spreading within its decision allocation rules.** As part of the governors office, the DCA was likely re-instituting the "picket fence" model by selectively spreading money to those towns that were facing urban growth but are likely to have planning skills access.

Grant Type

Under the Carter Administration, HUD policy guidelines required sensitivity to social policy programs. Since rural governments are funded by HUD discretionary funds, we would expect those social policy projects located within the rural towns are a top priority. Such towns often demonstrated social need (Mattson and Solano, 19986; Watson, 1992). Concomitantly, local officials could enhance their grant getting opportunities by applying for social grants. Is this a factor? **Equation 2** tries to tease out this information by determining grant type.

Table 8.2, Equation 2 gives us some indication of this policy behavior within the state/local policy domain. This equation explains 12 per cent of the grant allocation behavior by the independent variables. It notes that 104 of the 362 eligible towns obtain a grant for the time period. According to **Table 1**, grant type has a positive sign, indicating a measurement for benefit distribution for low and moderate-income family households. The positive intercept (1.4553) tells the reader that social policy grants are likely to have priority. At first this could be confusing. **Equation 1** told us that wealthier small towns were more likely to obtain a grant. But, poverty rates for the elderly in Florida are below the national level for such towns located on the fringe. It is quite possible that the newcomer elderly are utilizing the CDBG grant program as a means of shifting the cost of certain social services onto the federal government. Only a detailed analysis of each towns grant program would give us some sort of grant priority. Elderly community centers are eligible. It is quite possible by gross dollar amounts that these large-ticket items are distorting the grant allocation process.

Equation 2 gives us some additional insight into DCA's policy behavior. The equation tells us that smaller, somewhat less pluralistic, wealthier cities are adept in the grant getting game by shrewdly seeking these social oriented big ticket items such as passive parks and elderly community centers. For the town officials, they are appeasing at least three policy actors—the elderly, the minority population and Florida DCA. As public opinion polls note, Florida is a highly Traditional-Individualistic state when pertaining to life style issues (Dye, 1998; Parker, 1990). Although the elderly vote Democratic in national elections, they tend to split votes during local contests. Local officials may be using CDBG federal funds as a substitute for own source scarce tax dollars, as David Swain speculated. For Florida DCA, it was appealing because it could then adopt a **grant spreading** policy behavior and ease growth management requirements at the same time. Accordingly, smaller, fringe cities were acting rationally by substituting federal dollars for own source tax dollars to pay for growth pressures.

Block Grants and Growth Management

The block grant system was designed to give local governments greater discretion in policy grant behavior. It was assumed that the removal of certain fiscal and administrative barriers encourages greater participation by the smaller, rural towns. Our analysis of Florida's CDBG program has partially supported this belief.

Table 8.2 tells us that minority populated towns had an opportunity to obtain federal money. But, overall, this was not a significant variable. Income level does influence grant getting, with smaller, less needy towns obtaining a significant proportion of CDBG funds. Moreover, Florida CDBG programs appears to be subsidizing growing, suburbanizing counties along the urban-rural fringe. This may mean that Florida DCA planners are likely compensating for sprawl related issues in their CDBG allocations. If this is so, this could be tied to **picket fence federalism.** Apparently, the table equation implies the adoption of a policy behavior in which the Florida DCA may be providing federal dollars for social amenity projects for small towns facing urbanization. These towns are very likely substituting CDBG funds for "own source" tax revenues. According to Peterson (1981), by freeing up social welfare funds, these same towns then can rationally pursue other economic policies that will improve their tax base. Ramsey (1995) in her analysis of two southern towns suggests this behavior is tied to political cultural factors. Moreover, this data may mean that wealthier, urban-rural fringe communities can purse needed growth policies, without neglecting their low and moderate income neighborhoods. Politically, this shift to federal funding is quite acceptable within Traditional-Individualism.

Overall, this table on CDBG grant policy behavior suggest that the Florida DCA has conform to Congressional program objectives. But, the state agency has modified its decision rules to fit the unique political conditions within the state. During this time period, the Florida DCA was responsible for state legislative mandates pertaining to growth management. Florida DCA was acting in a bureaucratic rational framework by spreading dollars to smaller communities facing sprawl on the fringe. Yet spreading does not mean that benefits are being evenly or fairly distributed.

In both models, need was defined by low MFI, while bond rating was a surrogate for tax base. This analysis shows that need was not a factor. In fact, the opposite became the cases with wealthier, smaller communities with local leadership skills being winners in the grant getting game. Professional expertise gave a slight edge, most likely in grant preparation and application stage. Behind the scenes, the richer towns had the overall edge in the CDBG grant getting game, meaning that the richer towns are getting richer and the poorer are being left behind. The reason is quite simple. The richer towns are able to substitute (substitution effect) federal money for local money more readily.

Table 8.2 Logistic Analysis of CDBG Policy Behavior Florida (FY 1983–1990)

Community Attributes	EQ 1 Award Est.	St. Dev.	EQ 2 Type Est.	St. Dev.
INTERCEPT	1.2537	0.8907	1.4553	0.4198
SCALE	-0.9869*	0.4918	-0.6282	0.5962
MFI	1.7879**	0.8075	1.6338**	0.7595
FORM	0.5408	0.6292	-0.3764	0.5701
PLNG	-0.2386	0.6170	-0.7015	0.6000
DIST	0.9843*	0.5125	2.3948**	1.0948
MIN	-0.0195	0.0231	-0.4336	0.5721
ELD	0.0046	0.0302	-2.1239*	1.1983
Chi. Sq.	85.6243 (84 df)		74.5611 (85df)	
p > Chi. Sq.	0.1593		0.0050	
R.SQ.	19.81%		12.02%	
N =	232		104	

Source: FL DCA Files, CDGB FY 1983–1990; University of North Florida Center for Local Government Surveys (1989, 1992)
*Significance at the 0.05 level
**Significance at the 0.01 level

Chapter 9
ಸಂಗ
Financing of Florida's Public Projects

In the southern political culture model, Krane (1992:202) refers to policy planning as "what governments choose to do and what they choose not to do." Before the 1985 Florida Growth Management Act, financing sprawls under fiscal policy planning (capital budgeting, capital facilities planning, and fiscal management practices) had been a neglected aspect of the planning process, especially within rural areas. The Growth Management Act (1985) had hoped to alter this tendency. As noted in the survey, during times of fiscal stress, difficulties can arise due to Florida's narrow revenue base.

Shifting Florida's Tax Bite

On May 3, 2002, Florida Tax Watch announced Florida Taxpayer Independence Day. On this date Floridians finally begin to earn money for themselves. Indeed, the average Floridian household still worked more than one-third of the year to pay his or her tax burden. The tax burden is a reflection of a state's political subculture (Koven, 1988; Boeckleman, 1991; Hanson, 1991). Rural residents are less likely than urban residents to support nonessential types of public services by property taxes (Ch.10). At the same time, Florida has had a long history of assisting the private sector's land development opportunities by tax subsidies (Ch. 3). As a Traditional-Individualistic state

(Miller, 1991; Elazar, 1972), private sector interests tend to be dominant in public policy issues.

Fiscal Capacity tells us how likely the citizen-taxpayer is willing to assume certain public policy initiatives. Generally, it represents the mix of taxes that either a state or a community is willing to use to raise public revenues (Barro, 1986). Florida's fiscal capacity during our analysis was ranked at **104**, which implies that Florida governments were capable of generating tax revenues 4 percent above the national average. The state's tax revenue effort, or willingness to raise such public revenues, was ranked an **82**, indicating there was a political unwillingness to tap certain own source revenues (*U.S. Statistical Abstract Annual*, U.S. Bureau of Census, 1992; *Governing Source Book*, 2002).

At the state level, the **tax base** is commonly grouped into three broad categories: income, consumption and wealth (Hy and Waugh, 1995; Hyman, 1990). A progressive tax base should be a balanced tax base, which means the willingness to tax a wide range of items in all three categories. To do so, the citizens of the state adopt a variety of tax sources, assuring that no one population segment is overly burdened. A broad tax base allows for a shifting of the tax bite and a widening of revenue capacity. Florida does not have such a balanced tax base.

The **tax bite** is born by either local residents or businesses (Ferguson and Ladd, 1986:142-150). A simple definition for a tax bite is "how much a dollar intake" of a particular revenue source (MacManus, 1978). Intergovernmental revenues may be considered. A better way for public managers to understand the **fiscal tax capacity** is by focusing on a state's or a town's own revenue sources (MacManus, 1978:62). Knowledge of the tax sources provides a practical indicator for tax base dependency. Since cities are spatially fixed, our knowledge of revenue sources is helpful in determining each household/business' **tax burden** or **tax bite.** Traditionally, we divide the per capita's tax revenue of each category by the per capita's personal income. Thus, the **tax bite** is a comparison of "taxes collected locally in relation to the incomes of the residents of the city" (MacManus, 1978:95). In Florida, property tax, sales tax and user fees are the principal sources of revenues for local governments. In addition, certain selective or excise sales taxes—taxes on restaurant meals, or hotel and motel occupancy—are heavily used because of the state's tourist industry (*Florida Tax Structure*, Florida Legislative Committee of Intergovernmental Relations, 1991; *Local Government Financial Information Handbook*, Florida Legislative Committee of Intergovernmental Relations, September 2001).

The challenge to fiscal tax capacity is to devise a modern, progressive tax structure that is politically acceptable. A progressive tax rate structure should allow for tax revenue growth to increase in proportion to the size of the town's or state's economic base (Hyman, 1990:363). A state or municipality should adopt a balanced tax system, which is tied to all three sources of revenues—personal income, consumption sales and property. Overall, this is perceived to be a fair means of collecting "own source" revenues. In Florida, the demographic trend encourages an exclusion of the personal income at the state level, indicating hints of inequities, and causing serious political squabbles (Craig, 1992). A balance system is believed to be a fair system when there is a perception of balance among the three "own sources" of revenue (Snell, 1993:17).

Florida's official policy is to shift the tax bite to meet changing state economic circumstances. For instance, in 1960, state revenues were generally tied to the sales tax. There was no corporate or personal income tax, with a majority of revenues being derived from gasoline and from the "sin" tax—tobacco, entertainment and alcohol. At the same time, state expenditures were quite limited to education, roads, courts and prisons. By the middle 1980s, changing demographics required some broader range public service expenditures. A new tax policy was tied to in-migration factors, which included a modified corporate income tax structure. Even so, the sales tax was still the key source of revenues. In 1960, sales taxes took 1.74 percent of some residents personal income; by FY 2000, it claimed 5.2 percent of an individual's personal income, making the state's ranking to be eighth nationally. Without a broad tax base, the tax bite has remained on the individual citizen. That is, without a personal income tax and the inheritance tax, the state property tax and the sales tax are the principal means to balance the state's budget. Consequently, the sales tax comprises 56.1 percent of the total state revenues, making Florida's ranked fifth highest in a sales tax dependency ratio (Gold, 1990:30; *Florida's Tax Structure*. Florida Legislative Tax Equity and Reform Committee, November 1991; MacManus, 1995:211-221; *Governing Source Book*, 2002). The FY 2001/02 Florida legislative session has rejected any extensive reform pertaining to the **tax balance** issue. Rather, Florida has consistently adopted an **incremental** or **backdoor** approach, shifting the tax bite to the groups that are "least likely to have political clout to fight them—tourists, newcomers to the state, and college students." (MacManus, 1995:247).

Red Ink and the State's FY 2002 Budget Crisis

On per capita basis, the total tax bill for each man, woman and child reached $9,785 in FY 2002. Moreover, Florida Tax Watch ("Florida Taxpayer Independence Day," May 5, 2002) reports that the index for per capita taxes rose to 163.7, meaning that since 1990, the per capita's tax burden had risen by 63.7 percent for Florida taxpayers. Or, the total tax bill was 162 billion dollars, just more than a third of the state's estimated 480 billion dollars in personal income. Florida's legislature has little control over federal taxing and spending, but it does have considerable control over state revenue sources.

A "balanced" state tax structure should be of critical concern to Florida's local governments. Under the Florida Constitution, Florida is expected to adopt a balance budget. Since the legislature cannot impose a personal income tax and is restricted on estate and inheritance taxes (Article VII. Sec.5), these restrictions are partly to blame for its revenue shortfalls. Florida's revenue sources, therefore, is skewed toward consumption and/or fee taxes. But these types of taxes are insufficient to pay for sprawl. As early as 1987, Florida officials had estimated that to maintain the existing infrastructure levels would take $248 billion over the next decade. In addition, just to pay for estimated population growth, Florida would have to invest another $52 billion by the fiscal year 2000 (Clark, 1988:76-79; *New York Times*, November 14, 1987). In a study on the cost of public services for southeast Florida for the Florida DCA, Rutger's Dr. Robert Burchell projected the cost for infrastructure over the next 20 years to be $10.5 billion if current sprawl patterns continue ("Eastward Ho, Development Futures," February, 1999). Obviously, under current fiscal policy arrangements the state legislature effort to ease the local tax burden is unlikely.

Governor Chiles' Tax Reform Efforts

The narrow tax base dependency has its pitfalls for both Florida and its localities. **When economic downturns occur, there is no diversified cushion.** As both the 1991–1995 and 2001–2002 legislative fiscal histories illustrate, revenue shortfalls can lead to partisan squabbles and public service budget cuts, jeopardizing many Smart Growth initiatives. In October 1991, after it ruled that Governor Chiles and the cabinet did not have the constitutional authority to make budgetary cuts without the consent of the legislature, the Florida Supreme Court forced Governor Chiles' to call for a special legislative session. After a bitter battle, a compromise budget was made to the tune of $513 million in cuts, which was not enough. Again, after a shortfall for FY 1993, another partisan battle erupted between "the expansionary, revisionist philosophy of the governor and the more traditional, incremental approach of a majority of Florida's state legislators." After three special sessions, a "bare bone" budget was passed, in which many "community-oriented" programs were slashed, further impacting on the fiscal health of local communities (MacManus, 1995:228-233). By FY 1995, Florida had pulled itself out of the recession. But, by then, Lawton Chiles had transformed himself from a "liberal" to a "moderate-conservative" spender who proposed a budget with "no new taxes" that focused on "controlling spending" (MacManus, 1995:235). By 1998, things were back to normal, with the Florida Legislature contemplating tax cuts.

September 11th and the Florida Budget Crisis

In his first two years, Governor Jeb Bush was at the helm of a booming economy. By FY 2000, Florida ranked 4th in personal income levels, with the per capita income being at $27,836. Moreover, its unemployment rate was 4.9% or 20th in the nation, with an employment growth rate between 1996 and 2001 being at 17.3 % (*Governing Source Book*, 2002: 3-6). With the state's coffers overflowing, the Republican dominated legislature gave Governor Bush $1.5 billion in tax cuts, nearly the same amount of a budgetary shortfall the state faced by December 2001.

In the Spring 2001 the state began to slide into a recession. Unlike the early 1990 downturn, the FY 2001 recession was more traditional, hitting both manufacturing and the service-financial sectors. With the stock market bust, the recession had wiped out more than 40,000 jobs in the state, and the terrorist attack of September 11th just added to the state's fiscal woes. Indeed, as a state highly reliant on tourism, Florida was especially hard hit, with a 1.5 billion-dollar a tax revenue shortfall. Nationally, 44 states were suffering from 40 billion dollars in revenue shortfalls by the Fall of 2001. But the ailing economy was only one reason for most state's financial woes. Besides the Twin Tower Attacks, two policy choices played a key role. For most states there were generous tax cuts given in the mid 1990s, and the absorption of health care and pension costs for public employees. In addition, the federal government's policy shifts on Medicaid costs, forcing the state to pick up the tab. The Twin Towers terrorist attack had only complicated matters, causing a deeper recession than anticipated. With increasing revenue shortfalls and required constitutionally balanced state budget, state officials were beginning to adopt the bitter pill of retrenchment and budget cutting. In April 2002, the National Conference of State Legislatures reported that 40 states were forced to slash their budgets by 27 billion dollars in an effort to contain red ink. Or as Georgia Governor Roy Barnes was heard to remark at the National Conference of State Legislatures, the terrorist attack did not cause the problem, "but it quickened it and may have deepened it" ("Deficit Deluge," *Governing*, May 2002; "State Budgets Facing a Fall in Revenues," *The New York Times*, November 2, 2001; "States Make Cuts and Increase Fees," *The New York Times*, May 16, 2002).

In the Spring 2001 legislative session, the Florida lawmakers began to feel the revenue pinch caused by an expanding national recession ("Tax cuts key to shaping the budget," *The Florida Times-Union*, March 31, 2001). In the final hours, the legislators agreed on a $48.3 billion budget that allowed for a $175 million rollback in taxes, hoping that the budgetary shortfalls would only be short-lived (*The Florida Times-Union*, May 6, 2001). Florida Tax Watch was not pleased, indicating that there were too many pork-barrel turkeys passed (J. Saunders, "Tax watchdog cites budget turkeys," *The Florida Times-Union*, June 7, 2001). The World Trade Center terrorist attack meant any economic turn around was unlikely. Indeed, the Florida General Revenue Estimating Conference forecasted that the State's General Revenue receipts for the current year were expected to decline by $673.2 million or 3.4%. Furthermore, the anticipated revenue estimate for FY 2002-03 would likely be down by another $800.8 million, causing a budgetary shortfall of $1.3 billion. Governor Bush immediately called for a special 11-day session to deal with the pending budgetary crisis.

On the opening day, the two state legislative houses showed a philosophical split which was not tied to partisan party beliefs. The Florida Senate, with a larger population constituency, advocated tax reform. On the other hand, the House leadership believed that program expenditure cuts could cure the crisis. Therefore, the Republican House leadership called for $1.3 billion in program cuts, including about $490 million from public education and $505 million form human services. By contrast, the Republican Senate majority had a more modest proposal, which included about $797 million in cutbacks, and the repeal of the $120 million intangible property tax. The House Budget chief Carlos Lacasa (R-Miami) felt that the Senate's proposal, including dipping in the rainy day fund, was irresponsible. ("Budget crisis sees a rough start," *The Florida Times-Union*, October 23, 2001). After much posturing and bickering, the House accepted the Senate's plan to cut $1.1 billion by June 30th from state programs ("Budget cutting blueprint stirs doubts," *The Miami Herald*, November 1, 2001).

Throughout the special session, House Speaker Tom Feeney (R-Oviedo) and Senate President John McKay (R-Bradenton) was both hopelessly deadlocked, except for an economic stimulus package ("Senate passes economic package," *The Florida Times Union*, October 30, 2001). With 1.8 million of its 16 million citizens on Medicaid, lawmakers were cognizant of the difficulty in making any cuts that will impact on this segment of voters. Consequently, the final budgetary compromise had no true claimant of parentage. Or as Lt Governor Frank Brogan proclaimed, it was a budget that didn't go far enough, but the best budget compromise due to the circumstances ("State house sets to OK budget cut plan," *The Miami Herald*, October 30, 2001). Florida Tax Watch called the plan vague, making it uncertain how much each state program would be cut ("Guiding Florida Through Our Fiscal Storm," *Budget Watch*, November 2001). House Budget Chief, Carlos Laicize (R-Miami) declared his doubts that the compromise would get the state in the black ("Budget storm watch issued," *The Florida Times-Union*, November 2, 2001).

Apparently, state lawmaker Laicize was correct. As the recession had deepened, few tourists arrived at Disney World or the state's beach communities. Panama Beach City's Town Manager Richard Jackson reported that a 30% decline in local revenues derived from the state sources. Without a city property tax, this is a significant chunk of Panama Beach City's revenue source ("Panama Beach City worries it may have to endure budget cuts, *Panama City News Herald*, October 29, 2001). With many other town's facing similar problems, Governor Bush called for another special session. On November 27, to give an appearance of unity, the Governor and legislative leadership pledged to solve the budget crisis, which was now projected to be at $1.3 billion. Interestingly, Senate Majority Leader Jim King (R-Jacksonville) broke ranks by expressing his concern over the deep cuts in public education and health and human services, indicating all items were back on the table ("Special session to open," *The Florida Times Union*, November 7, 2001). At the Governor's urging, on December 2nd, the House Speaker Feeney and Senate President McKay met behind closed doors to patch up their feud. The Governor brokered an additional $1.05 billion cut from the state's $48.8 budget. But, there was still the intangible property tax cuts to resolve, which was House Speaker Feeney's (R-Oviedo) pet project (*The Sarasota Herald Tribune*, December 3, 2001). On December 5, House Speaker Fenney, who controls the agenda in the House, announced that he would take the highroad and allow each legislator to vote h/her conscience. Governor Bush announced that he had the votes to break any House deadlock. Apparently, he did his math. Many House Republicans agreed with their Republican Senate colleagues and voted for to put off the intangible property tax cut ("Florida House set to vote on delay on intangible tax," *South Florida Sun-Sentinel*, December 5, 2001). On December 17, Florida Governor Bush signed the state's reconciliation budget, with a proviso that the intangible property tax-cut on stock and bonds would not go into effect until 2004. Florida Tax Watch (December 17, 2001) felt the legislature did a better job this time with its attempt to balance the budget, particularly keeping the state's $941 million Budget Stabilization Fund from being raided.

The Fishkind Report and the FY 2002 Budget Crisis

With skyrocketing Medicaid costs, just three months after cutting $1 billion, the lawmakers were faced with an additional $1 billion shortfall. State Senate President John McKay took the initiative by proposing the Sales Tax Reform Bill (SJR 938), giving greater visibility to the debate over tax revenues enhancements. Based on a tax study by the consultant firm Fishkind and Associates, Senate President McKay proposed closing $4 billion in exemption loopholes, which would allow each typical middle-class Florida household to pocket an additional $247 in tax savings. Overall, the proposed tax reform plan would wipe out 92 service tax loopholes, extend the sales tax to thousands of businesses and rollback the sales tax rate from six cents to 4.5 cents ("Showdown set on sales' tax plan," *Palm Beach Post*, February 20, 2002). At the same time, the Senate finance committee proposed to increase property tax rates that county school boards can levy to offset the cost of paying to educate an additional 72, 000 students the next year. The tax increase would be about $80 on a home with a taxable valuation of $100,000, making the overall package a controversial piece of legislation ("New taxes. Expanded gambling eyed," *Pensacola News Journal* February 16, 2002).

With term limits facing both House Speaker Tom Feeney (R) and Senate President John McKay (R), both legislative leaders appeared ready to repeat their grudge-match of four months earlier. With the Democrats being in the minority and not having the votes, all they could do is offer rhetoric. Yet, the plan did have its merits. For many Floridians, who do not own a sport's sky box, take golf lessons, go to tanning salons, or regularly charter a fishing boat, it seemed to be a rational tax reform package. For many other Floridians, who do utilize specialized computer services or lawn-care services, it seemed flawed ("Taxes: the little guy," *The Florida Times Union*, February 10, 2002). To complicate matters, both Senator Jim King (R-Jacksonville) and Senator Daniel Webster (R-Orlando), who both are former House Speakers, were seeking Senator McKay's job. In all likelihood, Senate President McKay would have a difficult time passing such tax legislation.

Prior to the FY 2002 session, Florida Tax Watch began an analysis on Mckay's tax reform initiative. As the Legislature was beginning its role of governance, Florida Tax Watch issued a statement questioning the ability to raise neutral generating type taxes to close the existing deficit ("Modernizing Florida's Tax System," Special Report, February 6, 2002). Within five days, in another white paper, the organization noted that Florida tries to avoid duplicating and pyramiding taxation. Thus, Senate McKay is misguided in his claim that many of the special loopholes listed are exempted ("Florida Sales Tax Exemptions Overstated," Special Report, February 11, 2002). Then three days later, Florida Tax Watch suggested that Mckay's proposal was foolhardy and illusionary in it claim of sales tax neutrality, especially for those households and firms residing within the 51 counties with a local option sales tax ("Revenue Neutrality: Just an Illusion," Florida Tax Watch, February 15, 2002).

Even though the Florida League of Cities and the Florida Association of Counties defended McKay's plan, Florida Tax Watch's opposition gave justification for House Speaker Feeney to employed a rare parliamentary move. He convened the 120-member chamber as a "select committee of the whole" to debate the Senate plan, causing 17 Democrats to walk out of the chamber in protest. A final vote of 99-0 rejected the Senate's plan ("Florida House votes 99-0 to kill tax revamp," *Palm Beach Post*, February 21, 2002). Within a week there were Senate desertions. The most notable was Senate Majority Leader Jim King, who still believed that sales tax reform was more acceptable than raising property taxes ("King abandons McKay plan," *Florida Times-Union*, March 7, 2002). In his chambers, Senate President McKay announced he would delay his tax and budget plans, and wait for tax revenue figures from the state's Revenue Estimating Conference. Unfortunately, the state's revenue estimating groups prediction was not overly optimistic. For Governor Bush and the more conservative House Speaker Feeney, this decision to delay tax reform was welcomed ("Senate leaders split over budget," *Tallahassee Democrat*, March 7, 2002). In the final, frantic hours the Florida lawmakers passed a controversial redistricting plan, but no budget. As for McKay's tax reform package, the two houses reached a compromise. A Joint Legislative Committee would review all existing tax exemptions, and with voter approval, overhaul the tax code (HJR 833). For most legislators, the special commission on tax reform simply represented a political unwillingness to change tax policy that was perceived as a mechanism to raise more taxes in a tax year.

Without a balanced budget, a special session was required. To no one's surprise, the four-day session ended in a stalemate. No budget was passed to meet federal mandated health and educational requirements. While lobbyists pitched in "to feed lawmakers and any staffers" who wished to visit local restaurants, State Senator Jack Latvala (R-Palm Harbor) accused House members of acting like petty "adolescents" by refusing to accept the proposed compromise (L. Morgan, "Session of Chaotic Consistency," *The St Peterburg Times*. April 6, 2002). Consequently, on April 23, Governor Bush called for another special session. For two weeks, Lt Governor Frank Brogan tried to broker a compromise between the House and Senate leadership. The Senate would accept a $ 262 million corporate income tax breaks as part of the federal economic stimulus package. In turn, the House would agree on spending an additional $113 million for health and human services. Senate Majority Leader Jim King acknowledged that the budget clock was ticking to a meltdown. He pledged that he would help orchestrate the most "scripted special sessions in the history of the state." ("Lawmakers called back to session," *The Florida Times Union*, April 24, 2002).

On April 29, a second two-week special legislative session convened. During this session, 3.5 billion dollars of additional spending were proposed, with an additional 1.8 billion dollars for educational reform. For Governor Bush and the Republican leadership, the 6 percent pupil increases in appropriations were a political accomplishment. For the Democrats, it was keeping spending at existing levels, while increasing costs onto the lower middle-class. For the environmentalist, the special session meant diverting previous committed funds for the economic tax stimulus package. Or as House Minority Leader Lois Frankel (D-West Palm Beach) claimed, the Republican's special session was held to put their "corporate cronies first" and the environment and education second ("Legislature: Limit Vision," *The Florida Times Union*, May 3, 2002; "No Sales Tax Holiday," *The St Petersburg Times*, May 11, 2002). On May 13, the Florida Legislature ended its second special session by passing a budget that stripped needed monies from a popular land conservation program, raised college tuition, handed a tax break to corporations, and ended the sales tax holiday for "back to school" shopping. For a 50.4 billion dollar budget, in the Senate the vote was 25-11; and in the House, the vote was 81-35.

Thomas Dye (1998:Ch. 10, Ch. 11, Ch.12) writes that Florida's budgetary process is often in the hands of special interests, with lawmakers rarely responding to public opinion polls. With Florida's population growth outpacing the nation, qualities of life, education and the environment are policy concerns that are regularly at the top of all state polls. Though 103 House members pledged not to touch environmental program funds, they did to the tune of $200 million. Otherwise, the $262 million economic tax stimulus package would have been abandoned. These same legislators pledged to help working-class children. Yet they slashed community college programs and voted to end the "Back-to- School" Tax Holiday. Indeed, the special session took dollars away from school sneakers and backpacks, manatee protection and crime prevention programs to help Chrysler-Daimler build a plant in Jacksonville. Or as Bill Newton of the Florida Consumer Action Network remarked, "The Message was clear: $262 million for the corporations, zip for the consumer." ("No Sales Tax Holiday, *The St. Petersburg Times*, May 11, 2002; "Budget Goes Down to the Wire," *The St. Peterburg Times*, May 14, 2002). The governor has 15 days after the passage by both houses, often resolved by conference committee, the General Appropriation Act, otherwise known as the state budget.

Hoping to be the first Republican Governor to win reelection, Jeb Bush had to decide where to trim this 50 billion-dollar budget. With only 98 million dollars remaining in the rainy day emergency fund, lawmakers gave him little wiggle-room. Florida's Constitution gives the governor an opportunity to line-item veto. However, early in his term, Jeb Bush went after certain "turkeys" in the budget and faced the anger of the legislature. He did not wish to have a rerun during an election year. On June 4, St Peterburg State Senator Jim Sebasta (R) expressed the concerns of many Floridians when he was overheard to remark, "We are waiting in limbo...wondering if the governor will have a fat red veto pen or a thin red veto pen" ("Veto ax hangs over lawmakers local projects," *The St Petersburg Times*, June 5, 2002).

Environmentalists, knowing the Forever Florida monies were raided for a $262 million corporate tax break, had little hope that the funds would be replaced. On June 6, much to their surprise, Governor Jeb Bush's found $107 million in the budget to replace part of the raided funds. In the $50-billion state budget signing ceremony, Governor Bush declared that he was going to put "the 'forever' back in the Forever Florida program," saving the popular land buying program from the chopping block. Kathy Baughman of Florida's Trust for Public Lands felt this action gave the legislator a "big message." "I think they're going to think twice before they do it again." Bob Bendick, director of Florida's Nature Conservancy, called Bush's line-veto action " a good and courageous act on the behalf of the environment of Florida." Hillsborough County Commissioner Jan Platt, responding to the governor's line veto, felt it was 'fantastic'. For once, the Florida environment had "won one" over the legislature. Florida Department of Environmental Protection boss David Struhs, a Bush appointment, declared that this illustrates that a Republican Governor can be both an environmentalist and a fiscal conservative ("Bush shields fund for land," *The St. Peterburg Times*, June 6, 2002; J. Ash. "State Budget Grows Greener," *The Palm Beach Post*, June 6, 2002). Not every one was happy. By lopping off $107-million in pet projects, Governor Bush hit both sides of the legislative aisle. For instance, Senator Jack Latvala (R) who lost over a $1 million in Pinellas County infrastructure funds felt that the governor's action was somewhat arbitrary. With many of the veto projects being within the cultural and social service category, the vetos were felt disproportionately among Democrats, causing the Democratic leadership to claim that the veto choices were politically motivated. Or as Democratic Party spokesman Ryan Banfill observed, the bill signing was a campaign event. "The only things that were missing were balloons and a Bush-Brogan banner" ("Bush shields fund for land," *The St Peterburg Times*, June 6, 2002; C. Krueger, "Bush veto pares Pinellas programs," *The St. Petersburg Times*, Juen 6, 2002; J. Ash, "State Budget Grows Greener," *The Palm Beach Post*, June 6, 2002).

Municipalities with Few Tax Options

Typically Florida residents are willing to maintain existing local public service levels. That is, Floridians are willing to spend $95 per capita for local fire protection, ranking 10th nationally; $237 per capita for police protection, ranking 6th nationally; $95 per capita for parks and recreation, ranking 18th nationally; and, $335 for local streets and roadways, ranking 34th nationally (*Governing Source Book*, 2002:67-79). Even so, many Floridians feel that current public service levels could continue even with decrease funding (Beck and Dye, 1982; Beck, et. al, 1987). Beck and associates found that Florida citizens were willing to make public service tradeoffs for lower taxes, with older, white households being the deciding factor. Parker (1990) found similar results. During the 1990 budget crisis, Parker's Tax Policy

Survey discovered that a majority of citizens (69%) felt taxes ought to be reduced, believing that public services would not be impacted. During the same budgetary crisis, a Florida League of Cities poll found a majority of the registered voters (76%) surveyed believed that the state's quality of life could be maintained, even with taxes and programs being cut. Moreover, most residents surveyed felt that most public services ought to be shifted to the local level, the exception was highways and prisons (Florida League of Cities Poll, August 1991).

Political proximity (political voice) may be the factor for the belief that public services are better at the town level. Yet, the citizen-taxpayer is not off the hook. For decades, communities have relied on the property tax to pay for a large chunk of their municipal service budget. It is viewed as somewhat stable as a revenue source. Unlike other taxes, it doesn't go down when personal income or the ability to pay it goes down (Rubin, 1998; Bland, 1989). As tax revolts began to spread, national trends indicate a shifting from this source. Florida is no exception. In 1970, a property tax share of Florida's local tax collections was 39.2 percent, by 1990 it fell to 31 percent, with the average per capita local property tax being $734.30. (Snell, 1993:57; *Florida's Tax Structure*, November 1991, p. 86). During the 1980s, Florida residents invoked property tax limitations which have restrained the growth of property taxes for both businesses and homeowners. The Florida Constitution restricts the ad valorem taxes to 10 mills for municipalities. It is usually paid in one lump sum, which not only makes it highly visible to the elderly on fixed incomes but makes it quite burdensome. At the time of our study, of the 362 cities less than 50,000 people, the average effective millage rate was 4.16. In 1991, Florida nationally ranked 27th in a property tax burden, with local property taxes being 2.99 percent of an individual's personal income (*Florida Tax Structure*, November 1991, p. 87). By FY 2000, Florida had ranked 20th in per capita property tax burdens. However, even with restrictions, the property taxes rose to 3.5 percent of an individual's per capita income, a substantial rise from a decade before (*Governing Source Book*, 2002:37). This tax burden can be misleading. Under the state constitution, not everyone is treated in the same manner. Although the state legislature requires property to be assessed at 100% full market value, it provides generous homestead exemptions, especially to the elderly and veterans. Thus, horizontal and vertical equity, when tied to special exemptions, is distorted. In Florida, the most likely group to bear the burden is the middle-income, middle-aged cohort. For this reason, the citizen surveys have found that this middle aged, middle-class cohort is more likely to believe that the tax burden is too high and the costs exceed the benefits of local public services. Voting with one's feet, for this cohort, is still possible, if taxes become too burdensome.

Florida has a 10-mill rate for local government, creating fewer revenue raising options. For instance, at the height of the growth management initiative, fast-growing Broward County derived only one-fourth of its revenues from the property tax or $899.33 per capita, while Miami-Dade raised $858.66 per capita or only 27.4 percent of revenues from local property taxes (Lynch, 1987:362-63, *Florida Tax Structure*, November 1991, p. 86). By 1997, Broward County had rebounded to 31 percent, but Miami-Dade had declined to 21.6 percent. In 1990, Jacksonville-Duval, which has a 20-mill tax cap due to consolidation, had a millage rate of 11.53. With the per capita tax burden of $591.82, the Jacksonville-Duval region raised $178.6 million or 38.2 percent from this revenue source. By 1997, its millage rate was 11.1, and it derived only 21.5 percent of its revenues from this source or a $678.11 per capita tax burden (*Florida Times Union*, February 12, 1990:2; *Florida Tax Structure*. November 1991, p. 86; *U.S. Statistical Annual Abstract*, U.S. Bureau of the Census,1998).

For local officials, the best tax policy is one that is less politically visible. Therefore, Florida's municipalities have gone after just about anything possible, including taxes on liquor, cigarettes, meals and motel lodging. In the past, intergovernmental grants were used to offset shortfalls for public service costs. Until the Reagan Era this was standard operating procedure. Now the only logical policy option is to broaden the local service fee base, which can be highly regressive and uncertain. Under the Florida Constitution (Art. VIII), counties and municipalities are granted powers to tax and impose fees to pay for public services. In 1987, local taxes and fees had averaged $1,594 per capita in Florida, compared to $2086 per capita nationally. By FY 2000, without a state personal income tax, the local tax and fee burden was $2,663 per capita, which was still lower than the national $2,994 per capita's average. At the same time, the state legislature cut taxes, allowing for a drop from 10th place to 28th place (*Governing Source Book*, 2002). With fewer state revenues coming back to the cities, localities are forced to seek other revenue sources. For slower growing rural communities, property taxes apparently became a factor. A study of 31 non metropolitan Florida counties noted that property taxes composed of 34.3 percent of all revenues, with a $ 834.29 per capita taxes burden. Although another 54.1 percent of all revenues were derived from either sales tax or a non tax revenue source, without federal grants, these counties had to raise revenues from the property tax. With property rate caps, the only alternative was to increase appraisal valuations. Overall, the local tax structure of most small communities is tied to an admixture of property, local option–sales tax, user fees and intergovernmental revenues, making them quite susceptible to land development initiatives. (*Florida's Small County Study.* Florida ACIR Report, March 1991; *Florida Tax Structure* , November 1991; *U. S. Statistical Annual Abstract* 1989, 1998; *Governing Source Book* 2002).

Sales tax imposed on consumption goods is an alternative policy choice. By 1998, all Florida municipalities derived nearly 57 percent of their revenues from this source (*Governing*, March, 2000:22). For state and local officials consumption taxes are popular because they are less politically visible and because such taxes are administratively efficient: the vendor serves as tax collector (Bland, 1989; Raimondo,1992). From 1979 to 1990 The Florida Annual Policy Survey found that a majority of Floridians supported this form of taxes as a means to pay for public services at both the state and local level (Parker, 1990:22). As noted above, the mood among Floridians had not changed even with the existing budgetary crisis. The unwillingness by Floridians to adopt a personal income tax has had a long political history. Faced with state bankruptcy in 1949, Governor Warren proposed a "tax reform package," mostly directed at the business sector. In the ensuing legislative session all his proposals were defeated. Instead, the legislature passed a three-cent sales tax (Klay, et. al. 1992:12-13). In 1968 Floridians rejected a proposed income tax provision within the Balanced Budget Constitution. Instead, reformers had to institute another sales tax increase to four cents. With FY 2001/02 budget shortfalls, the state legislature again sidestepped the issue of reforming the tax system, giving Florida the dubious honor of being fifth highest in a sales tax burden. In the 31 non metropolitan counties, even though the local option taxes might not generate sufficient revenues, smaller counties still have opted for this revenue source, simply to avoid imposing either impact fees or increased property taxes (*Florida Small County Study*. Florida ACIR Report, March 1991, pp. 13-14). For the FY 2000, the sales per capita tax burden was $1330. In one decade, Florida moved from a ranking of ninth to fifth, indicating that the sales tax bite is getting worse for residents. With 5.2 percent of a resident's personal income is now tied to the sales tax, it is quite difficult to presume that tourism is really picking up the tab (*Governing Source Book*, 2002:36).

Many scholars think the benefits principle is not met by a general sales tax. Outside of selective sin taxes, it has been difficult for Florida officials to blunt criticism of the tax's regressiveness. Consumption taxes do favor those in the highest income categories over those in the middle and low income range. Thus, the **tax bite** increases as one's income level decreases (Simmonds, 1990; Craig, 1992). Four recent governors-Leroy Collins, Rubin Askew, Bob Graham and Bob Martinez—all have tried to reform the sales tax system. Each had met with political opposition similar to Senator McKay. Or as Jacksonville *Florida Times-Union* (February 12, 1990:2) columnist Randolph Pendleton writes, any tax reform effort "has been pretty much a chewing gum and bailing wire affair." The James Madison Institute ranked the Florida among the bottom third of states in per capita tax payments, claiming Florida's "low" tax burden has helped the state attract business and population growth ("Seeking Conservative Solutions to Government Spending," The James Madison Institute Special Report, 2001). This low ranking is obviously tied to Florida's unwillingness to impose a personal income tax. Even so, when there is no tax diversity, fiscal instability is quite likely. According to the James Madison Institute ("Seeking Conservative Solutions to Government Spending," 2001), most Floridians have no desire for a personal income tax.

Financing Florida's Public Facilities Under Sprawl

With no personal income tax and the heavy reliance on sales taxes, Florida is somewhat limited in its revenue sources to mitigate the sprawl. Between 1970 and 1985, the state's expenditure patterns outgrew its ability to raise revenues for infrastructure improvements, even when adjusted for inflation. Thus, it has been quite difficult for the state to provide funds for localities to meet the burdens caused by sprawl. Moreover, local governments also did not fare well during this time period, where public service expenditures grew by 7.4 percent and revenues by 1.5 percent annually, forcing many counties and municipalities to defer capital infrastructure improvements (Nicholas, 1988:110-115). The under funding of the infrastructure investment means a catch-up tax bill between 30 and 50 billion dollars (*Florida's Fiscal Future*, Florida Taxation and Budget Commission, 1992; *A Profile of Florida Municipal and County Revenues*, Florida ACIR Reports, 1989).

Throughout the 1970s, Floridians mistakenly believed that growth management legislation would solve the problem of infrastructure capacity. State and local planning laws pertaining to the "timing and phasing" of infrastructure and "carrying capacity caps" would assure that infrastructure would be built and keep pace with population growth rates. **ELMS Two** study clearly demonstrated that this was not the case, provoking the passage of the **1985 Growth Management Act (G.A.).** Known as the **Pay as You Grow Act**, it requires all of Florida's counties and municipalities to submit a "fiscal policy plan" that details how they will pay for their growth related infrastructure needs under **consistency** of **Rule 9J5**. If a community approves a development project in an area with inadequate levels of service—thus threatening potential reductions in state-mandated levels of service standards—Florida's Department of Community Affairs can impose a development moratorium. In this way, the 1985 Growth Management Act rejects growth on an installment plan. The **1985 Growth Management Act** tries to mitigate this backlog by requiring the citizen or the developer to share in the cost of construction of adequate public service levels (Ch. 163.3177, F.S.A.).

In FY 2000, Florida estimated that for the next twenty years it requires about 37 billion dollars to install, upgrade and replace infrastructures in order to ensure the continued provision of safe drinking water alone. This can be translated into $233 per capita, ranking Florida 10th among states (*Governing Source Book*, 2002:25). This can be misleading because population densities and growth rates vary between counties and communities. We noted that Burchell study ("Eastward Ho, Development Futures," Florida DCA Report, February, 1999) has estimated a 10.5 billion-dollar public service cost to accommodate the projected additional 2.4 million people for southeast Florida. Jacksonville is another typical city faced with such sprawl costs. Under the **1985 Growth Management Act,** its planning department estimated that the infrastructure bill for population growth related projects for the 1990s was 1.8 billion dollars, including $733 million for solid waste, $455 million for water and sewer service, $166 million for drainage and $118 million for road work. To offset this fiscal deficit and conform to the **concurrency requirements,** Jacksonville budget analysts estimated that the city must raise an extra $27 million a year in property taxes and retain the option gasoline tax. In addition, homeowners were faced with a fifty-dollar annual increase on their water/sewer surcharge to repair the city's existing storm sewer system over the next decade. Whatever the city could not raise in taxes, it would simply have to borrow (*Florida Times-Union*, March 5,1991:B-1). At the time, the reaction among city residents was obvious—a **tax expenditure cap** (*Florida Times Union*, May 31, 1991:1). With an expenditure cap in place, by 1997, Jacksonville's tax effectiveness rate was 1.11, which was below the national mean of 1.54. The city's per capita property tax burden was down to $510. But, Jacksonville's per capita debt was $7,316, substantially above the national $2,619 per capita average or the state's $4,371 per capita average debt. The City of Jacksonville passed a tax burden onto its future residents (*U.S. Statistical Abstract Annual.* 1998). In FY 2000, state and local combined debt were 75 billion dollars, with a national per capita rank of 19th or $5010 per capita, suggesting that the residents are quite happy to cause an equity burden issue (*Governing Source Book*, 2002: 40). That is, Florida's public officials have simply shifted the cost of services to a less visible category, and placed the burden on the next generation of Floridians.

Jacksonville's woes have been repeated in communities throughout Florida. The challenge to budget analysts is to find alternative methods of revenue enhancement. These alternatives must meet expenditure requirements for state mandated levels of service that do not create "disincentives to further economic development or...[fuel] a taxpayer revolt similarly to the one prompting California's Proposition 13" (MacManus, 1991).

Fiscal Policy Planning

Fiscal policy planning generates and presents information to improve the decisional basis for local officials. **Fiscal policy planning** is a systematic way of responding to a changing policy environment by allowing planners to strategically integrate the community's financial resources into the community's effort to promote intentional change (Streib, 1992; Mattson, 1991; Halachmi and Boydston, 1991). It's a mechanism to integrate the comprehensive plan into the community's overall financial management system (McKay, 1989:44). Fiscal policy planning encompasses at least three local governmental planning tasks: (1) the management capacity to forecast revenues and expenditures; (2) the ability to undertake a capital facilities planning program; and (3) the management capacity to devise a planning strategy for alternative revenue enhancement. Fiscal policy planning helps maintain the linkages between a city's comprehensive plan and it municipal budget by assisting in efforts to assure rational budgetary allocations to pay for public facilities and municipal service levels (Halachmi and Boydston, 1991; O'tool and Stipak, 1991).

Table 9.1 provides a breakdown of policy behavior in the earlier recessionary time period. In our 1988/89 survey for the Florida League of Cites, we had 66 towns respond, indicating a 42.3 % response rate. The follow-up survey by the University of North Florida Center for Local Government had 77 of the original 155 sample towns respond, giving a 49.6%

response rate. A principal focus was on cities within the 31 small counties with less than 50,000 populations, which is home to 5 percent of the states population. In addition, we were looking at those 16 counties located on the urban-rural fringe facing immediate growth related sprawl issues. In our survey, of the 77 communities, 41 towns indicated that they forecast revenues and expenditures, which is approximately 54 percent of those reporting.

Without knowledge of revenue sources, it is somewhat difficult to administer a current town budget or plan for future capital facility expenditures. For this reason, Chapter 9J-5 of the Florida Administrative Code, known as **Rule 9J5,** requires a financial feasibility plan as part of a community's analysis of the availability and adequacy of existing and future public facilities as detailed within the town's comprehensive plan. Part of this feasibility plan requires the town to forecast its revenues and expenditures for public projects, tying both financial management functions to the town's capital facilities plan (McKay, 1989:40-43). Contrary to popular belief, forecasting does not commit a city to a particular policy stance or set of public programs. Rather, forecasting allows for a community to make adjustments with regards to its tax base or its level of public expenditures. Forecasting allows a town to identify and adopt suitable alternative revenue enhancement strategies when needed for public service allocations (Reed and Swain,1990: Ch. 7; MacManus and Groth, 1989). It provides a realistic understanding of a town's tax base and tax structure. Without forecasting, any proposed budget is highly unrealistic. Klay (1977) notes that in rapidly growing smaller Florida towns, the forecasting technique had become an essential component to a small town's policy repertoire. Not to forecast is "to increase the possibility that needs, which soon become critical, will be overlooked; or that resources will be squandered on misguided projects." Unlike stable communities, sprawl communities are less likely to retain accepted lines of communication that are critical to public policymaking (Seroka, 1986; Keller and Wamsley, 1978).

Florida planners are trained to utilize projection techniques for population, employment and housing needs. We would expect that revenue and expenditure forecasting would at least be available within towns with planners. Over two-thirds of the towns utilize historic trend analysis. Moreover, if a town did forecast, it was to anticipate expenditure rather than revenues (Chi. Sq.= 11.08; df=1; p> .01; Cramers V= 2.99). The historic trend analysis is the least sophisticated and is known as the "best guess" or "sniffing in the wind" method. It presumes future behavior is tied to past behavior and past revenue history. Since 54 percent of the town's surveyed indicate access to planning knowledge, this is quite puzzling. One possible explanation is that planners, finance officers and city managers seek simple methods of prediction that will limit possible distortion of revenues. Known as "make it simple, but not stupid" rule, the town government limits its knowledge base "to those things that are familiar"(Gargan,1987; Klay, 1977,1991). Contingency studies can become troubling. Historic trend analysis minimizes the uncertainty within the policy domain. Forecasts become incremental, usually on the low revenue side. For the local publicly elected official, chances of forecasting high expenditure trends are minimized. There is a consistent effort to be safe in determining how much money can be spent for local projects, making it difficult to pay for innovative projects. **Historic Trend Analysis** has one glaring shortcoming. It is difficult in times of changing economic circumstances such as increasing fuel oil prices to predict revenues accurately (Reed and Swain, 1993:119-120).

By contrast, **Regression Line Analysis**, may be viewed as too technical by locally elected officials. There are two explanations which may indicate why Florida's small town officials are unwilling to adopt this analytical technique. The first explanation is that publicly elected officials did not trust or appreciate the technical aspects of regression analysis. As a statistical tool, several officials reported in the surveys that with a variety of possible outcomes they felt uncomfortable in the selection of any particular strategy. Secondly, other local officials felt that they would lose political and administrative control over the budgetary process. Regression analysis coupled with a performance budget was simply too technical and complicated approach for local officials who spent most of their political lives applying simple bargaining and negotiation strategies to accomplish public policymaking. At least with historic trend analysis, the city council can play the ABCs of politics—accommodation, bargaining and compromise.

In rapidly growing Florida communities, Klay (1977; 1991) reports that "crisis politics" is dominant. Both the politician and the locally appointed public official (i.e., city planner, city manager or city finance director) tend to see forecasting as a valuable tool if it will simplify one's political decision-making. Accordingly, most city officials do not wish volumes of undigested data. Instead, they want an answer that plainly illustrates the political tradeoffs. Therefore, mactans and Grothe (1989:390) claim that multi-year forecasts tend to trigger uncertainty and can be confusing. By contrast the simple historic trend-line model does not. "Politicos in distressed jurisdictions already have enough political problems without creating more for themselves with multi-year forecasts." For these above reasons the historic trend line technique is more popular for municipal expenditure projections.

Table 9.1 Breakdown of Florida Municipalities by Population Size (N=155)

City Size	Cities Surveyed 1988/92	Cities Responding 1988/89	1992/93
Village < 10,000	75	18	36
Small Town 10,000 to 24,999	34	16	20
Small City 25,000 to 49,999	23	15	7
Midsized Urban Center 50,000 to 100,000	23	17	14
Total	155	66	77

Sources: *Florida TIF City Survey (1989); **Florida DCA CDBG Files (1992).

Capital Facilities Planning

Even in times of fiscal stress, the 1985 state growth management program requires a capital facilities plan. **Capital facility planning** and **capital improvement programming** are different aspects of the fiscal policy planning process. Capital facilities planning looks at the capacity needs of existing infrastructures to determine the "long-range needs [as] related to particular categories of public facilities," especially in regards to the types of population to be served (Steiss, 1975: 9). Capital facility planning is the umbrella process for both the **Capital Improvement Plan (CIP)** and the **Capital Budget.** Capital facility planning, therefore, is a "systematic process" for recommending capital projects needed to attain the long-range development objectives of a community (Catanese, 1974: 44).

Capital facility planning is essential to a town's economic revitalization and viability. A capital facility plan provides the planner with a framework for knowing "which services will be provided, in what quantity, at what cost, over what time period, in what manner, and for whom" (Bryce, 1979: 41). By contrast, **the Capital Improvement Program** links the placement timing with the financing of new public facilities (Bowyer, 1993). However, the Capital Improvement Program [CIP] should not be confused with the **Capital Budget** which is part of the annual operating budget. The Capital Improvement Program (CIP) includes all the capital projects that the municipality intends to undertake for a specific period of years, to meet the public facility needs of the community (Bowyer, 1993). The Capital Improvement Program (CIP) is a schedule for all present and future capital facility projects within the community as required by the comprehensive plan. The CIP can be viewed as a multi-year capital budget that itemizes the timing and financing of needed capital projects. These projects are arranged in a sequential order "extending over a relatively long period and based on a schedule of priorities, and involves the assignment of a 'price tag' to their development over a more immediate time period" (Steiss, 1975: 9). In other words, the Capital Improvement Plan provides a long range, multi-year budgeting timetable for such capital projects as fire stations, swimming pools or public schools (Elrich, et. al. 1995; Bowyer, 1993). Unfortunately, many planning staffs ignore the linkage between the CIP and the Comprehensive plan as part of the town's budgetary process.

The **Capital Budget** process is the financial arm of the capital improvement's plan. In growth management it helps establish a yearly priority review of replacement needs of existing infrastructures as well as potential capital project needs. The capital budget is a multistage process. First, the planning staff considers each project, then the planner costs-out each project, and finally determines the method of payment for each listed project. Ideally, the capital budget is viewed as part of the city's municipal budget document that is expected to be implemented within the forthcoming year. As part of the city's budget document, it should provide information pertaining to financial aspects of project funding (Bowyer, 1993; Steiss,1988; Bryce, 1979). In times of recession, capital budgets are especially vulnerable because they are funded by three major revenue components—own-source revenues, intergovernmental grants and debt financing. In Florida, own source revenues tend to vary and are not homogeneous, with sales and property being the principal sources. During times of fiscal stress, own-source monies normally allocated to the capital budget are transferred, usually to maintain existing public service levels due to revenue shortfalls (see Ch. 10). State aid also declines, with the legislature cutting back expenditures to balance the budget. And, the debt issuance's declines due to the vagaries of the fiscal health of the cities tax base. In our survey during the 1990s recession, 59 of the responding cities (76%) indicated an active capital budget process. Apparently, city form was not a factor. According to **Table 9.2** there was no significance when correlated to city form. Neither a council manager nor a mayor council form of government played an influential role in capital budget adoption. That is, both forms played a similar role with both acting in a similar manner during the period of fiscal stress.

Capital Improvement Planning (CIP) is a valuable fiscal policy tool for long-range public project planning (Bowyer, 1993; Steiss, 1975). A capital improvement plan is a performance indicator for planning management sophistication. Cities with a CIP are more likely to possess planning expertise (Doss, 1987) and have better financial management capacity (Erlich,1995). Our updated survey indicates that, among the 77 Florida communities, only 42 responding towns (54%) had a capital improvement plan **(Table 9.3)**. This is somewhat confusing and contradictory to the capital budget findings. When investigating city form, the undated survey found that there was a level of significance (Chi. Sq.=6.91, df=1; p>.01; Craver's V=.298). **Table 9.3** suggests that a town manager community is more likely to exhibit capital improvement planning policy behavior, supporting the planning management thesis.

The **1985 Growth Management Act** does require a capital improvement plan for infrastructure that is consistent with neighboring jurisdictions. Moreover, it requires the town to provide a financial policy strategy for anticipated capital projects needed to meet future population growth and land development. The council managers' towns are more likely to have adopted both policy tools. On the other hand, as **Table 9.2** indicates, there is no significant difference between city form; that is, a mayor council city is just as likely as a city manager form to have a capital budget. This is what we would have expected from enforcement of the **1985 Growth Management Act.** The finding in **Table 9.3** tells us that professional capacity is a factor among smaller cities, supporting our earlier contention that management capacity is essential for policy innovation.

User Charges, Dedications And Impact Fees

In rapidly growing regions, Florida's local governments are turning to non tax sources to pay for suburban sprawl. Increasingly, developers are being asked to pay a share for the streets, parks and public utilities. **Table 9.4** illustrates that Traditional Individualistic policy behavior still remains' viable. In our analysis of Florida League of City communities, it was found that the faster growing, "spill over, leapfrogging" urban-rural towns are more likely to rely on impact fees. This suggests that after 15 years of growth management planning, this tool has gain worthy acceptance by urban-rural fringe community leaders.

User Charges or Service Fees

With the decline in the availability of federal dollars, local governments have little choice but to raise revenues from alternative sources. One such promising means is to shift the cost of sprawl onto developers and new homeowners. Roberts (1986) points out that Florida's political climate makes property taxes highly unacceptable. Moreover, service user fees and impact fees are beginning to be seen as an extension of the "well-established practice" of dedications as part of "on-site costs" in most subdivision regulations. For local officials suburban sprawl in times of revenue shortfalls means a shift to non-tax revenue sources such as service fees or user charges. For FY 2000/01, Governing magazine reports that Floridians paid a total of $1447 per capita in service fees and other user charges, ranking Florida 8th among the states. These officials are willing to adopt such fees, discovering it to be a cash cow, with about 24.6 percent of all local revenues derived from such sources (*Governing Source Book*, 2002:38). No longer is the idea that "growth for growth" sake is a feasible option for cash-strapped local governments.

Table 9.4 tells us that Florida's rural, small towns adopt a "growth by the installment plan." Whereas small towns in the rural-urban fringe are adopting impact fees, this is not the case in the rural areas. The "pricing" of public services by **user fees** is the policy approach. User fees are design to cover additional expenses that local government incurs when providing a municipal service. A user fee normally represents a "payment for services that would not be provided" if a charge was not adopted. In most cases, local government establishes a fee schedule rate that is intended to cover the cost of supplying the particular public service. The pricing schedule will vary according to output, distribution, need and demand. As a pricing mechanism, user fees are believed to reveal citizen preferences. A user fee is a "rationing" tool because the citizen will purchase only the amount that he prefers or can afford, eliminating the possibility of squandering consumption. For municipalities this means that public goods delivered under these conditions should correspond to the preference demands of its residents (Bland, 1989; Raimondo, 1992: 205-210).

Property tax revolts have made user charges quite popular as a source of income for local governments (Downing, 1999; Netzer, 1992). Tied to the benefit principle, the tax burden shared by the homeowner and the businessman is now shared by those who directly benefit from the particular service, helping to reduce the municipal budget (Clark and Ferguson, 1986).

Bland (1989:108-109) discovered that the per capita's property tax burden declined by 16 percent while the user fee per capita's tax burden increased by 40 percent among small cities (< 50,000 persons). Smaller cities, lacking a diversified tax base, have no choice but to shift efforts for own source revenues to user fees. In most cases, municipalities had focused their efforts on establishing service fees on utilities or public services that are not considered to be ordinary functions of local government (Mattson, 1994, 1990; Downing, 1999; Netzer, 1992; Bland, 1989; Frank and Rhodes, 1987). In short, user fees are popular because:

(1) user fees are tied to the benefit tax principle, meaning those who pay are obtaining the direct benefits from the use of the production of such a public good/public service;
(2) user fees can eliminate untidy local political squabbles, allowing all interested game players see themselves in a win-win situation;
(3) and, user fees can compensate local governments for the production of certain public services that are not normally considered part the local government's repertoire of public services at near cost.

For each of these reasons, Florida's small town officials have selected this policy option as a viable means of alternative financing of municipal services. As noted above, 24.6 percent of all revenues are collected in this manner.

Table 9.2 Capital Budget Adoption, by City Form

City Form	Capital Budget Status No	Capital Budget Status Yes	Total
Mayor Council	11	30	41
City Manager	9	27	36
Total	20	59	77

N= 77; Chi Sq.= .313, df= 1 P = no significance
Source: UNF Center for Local Government (1988; 1992)

Table 9.3 Capital Improvement Planning, Adoption by City Form

City Form	Capital Improvement Plan Status No	Yes	Total
Mayor Council	24	17	41
City Manager	11	25	36
Total	35	42	77

N = 77; Chi Sq. = .6.91, df = 1 p > 0.01. Cramer's V = .298
Sources: UNF Center for Local Government Surveys (1988; 1992)

Impact Fees and Required Dedication

Until the 1970s, most private development was subsidized by municipalities under the installment plan, where local governments accepted the "build now, and pay later" method (*Florida Trend*, 1988:31). With the rise in anti-growth sentiment, this strategy became no longer politically viable. Instead, sprawl-impacted communities have shifted the burden onto the builder, justifying such policy behavior under the "privilege to build" doctrine. **Table 9.4** notes that development impact fee category is becoming quite popular in smaller Florida towns and counties. For instance, Hernando County Commission ("Building Impact Fees Increased," *The St. Petersburg Times*, November 2, 2001) had approved a revision of its impact fee schedule. The single-family home builder fee for schools has jumped from $1,173 to $2,406, and for roads from $1, 237 to $1,845. There are at least three reasons for growing popularity of impact fees. Firstly, impact fees protect existing citizen-taxpayer residents from additional costs. Secondly, impact fees allow the community to gain a grip on infrastructure installation costs. Thirdly, impact fees force the developers to think smart. That is, a developer is forced to be "economically prudent" when making investment decisions (Nelson, 1988).

Impact fees are functionally similar to **required dedication** or **in lieu fees.** Both require payments for capital facilities' projects. Yet, there is a key difference. **Required dedication** or **in lieu fees** are predicated on the developer funding infrastructure improvements only on-site. By contrast, impact fees can be applied for both off-site as well as on-site public facilities. Originally, required dedication fees were tied to conditions associated with a subdivision plat's approval. The municipality would grant subdivision plat modifications upon the developer's agreement to provide or dedicate such improvements as street lighting, street curbing or drainage improvements. Overtime, the **"in lieu"** fee was devised as a refinement, in which a developer could substitute money payments for dedication requirements (Juergenmeyer and Roberts, 1998:Ch. 7; Frank and Rhodes, 1987).

Impact fees are also part of local government's repertoire of police powers. In FY 1985 alone, a total of $342 million was raised in impact fees by Florida's municipalities (Nicholas, 1988:116). No doubt, **The1985 Growth Management Act (GMA)** has stimulated the greater use of impact fees. **The 1985 Growth Management Act** did not specify nor require an impact fee as the method to pay for infrastructure development, but it does "encourage local governments" to utilize it as a planning tool (Ch. 163.3201 F.S.) The underlying rationale for impact fee adoption is an equity argument. If a proposed development requires the expansion of public facilities, impact fees are believed to be justified to accommodate that needed expansion. Known as the "but not for" concept, the premise is those existing facilities would not have to expand but for the proposed development. Therefore the new development should pay for the needed expansion (Juergenmeyer and Robert, 1998: 390). Or, in the case of Florida, funds contributed by the developer are "expressly designated and used to accommodate impacts reasonably attributed to the proposed development (Ch. 380.06 [15]).

Florida case law goes beyond the narrow interpretation of 'exclusiveness of benefits' position. Benefits derived from impact fees can spread to others than just those who have paid the fees, "as long as the fee does not exceed the cost of the improvements required by the development which is the source of the fee." (Hollywood, Inc. V. Broward County, Fla. App., 1983). Or as Nicholas (1988:124) claims, the relevant questions for any impact fee are "whether the new development caused the need for the improvement and whether the new development will benefit from it." In other words, the local government must not only establish the impact fee schedule as a valid exercise of police powers, but also establish that the new development has created the need for an expansion of public facilities (Jordon v. Village of Menomonee Falls, Wis. 1965; Wald Corp. v. Metropolitan Dade County, 1976; St. Johns County v. Northeast Florida Builders Assoc., Fla. 1991).

Known as the **rational nexus** test, Florida's impact fees, as exactions, must achieve equity by demonstrating a "reasonable relationship" to the needs created by the new development. Moreover, the fees imposed do not exceed the cost incurred by the community; and, the exaction fees collected are specifically earmarked and are spent directly for the collected purposes (Contractors and Builders Association of Pinellas v. City of Dunedin, Fla. 1976; Broward County v. Janis Development Corp., Fla.1975). By doing so, the local governmental entity is demonstrating a valid exercise of police powers because there is a "reasonable connection" between the need for additional facility capacity, and the new development is paying its "proportionate share" of such public service levels (Juergenmeyer and Robert, 1998:391-398).

Under the rational nexus test, capital facility improvements do not have to be exclusively for the benefit of the new development paying the impact fee. The relevant issue is whether the new development has caused the need for such improvements. Under the **substantial benefit's** criterion, the impact fee is valid if the newcomers are likely to use the public facility and the public facility is within reasonable travel distance for expected use. Based on this criterion, Florida courts upheld the use of impact fees for the expansion of local park systems (Hollywood, Inc. V. Broward County, Fla. 1983; Town of Longboat Key v. Lands End, Fla. 1983) and for road improvements (Home Builders Association v. Board of county Commissioners of Palm Beach County, Fla. 1983). In each case, the local government's planning departments had to substantiate the "reasonableness of the connection" by providing technical data that justified the need for the capital facility improvements (Juergensmeyer, 1985:34-40).

Impact fees are deemed less desirable by Florida's smaller communities **(Table 9.4)**. Small town officials may be somewhat "skittish" about adopting an impact fee ordinance. To avoid legal challenges, an impact fee ordinance requires considerable documentation. Indeed, the formula problems associated with the reasonable relationship between the assessed development fee and the benefit spread can be complicated. The level of professional capacity of small towns may be the explanatory factor for the lack of impact fees. Another explanation may simply be the desire by small town officials not to discourage growth. For these two reasons, small town officials may have retained the growth by installment plan policy option.

Table 9.4 does tell us that rural small town officials do not see impact fees as a viable policy option. Instead, **user fees** are the more plausible option. The attractiveness of user fees may be tied to the fact that they are less complicated to implement. Besides, user fees are targeted to those who are using the public service and are paying in proportion to the benefits they derive from it. Other residents who don't use it are not subsidizing the public service from the general taxes. In fiscally stressful times, user fees encounter less opposition from the citizen-taxpayer, exhibiting a Traditional

Individualistic political cultural trait. Under the "Full Cost Accounting Provision" of Bush's Florida Growth Management Study Commission had recommended the adoption of a broad range of user fee strategies. Unfortunately, the budgetary crisis has sidetracked this and many other reforms (Smitt, "The Novel Full Cost Accounting Provision," *The Tampa Tribue*, April 6, 2001).

Discussion

The 1985 Growth Management Act was passed by the legislature in response to the mounting cost of public sprawl. Each county had to devise a financial feasibility plan to assure adequate levels of the infrastructure. We found, during the fiscal crisis of 1992, smaller communities were unwilling to innovate. Only 54 percent had a capital facility planning procedure and/or were willing to implement capital facility projects. And, fewer were willing to impose any fiscal policy tools, claiming the recession and budgetary crisis was a factor. It is quite possible that this reluctance to implement an aggressive financial planning management program may be partly due to a lack of financial/planning management capacity and partly due to the fiscal stress faced by many of Florida's cities during this period (1988-92). The Traditional-Individualistic political culture, with its conservative fiscal

Table 9.4 The Breakdown Of Alternative Fiscal Policy Planning Proposals Among Florida's Smaller Communities

Proposed Strategy	FY 1988/89*	FY 1992/93**
Retrenchment	47	55
Raise User Fees	43	51
Raise License Fees	9	14
Utilize Impact Fees	7	10
Raise Option Sales Tax	5	7
Utilize Debt Financing	5	7
Raise Millage Rate	0	2
Dedication (In Lieu Fees)	0	2

Sources:
*Florida TIF Study (1989), N=49, 132 city subsample in 47 non-urban county survey
**UNF Florida Needs Analysis Survey Update (1992), N=62, 132 city subsample
The N indicates the number of responding cities for this particular question.

tendencies, had also played a role. In FY 2001, with another fiscal crisis at hand, the state legislature under pressure from its local constituencies sidetracked Governor Bush's more modest proposals within the Florida Growth Management Study Commission report. At the state legislative level there has been little political will to experiment in times of budgetary shortfalls. Therefore, can we expect any alternative policy behavior from small communities? I think not. With fewer dollars available from the state, fewer dollars coming in from tourism, local governments are willing to undertake planning projects that require extensive financing.

I contend that the policy architects of the **1985 Growth Management Act** had ignored the inherent Traditional-Individualistic policy behavior among local communities. This political cultural sentiment exhibited itself in both the FY 1995 and the FY2001/02 legislative sessions. In 1995, the legislature made changes to the growth management legislation which stressed local planning solutions to the financing of public projects. Florida's current budget crisis (FY 2002) is only likely to aggravate an already fiscally sensitive statewide problem. The policy behavior of the state legislature during the present budgetary crisis indicates little sympathy toward growth and environmentally related issues. Academic scholarship suggests that legislators function according to one's job role, the rituals of the institution and the political orientation of their respective constituencies. Each legislative body tends to jealously guards' it institutional prerogatives. Former Democratic Governor Askew discovered this first hand. In 1975, the State Senate did not appreciate his meddling into its procedural affairs. The then Democratic Senate President blocked Askew's social services secretary appointment and then scold the Governor Askew. Governor Bush has encountered a similar fate in his efforts to obtain Phil Handy's confirmation as state educational board chair. For many senate Republicans, Bush appears to have neglected education, a powerful local constituency, and decided to take him down a "peg or two at Handy's expense." (Dyckman, "The State of the State in Tallahassee," *The St. Petersburg Times*, March 31, 2002). Nor was immunity granted to Governor Chiles when the Democrats were in power. During the 1991/93 Recession, Governor Chiles attempted to push a tax/budgetary reform agenda. State lawmakers simply closed ranks and guarded their prerogatives. For political cosmetic purposes, they did close some loopholes, and made some minor administrative budgetary changes. Overtime, Democratic Governor Chiles was forced to dismantle his tax and budgetary reform efforts. In turn, the legislature was able to go about its business in the same old manner.

During the early Chiles Administration, the House was somewhat more liberal than the Senate. Yet, neither house is very liberal when compared to a Frostbelt legislature. Indeed, today's Florida Senate is more moderate than the House. Serving four years and having a larger population base may be the reason. Legislative Term Limits provide for an alternative explanation. Prior to 1992, the incumbent reelection rate was about 90 percent, giving the county courthouse politicians considerable power within the legislature. But public confidence was waning. The statewide "Eight Is Enough" referendum changed the incumbency rate, manifesting the lack of public confidence for state officials. Now legislators and cabinet official face an eight-year term limit (Dye, 1998:99). This has weakened the local party apparatus for both Republicans and Democrats. It may have also helped ensure the emergence of dedicated conservative insurgent at the grassroots, making it more difficult to instill party discipline among Republicans.

The impact of term limits on legislative policymaking is making its appearance. First, among House members, half are first term freshmen with no institutional memory. As newcomers, it takes them at least one annual session to merely understand the House's rules and procedures, making them less independent. Secondly, with half the party leadership not returning in 2003, the special sessions appeared to be lame duck sessions, causing a further breakdown in party discipline. Thirdly, with a limited house staff for advice, the Florida House members are becoming increasingly susceptible to lobbyists. On the other hand, the Senate, with 39 members previously serving, was less susceptible. Senate President McKay was able to maintain some loyalty on the sales service tax issue. But, with one in four leaving after the FY 2002 session, many key GOP lawmakers became dissenters. "They no longer are responsible to those who elected them." They were free "to act on their own impulses." This is the downside of term limit reform ("Legislature: Limited Vision," *The Florida Times Union*, May 2, 2002; M. Dyckman. "The State of the State in Tallahassee," *St Petersburg Press*, March 31, 2002).

The complexity of social and environmental alignments only complicated the politics in the legislature. The two chambers were not simply a division between Republicans and Democrats, with the Republicans in control of both houses. In fact, the impasse between the House Speaker and the Senate President was not over deep-seeded ideological differences. Both legislative Houses are highly Traditional-Individualistic, reflecting the dominant civic core vales of their constituencies. Instead it was over intra party rivalries, tied to factions and the loss of party discipline. Adding to this splintering, there was a determined cadre of special interest lobbyists that seems to flourish within this style of plural-executive governance. The fiscal crisis had only complicated matters. The budget pie got smaller. Apparently, many Floridians feel they are overtaxed, and believe that the current state tax structure is adequate ("Panel recommends sales tax review," *Pensacola News Journal*, February 15, 2002). House member Randy Bell's (R-Titusville) perspective may simply be a reflection of the dominance of Traditional-Individualism within the two houses. "Our tax system is a good one." It is good because "it has more than funded the population growth and demographic shifts of recent years while allowing historic amounts of dollar in tax relief...." For Randy Bell, there is no real lack of money. Instead he believes that it is a "lack of discipline" in regards to state and local governmental expenditures ("Tax reform effort badly flawed," *Florida Today*, February 22, 2002).

Whenever possible the Legislature has shifted the tax burden of growth management onto the tourist or the relocated residential home owner. What if the tourist doesn't come? What if the newcomer/home buyer decides to move elsewhere? When tourism is up, and homebuilding is up, there are few rain clouds on the horizon. Under such conditions, the Sunshine State can fiscally function fairly well. However, a narrow tax base is not designed to weather a long term thunderstorm. It simply lacks the fiscal cushion. Since national recessions are inevitable, another Florida budgetary crisis is likely to occur. If past fiscal stress policy behavior is any indication, the same policy behavior is likely to be adopted again. Although there will be new players at the state level, if past legislative policy behavior is an indicator, then there will be greater impact on the fiscal health of local Florida communities and greater impact on Florida's fragile environment during the next fiscal stress situation, making it necessary for better fiscal policy planning management in the future by local governments.

Chapter 10
Municipal Services and Small Florida Towns

Conventional wisdom holds that one can gain a clear understanding of a community's priorities merely by focusing on budgetary policy outputs. Although budgetary allocation has helped us to understand how the budgetary process operates, small town budgetary allocation behavior does have its limitations, especially in the realm of coalition building among diverse groups (Rubin, 1982; Honadle and Sokolow, 1984; Clark, et. al., 1986). An alternative approach is the investigation of municipal service priorities (Koven, 1988; Mattson, 1990). For small towns, where population scale precludes specifying which client or ethnic group has directly obtained the benefits, an examination of the priority ranking of municipal services is possibly a better indicator of local policy planning behavior, correcting for the difficulty of investigating internalize derived group benefits from policy outputs.

Public Goods and Fiscal Stress

Small town planners are resource allocators. Furthermore, a small town planning agency is characterized as a publicly funded organization, which is operationally defined as an administrative structure that: (1) is highly depended upon budgetary cycles; (2) tends to have vague, if not conflicting and/or multiple program missions; and (3) is by nature an institution that is expected to help assist in the provision of public goods.

Municipal services are a form of **public goods** that are defined with the following attributes. First, they are public or municipal services that can be consumed by all members of the community. Second, exclusion is difficult because each citizen taxpayer/ voter has the ability to consume them without diminishing the consumption availability to any other citizen- consumer, regardless of whether that other individual consumer is a local taxpayer or not. In theory, these two attributes are highly relevant for municipalities because such attributes may make it too costly to exclude those who do not directly pay for the municipal service in the form of taxes. Such persons who benefit from the public service are known as a **free riders** (Savas, 1987; Buchanan, 1984: Ch. 19; Moore, 1978). **Free riders** pose a problem for small towns with limited resources. Streets are excellent examples of such a public good. Because of the characteristics of joint consumption and non-exclusion, it is quite difficult for the local government to prevent the benefits derived from joint consumption by all travelers who pass through the community. For example, constant truck traffic can "tear up" local roads. But, road repairs must be borne by local taxpayers.

Large metro centers have substantial flexibility with regard to their municipal budgets. Most rural communities do not. In fact, if rural communities were to adopt such urban oriented budgetary behavior for road repair, these rural towns would be likely to incur huge deficits, placing themselves in fiscal jeopardy. Too often, small towns must adopt a "make do without" policy choice. This chapter will focus on three aspects of this problem. First, we will discuss the concept **fiscal stress** and consider some of the ways it has been addressed. Next, we will evaluate the issue of **essential** versus **nonessential** municipal services so that we may understand how priorities are being established by small Florida communities. Finally, we will examine how smaller Florida cities are coping with the policy pressures of **The 1985 Growth Management Act**.

Defining Fiscal Stress, Privatization and Retrenchment

Fiscal strain means the inability of a local government to maintain existing service levels and meet the demands of urbanization (Clark and Ferguson, 1983). **Fiscal stress**, however, is viewed in a more narrow context. It is defined as the gap between existing public service needs and the expectations of residents for certain public service levels. This is equated in terms of maintaining municipal service expenditure levels and the ability to raise needed revenues to meet those expenditure levels. Therefore, **fiscal stress** is the point where budgetary expenditures consistently outstrip the ability of the community to raise revenues. **Fiscal stress** does not mean **fiscal distress**, which is the point at which a municipality can no longer pay for specific municipal services at existing cost levels. As a consequence, existing municipal services cannot be expanded or new programs created without raising taxes. Under conditions of fiscal distress, although the desires for existing municipal service levels remain, the local citizen-taxpayer is unwilling to pay for these existing municipal services out of additional tax levies. Subsequently, since raising taxes is not a viable policy option, local officials must seek an alternative strategy (Mattson, 1990; Pammer, 1990; Stein, 1990; Blitz and Pilegge, 1987).

There have certainly been no lack of attempts to explain and identify general patterns of response to situations of fiscal stress (Rubin, 1982; Weinberg, 1984; Mattson, 1990). Levine, et. al.(1981) documents the expected relationships between varying types of revenue change and accompanying patterns of political activism from specialized interest groups. Accordingly, all large cities undergo three sequential phases of fiscal stress/distress ("no revenue growth," "moderate revenue growth," and "severe decline"), which influence local municipal policy making. Each strategy is designed to share the pain" in the provision of public goods and services. Under **no revenue growth**, a municipality will cover fiscal difficulties through a series of stop gap measures, but no actual alterations in resource budgetary allocations will emerge. By contrast, when the situation of **moderate revenue decline** develops, unions or citizen groups will mobilize to protect their own areas of self interest. Subsequently, short-term adjustments, such as hiring freezes will be adopted. However, by phase three when **make do with less** no longer suffices, fiscal distress will manifest itself. Public officials will then issue **across the board cutbacks** edicts, hoping to limit the political fallout on funding priorities. It is only at this phase that public officials are willing to adopt drastic policies, including **target cuts, privatization** and **centralization of policy power**. While the authors' model was not entirely substantiated by their own case study research, their emphasis on **stretching techniques** and the role of **centralized decision-making** have served as foundations for evaluations of policy priorities in times of fiscal retrenchment.

Public officials, rather than the general public, play the deciding role in determining policy strategy during fiscal stress(Rubin, 1982; Weinberg, 1984).

When revenue enhancement strategies are not politically feasible, "stretching" techniques are utilized: 1) reducing existing public service levels (cutbacks); 2) shifting a municipal service to the private sector (load shedding or service shedding); 3) contracting the municipal service out to the private sector or another governmental entity (contracting out); or 4) shifting the responsibility onto a voluntary private agency or organization (co-production). Collectively, each of these strategies imply an expenditure reduction on part of the local municipality. Moreover, the last three strategies usually fall under the rubric of alternative service delivery, suggesting that local officials have concluded that privatization of municipal services has become necessary.

Privatization is a policy option that can be highly seductive. Privatization in its three distinct forms (load shedding, contracting out and co-production) allows for the public policy outputs to be provided under some sort of public-private agreement. For the municipal government this policy choice can minimize the municipality's expenditure obligations while maintaining existing service levels (Hilke, 1992; Stein, 1990; Barnekov, et. al., 1989; Morgan and England, 1988). Or as Donahue(1989: 136) remarks, privatization is a tactical "gambit for easing back on city services that the citizens simultaneously insist upon but refuse to pay for it."

Advocates of privatization contend that citizens have either (1) scope of public choices expanded or (2) service quality improved without eliminating the full range of public services (Stein, 1990; Donohue, 1989; Savas, 1987). But privatization should not be casually adopted for two reasons. First, there is a potential for loss of program flexibility and public accountability. Second, Cost shifting onto the resident can lead to social inequities. Thus local governments are frequently reluctant to take the somewhat painful step of managing governmental activities by privatization (Calder and Mattson, 1990; Barnekov, et. al. 1989; Moe, 1987; Ferris, 1986).

Defining Essential and Non-Essential Public Services

When faced with the prospect of reducing government responsibilities through privatization options, communities must assign priorities to the various services provided in order to distinguish essential from non-essential services. In nonmetropolitan communities the optimal mix and level of locally delivered services is determined by the "willingness to pay" criterion. Despite this "willingness to pay" criterion, small town officials find it difficult to determine true "taxprice." As noted, small town, white Florida residents tend to be conservatives, who wish to keep taxes low. Moreover, many have converted to Republican policies that emphasize limited government. This Republican outlook makes it increasingly difficult for local, rural Democratic officials to gauge local municipal budget priorities.

The public choice perspective provides a means for understanding local municipal budget priorities. If a household will choose to locate its residence by comparing the tax burden, then a rational individual will choose h/her place of residence where the best combination of a municipal service-amenity tax package exists (Tiebout, 1956; Schneider, 1989; Lyons,et. al., 1992). Throughout Florida, communities are in competition to attract households. If a newcomer is dissatisfied with the municipal service tax package, he or she as a citizen-taxpayer can select another town nearby that will provide a level and/or mix of services that best corresponds to h/her preferences. This is known as the concept of **citizen-consumer sovereignty**.

Citizen-consumer sovereignty simply means that the citizen-taxpayer is informed of alternative municipal service-amenity tax packages. Subsequently, the citizen taxpayer/consumer will maximize and match municipal service preferences (Lyons, et. al., 1992: Ch. 5; Stein,1990: Ch. 2; Schneider, 1989: Ch.3). Schumaker (1991) claims that citizen preferences are tied to a community's dominant political culture. Subsequently, in a pluralistic society, citizens will **vote with their feet** by selecting the community that best matches h/her tax expenditure policy choices (**policy congruence**). Policy congruence is more likely to be realized in large urban areas, where there is an existence of multiple local governments (Hirsch, 1964; Sharp, 1986; Schneider, 1989; Lyons, et. al. 1992). It is the possible to "simulate an efficient local market for public goods in which metropolitan residents 'shop around' to locate a community where service/tax bundle offered by local government most closely approximate individual preferences" (Schneider, 1989: 12).

Small town residents rarely are able to enjoy the same policy opportunities. Firstly, small towns have a limited economic base, which precludes the provisioning a wide array of municipal services. Secondly, small towns rarely are able to spawn the development of specialized interest groups needed to stimulate the demand for a variety of public services. Thirdly, the population scale is more likely to encourage a highly personalized political perspective that tends to engender elite-dominated politics. Finally, the spatial distance between population centers may preclude full mobility of households and firms (Swanson, et. al., 1979; Exoo, 1984). Given these four aspects, the traditional methods of "taking the pulse" of the several communities (referenda, surveys, lobbying or public hearings) may be imprecise.

Policy planning presumes that selected policy choices are incrementally determined by the majority of citizen-taxpayers (Downs, 1957). Or as Hirsch (1964) notes, political proximity is a key component in determining true policy preferences. For this reason, the small town dweller may have a **fiscal equivalence** advantage over his urban/suburban counterparts. That is, the policy choices selected will correspond to both the benefit areas as well as the political boundaries of the community (Lyons, et. al.1992; Raimondo, 1992: 40-61). But, as Peterson (1981) points out, all cities are constrained in their service policy choices. Due to fixed spatial boundaries, most cities must guard themselves from "raids" of other cities on their industrial and household base. Rational fiscal policy planning expects a city to provide a wide range of essential services that will enhance its economic base. At the same time, there should be a strong disincentive to use scarce local resources for non-essential services. Or as Stein (1990: 18) notes, "Expenditures on redistributive services are not a function of demand but simply a matter of available fiscal capacity and the charitable inclinations of the city."

Small towns generally exhibit informal patterns of leadership. This informal character of policy-making is shaped largely by the town's political culture. If scale is an aspect of fiscal equivalence, then the small town is more likely exhibit true policy congruence. Accordingly, in rural areas, where a long standing local business elite has held sway over local governance, political proximity has aided in the development of a pattern of informal procedural networks that is dominated by this elite (Keller, 1978; Swanson, et. al., 1979: Ch.5; Wikstrom, 1993).

Essential public services are municipal services that are critical to the effective functioning and/or proper maintenance of a community. This implies that an essential municipal service is a collective public good. That is, the municipal service benefits are available to all citizen-consumers of the community, regardless of whether the recipient has paid taxes. No doubt, some citizen consumers are "free riders" under the "essential service umbrella." The overriding objective of essential service provision is to create a safe, civil society which supercedes the exclusion principle (Mattson and Twogood, 1991). The **principle of non-exclusion** refers to the fact that certain public services are simply too difficult to prevent anyone from deriving a benefit from their use (roads, traffic signals, and police protection).

An **essential service** is normally financed by the city out of its own revenue resources. By doing so, the city officials can establish parameters for both political responsiveness and political proximity. Due to production costs, however, a municipal service may be contracted out but not completely privatized. The cost for an essential service is still paid from public tax dollars. An essential service may be classified either as a **caretaker** public service [i.e., police or fire protection, traffic lights, solid waste disposal, etc.] because the service protects, promotes, and/or manages the health and/or safety of the public; or, as a **promoter** type service [i.e., street maintenance, street lights, water/sewer service, etc.], because the service economically enhances the proper maintenance of the city.

In contrast, a **non-essential public service** is not deemed to be critical to the effective functioning and/or proper maintenance of the municipal government. Although highly useful to the overall community's quality of life, if not directly produced or financed by the city council, the community's social and economic activities will not come to a screeching halt. Additionally, a non-essential municipal service is a less visible service. There are two classifications. **Amenity type** services such as libraries, zoos, museums or swimming pools are recreational and/or cultural type services. Often these services are classified as a merit good that is rationed by some sort of "patronage" user fee. By contrast, **management-support** public services (building inspection, legal aid services, planning, etc.) are also desirable, but are not deemed critical to the effective functioning of a community. Such services are frequently funded by an outside source [intergovernmental aid or intergovernmental compact].

Public Services and the New South

Small southern towns will rarely exhibit the political will to accept social innovative risk taking. Moreover, locally southern elected officials tend to operate within a highly personalized decision-making setting, where these part-time civic-minded politicians have a strong desire to avoid conflict (Wikstrom, 1993; Ramsey, 1995). Finally, small towns rarely have the budgetary slack for innovative management activity. With limited budgetary revenues, local professional staff have few "stakes" or "goodies" that they may utilize to orchestrate incentives to induce management innovation. With few budgetary goodies, there are fewer opportunities to "spread the benefits" over the entire community and thereby encourage negotiation and bargaining among policy actors to assure innovation adoption (Mattson and Solano, 1986; Benton and Daly, 1992). In times of fiscal stress, the politics of retrenchment does not mean bargaining for the optimization of public services; rather, it means the deferment or cutting back of nonessential public services.

The South has always had a political history of limited scope in public services. In Jeffersonian-Jacksonian period, the individual, not the government, was expected to assume responsibility for basic services. At the time, a legal moat surrounded private property. Under the **public purpose doctrine**, Traditional-Individualism dominated the southern town building process, with private property rights well-defined. It was a time when municipal government stopped at the property line. Or as Warner (1995: 26) remarks,"If toilets, fire barriers, windows, stairs and central heating were to be installed, the landowner had to do it, and execution therefore was dependent upon his financial capabilities and his personal willingness to modernize." According to Goldfield and Brownell (1979: 167), there were two reasons:

> First, government intervention implied an interference with private property and the regulation of living habits, two areas in which Americans insisted on privacy. Second, active intervention meant fiscal support. Once state-granted charters were amended to approve revenue-raising powers, the burden of supporting new programs fell upon the leaders themselves, since property tax was the greatest source of revenue. Local government which consisted primarily of the community's business leaders implemented plans only when the benefits to the city's economic growth out-weighed the costs to the property holders.

State courts could invoke the doctrines of public nuisance and/or police power to prevent an individual from using h/her property in a detrimental manner either to the public safety or the public order. Property owners could "face potential liability for acts that inflicted injury on the community" (Ely, 1992: 60-61). If government did intervene, it tended be in a cautious manner. Ordinances enacted were often piecemeal and far from being comprehensive, with fire codes and sanitary improvements as the two principal justification for governmental intervention (Hammack, 1988). The nineteenth century town street was mostly comprised of dirt, which was muddy in the wet season and dusty in the dry season. Lack of storm drainage was a frequent complaint among citizens, especially in the yellow fever prone coastal towns where standing pools of waste remained commonplace (Larsen, 1990: 55-57; Crooks, 1991: 12). Even in sophisticated urban centers, town residents were often dependent on springs and wells for their drinking and privies to dispose of their human waste. Ordinances enforcing cleanliness were frequently ignored, with garbage and litter cluttering vacant lots and all but the main thoroughfares. Local residents often discovered that streets were "not only offensive to their eyes, nose and ears, but also a threat to health" (Leavitt, 1986: 24). Horses were especially troublesome, as there was likely to be one horse for every four citizens. It has been estimated that in a single working day, " a thousand horses deposited about five hundred gallons of urine and ten tons of dung on the streets." (Larsen, 1990: 84). Hogs, goats, and vultures were allowed to forage in the streets as a means of coping with the garbage, but these animals mostly succeeded in transforming "one form of sidewalk pollution into another." (Bartlett, 1998: 56).

Towns and cities with their unpaved streets mired in horse manure, inadequate or nonexisting water supplies, malfunctioning privy vaults, stagnant pools of water, and open sewers were likely to experience periodic epidemics of typhoid, cholera, and yellow fever (Leavitt, 1986; Crooks, 1991). Existing health boards were ad hoc, reactive entities. Once the epidemic seemed to run its course, the health board was disbanded, with "the town council applauding its efforts." Its members resumed their regular occupations, "remaining like a militia ready to act instantly at the onset of the next pestilential episode." Apparently, this laissez-faire style to health enforcement fit neatly with the nineteenth century notion "that city government existed only to allow individuals the opportunity to engage in commerce and manufacturing" (Marcus, 1991: 56).

After Reconstruction a "New South" emerged. As the towns grew, civic associations came to believe that their towns could no longer afford to ignore the problems of sanitation. Unpaved, dirty streets pointed "to a disorderly community and possibly an unhealthy one," and both aspects of town life were bad for business (Goldfield and Brownell, 1990: 155). No farmer wanted "to trade cotton or tobacco for yellow fever or cholera" (Goldfield, 1977: 68-71). However, there was no national organization to which communities could look for guidance. The commonality of public health related problems apparently led civic groups in countless American cities to adopt similar courses of action. Throughout the South, civic groups demanded the authority to establish health departments with the task of enforcing the city's health or sanitary codes on a year-round, full time basis. Because of their private makeup, local officials readily agreed (Marcus, 1991: 33-37).

By the 1890s, these early chambers of commerce, known as boards of trades, pushed their respective city officials to regulate everything from garbage collection to privy inspections under the expanded a definition of the police power doctrine. Outside of police and fire protection, the public health issue became the next important policy issue. By funding public health activities from taxes, these local boards of trade established a precedent for regulatory activity in other spheres of urban life (Goldfield, 1977: 72). Even though badly underfunded, privately sponsored city health boards gradually "acquired greater control over sanitary concerns" by maintaining public infirmaries and making nuisance inspections (Larsen, 1990: 41).

On the eve of the Great Depression many southern cities remained streetcar towns, where home place and work place were functionally intertwined, with most of them serving as minor regional economic centers (Harris, 1976; Silver, 1984; Larsen, 1990; Crooks, 1991). Grady's New South doctrine of modernization was not new (Rabinowitz, 1992: 30-34; Wright, 1986: 4-16; Goldfield, 1982: 120-130). It had been the Bourbon blueprint of linking the Old South to the industrial North. "In physical size, population, quality of municipal services, wealth, and actualization of industrial potential" this blueprint, however, meant that southern cities would still lag far behind those northern cities (Silver, 1984: 49). Nevertheless, local political elites were unwilling to give up the Old South. Although public services improved, they were not uniform. Not all streets were cleaned and not all houses were served with improved water and sewer systems.

Income and racial segregation remained intact. Municipal service delivery was allocated and measured "in terms of property values and property maintenance rather in terms of assistance to persons." A Market Equity allocation model emerged in which business community's leadership operated "upon the apparently unquestioned assumption" that they should be given top priority (Harris, 1977). Consequently, even into the 1960s, municipal services to the poorer neighborhoods of any southern community was frequently either inferior or non-existent (Lineberry, 1977; Silver, 1984; Helig and Mundt, 1984; Button, 1989). At the height of the Progressive Era, life in southern black neighborhoods were especially miserable, reporting the highest mortality and tuberculosis rates (Harris, 1977; Crooks, 1991: 50). The poorer Black neighborhoods appeared "as they had in the 1850s: dirt roads, outdoor facilities, poor drainage, and farmed 'double-pen' houses or 'shotgun shacks' that differed little from sharecroppers' dwellings." (Goldfield, 1982: 112). Besides, under "market equity" rules, the white middle-class taxpayer paid the greater proportion of a city's revenues, and considered it unfair that their tax money should go to benefitting the poorer neighborhoods (Harris, 1977: Ch. 8; Silver, 1984: 31-54).

From Progressivism to the Depression

The railroads had become the predominant factor in the creation of Southern interior urban centers. During the Gilded Age, the South nearly doubled its track mileage. Yankee investors had consolidated the railroad network into 31 independent lines, with three-fourths of the track mileage outside Texas controlled by five Northern corporations (Wright, 1986; Rabinowitz, 1977). This steady flow of Yankee dollars assured the expansion of rail links into the Southern hinterland. Even during the Panic of 1893, Florida's rate of new track construction remained above the national average. In fact, in the last decade of the Nineteenth Century, the total track mileage jumped from last to fifth place in the region (Rabinowitz, 1977: 106: Tebeau, 1971).

The major Florida port cities, of course, still played a vital role in the region's economy, but newer hinterland communities began to rival these port cities. Prior to the railroads, a journey to towns along the Old Spanish Mission trails was quite arduous, especially when trying to cross the many rivers. "In the early days most rivers could only be crossed by ferry boat. If the operator was sleeping, drunk, or just obstreperous, travelers had to cool their heels until he was ready" (Waitley, 1997: 350). Railroad technology improved the flow of people and commodities. As the rail system expanded so did local trade areas, ensuring "that all manner of products from precut beef to stone crushers could be sold nationally" (Warner, 1995: 91). Railroads shifted community hierarchy, allowing many former bi-passed country courthouse hamlets to diversify. Towns such as Crestview and Sanford began to be directly connected to seaport towns (Fernandina Beach, Jacksonville or Pensacola). Consequently, they became thriving mini-trade centers for the shipping of cigars, citrus, cattle, phosphates and turpentine (Tebeau, 1971).

Yankee dollars made town expansion boom a reality. At the beginning of the Twentieth Century the old seaports of Jacksonville, Pensacola and Tampa had joined Key West on this list. Yet, Jacksonville, as Florida's premier metropolis with twenty eight thousand souls, was still smaller in size to its regional, seaport competitors—Savannah, Charleston, Mobile and Norfolk. Eventually northern "carpetbag" investment, at least for Florida, paid off. Over the next three decades, 14 Florida cities obtained populations levels above 10,000, and three cities—Jacksonville, Miami and Tampa— reaching population levels above the one hundred thousand mark (Arsenault and Mormino, 1989; Larsen, 1990; Stephenson, 1997: 30-34).

The blessings of population growth had its price. It required imaginative leadership with the political will to expand public services and raise property taxes (Stephenson, 1997). Urban Southern Progressives had this political willingness to shift "the emphasis from the preachments of pure individualism and governmental inaction" toward government's duty to act "for the benefit of community development" (Crooks, 1968: 208). On the eve of the Twentieth Century, in the North, Progressivism meant social, political and economic reform. In the South, however, it meant something else. It spoke in terms of economics (Crooks, 1968, 1991; Harris, 1977; Silvers, 1984; Larsen, 1990). For Southerners, Progressivism meant regaining control of Yankee dominated "monopolies." Southern state legislatures reorganized or established commissions to regulate banks, railroads, public utilities and insurance companies, while southern city councils tightened the franchise agreements of publicly sponsored utilities and streetcar companies (Rabinowitz, 1977, 1992; Link, 1986). In many respects, Southern Progressives' were deeply outraged at Yankee "corporate wrongdoing." But, they were not socialists. They undertook reform, "not to dismantle modern economic institutions," but rather to ameliorate and improve "certain conditions" that had befallen them (Link, 1986: 21-23).

Public Projects in the Gilded Age

As the towns expanded, Southern Progressivism meant the expansion of local public services. It meant providing drinkable water to and removing the sewage away from the homes and businesses. It also meant modern fire protection, as the "Jacksonville 1901 Fire" had demonstrated (Crooks, 1991). Since the Old Guard-dominated private sector failed to do so, the Southern Progressives demanded their cities assume this role. Such a role was quite costly, causing many to go into heavy debt. For instance, public water distribution systems for towns along the Southeastern Atlantic coast, which depended on artesian wells and pump stations, cost nearly a half million dollars (Larsen, 1990: 86). As local officials were urged by Northern investors to improve water systems, towns had to float bonds and raise taxes. Towns had no choice, if they wish to grow. By 1902, Jacksonville had constructed its own municipal electric power and water distribution system. Tampa, which grew from 720 to nearly six thousand inhabitants in one decade, approved bonds totaling $95,000 for streets and sewers in 1889, and then approved an additional $100,000 in 1891 for a water system (Rabinowitz, 1977: 111; Crooks, 1991). St. Petersburg, Florida floated more than $1.3 million in municipal bonds to pave streets, install water mains, build a sewage system, and acquire land for parks, hoping to make it the Eden of the South (Stephens, 1997). Throughout the Florida, the bulk of public expenditures went for the improvement of basic types of municipal services to spur land development (Frazer and Guthrie, 1995).

Southern leadership focused their expenditure efforts for the benefit of their most influential property owners. Middle and Upper-class neighborhoods were protected. Indeed, their streets were "cleaned, lighted, and repaired", and their homes were cleared "of refuse and garbage" by public funds (Harris, 1977: 146). By doing so, municipal service delivery policy remained within the context of a "Traditional-Individualistic" policy choice. Outside of public health and safety, a civic culture prevailed which implied that those who directly bear its cost would directly benefit from the public improvements. No doubt the tax bite increased, but not as dramatically as for ethnic political machines that dominated cities of the North. If taxes were raised, it benefitted the land-based elite of the community.

The tax expenditure burden tells us not just "how much the government takes from its people" but also what the people "gets" for this tax burden (Bryan, 1981: 58). Since federal law did not require reporting of such disbursement during the Progressive Era, we can only speculate the actual burden. But, if data for 1932 is any indication, the tax bite was heavy. Nationally, in 1932, total revenues collected for the states, the counties and all subdivision over twenty five hundred persons was $71.09 per person, with an average public expenditure or "pay out" being $76.80 per person. This suggests that according to the national baseline, the average citizen got more than h/she had to pay. For Florida this was not the case; **more money was collected** by the state, the counties and the cities than was **distributed back** to its residents. In 1932, the total amount of tax revenues collected was $70.17 per person, with the mean average public expenditure or "pay out" of only $64.68 per person. The difference went to pay off public debts.

In 1912, the national per capita gross debt for all counties and municipalities above 2500 persons was $39.37, and by 1932 it was up to $141.17. In 1912, Florida's per capita gross debt was $22.72, and by 1932 it rose to $337.74 per capita, indicating nearly eight thousand per cent increase. Obviously, this increased debt burden was tied to the massive catch up in public works caused by the land speculation boom of the twenties (U.S. Bureau of Census, *Historical Statistics on State and Local Government Finances, 1902–1953*; U.S. Bureau of Census, Statistical Abstracts, *Government Finances, 6F (4)*, Annual Series). Yet, Florida's state constitution prohibited "rainy day" set asides. Thus, future residents had to assume a heavy per capita tax debt burden to offset shortfalls caused from a very antiquated tax-revenue structure.

Civic Engagement and Municipal Service Outputs

Florida governmental units tend to look upon the **benefit received** principle as their guideline for both revenue/expenditure policies, which emphasizes that each taxpayer should be taxed according to the level of service benefits h/she derives regardless of one's ability to pay . For public service delivery the **benefit principle** provides some notion of tax efficiency in that "each individual consumes no more services than he pays for at the price necessary to recover the costs of producing the service"(Peterson, 1981: 71). It presumes some sort **fiscal equivalency** or **fiscal correspondence** is obtained in the community where each "individual pays, and exactly pays, for any benefits received as a result of the provision of a public good/service" (Raimondo, 1992: 110).

A community which is populated by households and firms who have similar preferences should have a similar bundle of public goods and services. Consequently, there should be a diversity among communities, with each comprising households and firms that are willing to share the costs of this specific bundle of public goods and services. Accordingly, local governments are organized to provide for the multiplicity of demands for such a diverse range of municipal services. Equity is therefore based on the satisfaction levels due to this **"shared community interest"** (Raimondo, 1992: 56-61; Lyons, et. al., 1992: 46-114; Schneider, 1989: Ch.3). It is assumed that households and businesses exhibit a variety of tastes or preferences for public services, with some having a greater preference (satisfaction level) for ballparks to libraries, or for police protection to library services. Whatever their preferences, as Schneider (1989: 8) observes: "As rational consumers, buyers want to purchase products offered in the local market for public goods at the lowest costs. Indeed, this diversity in the preferences at minimum cost , are preconditions for the operation of the local market for public goods."

For Tiebout (1956), **like minded people** did not have any racial or ethnic connotation. Instead, **like minded people** simply means that city residents could be classified according to their willingness and ability to pay taxes for specific public services. Buchanan (1987: 174-176) writes that individual citizens collectively make local fiscal choices. They determine "the size of the public sector, along with the distribution of the costs and benefits." Not that each of these like-minded taxpayers makes the day to day policy choices; instead, it is the office holder who selects "specific fiscal outcomes that he predicts will 'satisfy' a sufficient number of citizens." Political proximity becomes a key component. Certain municipal services [police, fire, libraries, parks] can be "more effectively realized" at the local level. Accordingly, community leaders are willing to sacrifice tax dollar efficiency to provide these municipal service preferences, especially those services that are highly visible and directly impact on the citizen/taxpayer (Hirsch, 1964; Stein, 1990). In addition to size of population and composition of the community, socially derived factors appear to influence municipal tax expenditure priorities. For instance, neighborhoods with higher socio-economic status and higher proportion of home ownership spawn greater civic participation rates. Moreover, these same higher income neighborhoods demand more "particularized" or self-interest public services (Lineberry, 1977; Jones,et. al., 1980; Sharp,1986; Coulter,1988; Stein, 1990; Lyons, et. al. 1992).

Civic engagement is critical to municipal service delivery. Personal governing skills give higher income citizens greater political proximity or political voice (Coulter, 1988; Helig and Mundt,1984). Political skills and income assume to go hand-in-hand. Higher income neighborhoods tend to gain access to local resources (tax expenditures), meaning the pothole on their street will be filled promptly after a telephone call. "Voice" tends to be used as the first option, whereas "voting with one's feet" is the option of last resort (Lyons, et. al. 1992; Sharp, 1986). Political proximity to a small town's city hall has become a key factor for the decision to "vote with one's feet" from the "big city."

Sprawl and the Cost of Municipal Services

Not every public officials sees new residential development and commercial growth in terms of municipal service delivery costs. As Anderson (1998: 17-19) points out, in community after community, as a general rule, land use growth costs more than the revenues it generates in terms of the increase in population density, the rise in the level of public service demand and the changes in land development from compact to nodal and/or corridor pattern. This increase in costs to local government manifests itself in terms of either increases to existing tax or debt levels (Ch. 9) and/or the need to improve infrastructure and municipal service delivery levels. In addition, neglect to such public service delivery levels can be viewed as an additional cost—the cost of municipal service delivery reductions or infrastructure/municipal service deficits.

A major source for higher public service levels is **leapfrog** development. For instance, utility service is tied to population density, a scattering of dwelling units along a rural strip corridor can double infrastructure development costs per unit dwelling unit (Anderson, 1998: 18). Land development generally increases both revenue and costs within a community. Several studies done in the late 1970s discovered that revenues did outstrip expenses for public service provision, if we ignore the cost of deferring infrastructure investments (Kelly, 19993: Ch. 9; FLA). However, a recent study of South Carolina's low-density, land consumption corridor sprawl found that if unchecked, the statewide public service and infrastructure costs for the period between 1995 and 2015 are likely to exceed $56 billion, or $750 for each resident (Edelman, 1999: 6). New developments of all kinds–residential, commercial and industrial create demand for additional infrastructure in the form of upgraded roads, utilities and public facilities such as—schools, fire stations, libraries, etc. Although the impacts may differ between type of residential, commercial and industrial development, the operation, maintenance and upgrade of infrastructure and public services in the long run tend to outstrip revenues derived from taxes generated by these new developments. For instance, a study of Fayette County, Kentucky by the American Farm Trust (1999), it was found that this form of development can be quite costly. For every tax dollar generated by such rural corridor development, it costs the county a $1.64 in public service delivery. By contrast, farmland and open land cost the county only twenty two cents in public services for every dollar contributed to property taxes.

Peiser's (1984) study of planned versus unplanned development give a reader a different perspective. In his study of a Houston site, he discovered that there was varied public utility savings for a planned subdivision, when he held the dwelling unit mix and population constant. James Frank (1989) in an effort to synthesize data under the "cost of sprawl" guidelines also found capital costs for infrastructure varied according to type of development and distance from existing nodal development. In James Duncan's (1989) analysis of differing types land uses, he found that public service costs varied. In this Florida study, it was discovered that scattered, leapfrog development was the most costly, or $23,639 per capita. Other than an actual, in-place compact development, the contiguous development pattern was the least costly type of residential development for public service provision. Overall, each of these studies may be somewhat erroneous. Low-density developments on the fringe are frequently subsidized by a myriad of federal, state and city tax and franchise policies, giving an comparative advantage to those land consumers who can afford to purchase a larger, more expensive dwelling unit beyond the central metropolitan core (Daniels, 1999: Ch. 6; Anderson, 1999: 21-25).

Privatization and Public Services

During this study period (1988–1992), Florida was facing a $1 billion revenue shortfall. Given the legislative and state constitutional mandates (Simmonds, 1990; MacManus, 1992, 1995), most Florida cities anticipated continual municipal service obligations under growth management policies. In Chapter 8 we noted that the Florida DCA has assisted small towns facing sprawl by allocating CDBG funds. Yet, not all small towns have applied. In our 1992 survey, there was an increase in towns below 50,000 people reporting financial difficulty. Between 1988 and 1992, the number rose from 19 to 26, with the majority of these towns falling below 25,000 residents. It is not the intention of this study to dispute whether certain indicators provide an explanation for fiscal stress. Instead, it is the intention here to discover how Florida's smaller communities were coping with municipal services delivery while under growth management mandates. For this reason, there has been no attempt to control for certain factors (unemployment rates, business failures, etc.) that are believed to be indicators of fiscal stress. Rather, this analysis focuses on what type of municipal service delivery priorities were adopted to cope with sprawl and to meet the growth management guidelines.

Municipal Services and Growth Mandates

There is a relationship between public service provisioning and the intensity of landuse development. As Knapp and Nelson (1992: 99) have remarked, "Land cannot be successfully urbanized until it offers essential services, including access, shelter, water supplies and waste removal, often collectively referred to as 'infrastructure.'" Too often, there is a hidden cost the citizen-taxpayer, which is the unwillingness for public officials and residents to pay the cost of building and maintaining adequate "threshold levels" of public services. Indeed, up to the mid-1980s, Florida's local officials paid little attention to the finer details of infrastructure maintenance and provision, hoping that any piecemeal strategy would suffice. Yet, development continued in its leapfrog fashion, causing undesirable consequences. For instance, by 1990 60 percent of the household residents in the City of Jacksonville were utilizing on-site septic systems, including this author. By then, Sarasota County had issued 45,000 septic system permits, and granted franchises for 49 water supply systems and 115 package waste-water treatment systems (Porter, 1997: 117). Or as Siemon (1989: 13) notes, Florida had experienced a capital facilities overload, with an estimated deficit shortfall between $20 to $30 billion just "to maintain, never mind improve," the existing public service levels. By 1990, it was estimated that this form of scattered and linear form of development was costing Floridians $16,628 per capita. In other words, unbridled growth did not bring in adequate revenues to pay for the cost of public service provisioning (Duncan, 1989: 15-20).

Koven (1988: 97) writes, "It would be unrealistic to assume that all cities are guided by an identical set of values and political predispositions. Intuitively, one would imagine the political views of people in one city would differ from the political views of people in other jurisdictions." By controlling for the scope of services, Traditional-Individualistic cities were more likely to assume responsibility for only essential services, were less dependent upon intergovernmental revenues, and more likely to rely on fees or charges as a source of revenues (Koven, 1988). But, political ideology alone doesn't explain why there is variation in municipal policy behavior. Other factors do come into play. For instance, demographics is a critical factor. Button and Rosenbaum (1986) found that in their ten-year study of small Florida city budgets age, ethnicity and population density were factors in municipal allocation behavior, with high concentration of elderly being an important determinant in municipal service preferences. Moreover, poorer neighborhoods are found to prefer greater expenditure levels for trash removal or park improvements, while wealthier neighborhoods prefer greater expenditure levels on amenities (Jones, et. al,1980; Lineberry, 1977; Levy, et.al. 1974). Variation in income levels can also explain the differences in expenditure preference levels for the same municipal service (Sharp, 1986; Coulter, 1988; Lyons, et. al. 1995). Furthermore, research suggests that administrative delivery rules will differ with the nature and type of municipal service. That is, budgetary allocation for specific municipal services are tied to the linkage between neighborhood characteristics and the administrative decision rules of a particular municipal agency. For instance, wealthier neighborhoods tend to get favorable budgetary allocation for library resources simply because the decision rules are based on user rates, meaning that middle-to upper income neighborhoods are more likely than low- to moderate income neighborhoods to check out library material, indicating agency decision rules tied to circulation rates (Levy, et.al., 1974; Lineberry, 1977; Jones, et. al. 1980).

The scope of municipal services should be determined by the needs and preferences of all the community's citizens. In reality, federal and state mandates have altered this conventional belief. Because of community scale, the distribution of rural municipal services are not as complicated as their urban cousins. Furthermore, since Hawkins vs. The Town of Shaw (U.S. Court of Appeals, 5th Cir, 1971), an unequal distribution of public services due to demographic characteristics should not a factor, especially in small Florida towns (Price, 1980). Instead, state legislative mandates appear provide the impetus for any special problem associated with a typical Florida small town. Relying on property taxes as their principal source of revenue, Florida's small towns do not have the budgetary flexibility to meet state growth mandates. Indeed, since locally generated revenues depend of local economic activity, unfunded growth management mandates may have preempted local policy initiatives (MacManus,1992).

As more people move to the urban-rural fringe, state planners believe that growth management mandates will encourage higher density of development of land that was skipped over during the first wave of leapfrog development (Kelly, 1993; Fischel, 1991; Dowell, 1984). The rationale behind such a belief is that land markets do not work perfectly. Developers do not see nor do they care to take "into account the cost and benefits they might confer on others by their decisions concerning the precise use, density, design and timing" of proposed land developments (Chinitz, 1990: 6). As unguided sprawl continues, often a consensus emerges among residents that traditional land use controls—zoning and subdivision regulations—which are undergirded by self-interest tend to assist in the proliferation of low density sprawl, increasing the cost of land, housing and public services (Daniels, 1991; Anglin, 1990; Baldassare, 1986, 1981; Gottdiener and Neiman, 1981).

The intensity of land use change influences public policy outputs. Homeowners in fast-growing communities are more likely to express concerns about the cost of public services, the pollution and traffic congestion, regardless of political ideology. Furthermore, these same homeowners are more willing to support greater governmental intervention as a means of protecting the community's quality of life (Gottdiener and Neiman, 1981; Baldassarre, 1981; Anglin, 1990; Bollens, 1990). Lance deHaven-Smith (1991) claims that growth management sentiment is tied to the "visibility" of the dramatic departure of existing natural patterns of land use. Consequently, there is strong local support to "do something" to protect one's quality of life is in direct proportion to the real or imagine threat" that may occur to one's life-style. For instance, Vogel and Swanson (1989) report that Gaineville's anti-growth coalition believed that their actions to minimize the cost of public services were not tied to self-interest of keeping property taxes low. Instead, by putting a cap on growth, Gainesville residents would protect the town's inherent quality of life features. For most Floridians, a "Vision of the Good Life" means residing in a less densely populated area within proximity to water and recreational areas, combined with adequate public service levels and low taxes (Auderic, et.al. 1990: 474-75).

The passage of Florida's 1985 Growth Management Act was to bring order to local public service expenditures. The intent of the Act was to encourage **Smart Growth**, containing the rising costs of public service delivery by discouraging land developers from leapfrogging to alternative sites in adjacent communities. In any compact growth scheme, there are two fundamental objectives. The first objective is to assure that there is less conversion of land "to urban uses, leaving more land in a pristine, natural condition" (Audirac, et. al. 1990: 476). The second objective is to assure that the overall development of public facilities take place in an orderly, timely and cost efficient fashion. In Oregon, this objective meant that public facility expansion was designated to accommodate existing areas of urban development while discouraging the extension of public facilities and services onto the urban-rural fringe until the suitable land is exhausted (Knapp and Nelson, 1992: Ch. 4). In Florida, however, this objective at a local level means the placement of public facilities where it is needed to support and accommodate newly "developmental sprawl," which is a much different perspective.

Public Services Policy Behavior

Smaller Florida communities tend to have fewer policy budgetary policy options to cover revenue costs tied to the 1985 Growth Management Act. In study of fiscal constraint caused by state growth mandates and federal cutbacks, Wolensky and Enright (1991) found the two most viable options adopted by small Wisconsin communities was : retrenchment or user fee adoption. Of the two, retrenchment is simply the shifting of responsibility for the production and delivery cost of the municipal service onto the individual taxpayer or some other governmental or nonprofit entity. In our survey we asked (1) whether publicly appointed local officials (planners) were "willing to pay" for specific municipal services out of their city's revenue sources, and (2) what alternative strategy should be adopted in an effort to maintain current municipal service levels? It was assumed that the planners had "the pulse" on their local policy setting and their responses were surrogates for the policy preferences of their respective city councils.

From existing research, most Florida communities under scrutiny are expected to have the following fourteen services within their repertoire.

Therefore, in **Table 10.1** the responding planners were asked to rank each municipal service in order of importance, based on the **willingness to pay** for public services out of the city's own tax dollars. If we assume in times of deep financial crisis that the first ten ranked services will be retained by the community, then the responses in **Table 10.1** provide some insight on local policy choices among residents of Florida's small towns. This table illustrates not only areas that are likely to be retained in times of fiscal stress, but also the policy shifts over the two time periods. The table first notes that all seven of the essential public services are likely to be retained. Moreover, four of the top five ranked services during the first survey period were designated essential type services. The only non-essential service to be included was planning, which—given the state mandates of the 1985 Growth Management Act—could hardly be ignored. When the small town completed its comprehensive plans for Florida's DCA, many cities downgraded this municipal service activity, defeating the legislation's intention. Furthermore, if we assume that in times of deep financial crisis the first ten services are most likely to be retained, all essential services would be in-

Table 10.1 Funding Priorities of Municipal Services Among Small Town Florida Public Planners (Willingness to Pay Out of Taxes)

Municipal Services	1988/89*		1992/93**	
	Rank	Mean	Rank	Mean
+Water/Sewer	1	3.78	3	4.29
+Street Repair	2	4.37	4	5.69
+Police Protection	3	4.47	1	2.18
Planning/Zoning	4	4.91	10	7.92
+Fire Protection	5	5.27	2	4.06
+Solid Waste	6	6.69	6	6.31
Parks/Recreation	7	7.18	8	6.93
+Trash Collection	8	7.77	5	5.94
Building Inspection	9	8.49	9	7.91
+Tax Collection	10	8.54	14	11.97
Street Lighting	11	9.38	11	8.16
Ambulance/EMS	12	10.18	7	6.46
Library	13	10.77	12	9.31
Elderly Care	14	11.27	13	11.08

+Indicates Essential Service
*Florida TIF City Study (1989); N=49, 132 city subsample
**Florida Needs Analysis Survey (1992); N=63, 132 city subsample

cluded. Such important quality of life services as library facilities, street lighting, park maintenance and ambulance services appear to be susceptible to cuts.

Most of the essential services fall within a **caretaker** or **developmental** category. Stein's (1990: 59-67) national survey on privatization found that rarely are these services jettisoned by the community. Both Button (1989) and deHaven-Smith (1991) discovered that maintenance of essential services were paramount among the Florida communities they investigated. This survey finds supporting evidence, as noted during the second survey period. There seems to be an agreement that developmental services, with the exception of street lighting would be retained. In a comparison between small cities and large Florida cities, Mattson and Twogood (1991) found that smaller cities were more likely to be politically sensitive to elderly services, hypothesizing that political proximity was a factor in smaller communities, where the elderly can exercise considerable clout. This updated survey supports this contention, as Ambulance/EMS moved from 12th place to 7th place over the two-timed periods. Yet, elderly care remained stable in the rankings. The variation between these two closely identified services may be tied to the social status. As newcomers who are proportionately wealthier than their fellow urbanites, these older citizen-taxpayers may expect Ambulance/Ems as part of their municipal service/tax package bundle, especially if they are a former urban/suburban Midwest or Northeast residents. In fact, the Ambulance/EMS service is the only non-essential service that achieved a major priority ranking revision.

Table 10.2 examines the extent to which small cities are likely to adopt retrenchment strategies during this time period of analysis. Nationally, three widely accepted policies have been load-shedding, contracting out and co-production. Of the three distinct forms, load-shedding or service-shedding is the purest form of privatization. In this form the local government simply abdicates responsibility for the production, payment and delivery of a municipal service. In other words, the public service is shifted to the private sector, meaning the individual takes responsibility for seeking and obtaining a particular load-shedding service. By contrast, on the other-end of the public service delivery continuum is co-production, an approach which implies joint production of municipal services by the citizen and municipal employees. Falling under the rubric of **volunteerism**, it is when "citizens freely provide their services to government for the provision and production of a wide range of services benefitting non-volunteers." (Stein, 1990: 51). As a municipal service category, it promises to maintain existing service levels keep taxes low, and expand the role of the citizen-taxpayer from a passive consumer to one of active producer of a municipal service. The middle course is an approach known as "contracting out," which simply means the local government enters into a legal contract with the private sector to provide a designated service for a specific time and cost.

Rising population densities tend to have a positive correlation with the demand for public services. As population increases, the demand for the scope and range services are likely to intensify (Duncan, 1989; Frank, 1989). Rural residents are more likely to make do with fewer services. In a study of citizens and local officials in eight rural Alabama counties, it was found that spending patterns were similar among both groups. Essentially, they were willing to tax themselves for "essential type" services. The only exception was Ambulance/EMS. In general, local residents were satisfied with the service delivery levels in context to the taxes they paid (Molnar and Smith, 1982). In a statewide survey of Kentucky communities, Warner and Burdge (1979) compared small towns located both within metropolitan

Table 10.2 Municipal Service Privatization Strategies, Small Florida Cities (FY 1988/FY 1992)*

	Contract Out		Load Shedding		Coproduction	
	FY88	FY92	FY88	FY92	FY88	FY92
Essential						
Police	3	2	0	0	0	0
Fire	6	5	0	1	40	44
Street Repair	8	9	0	1	0	0
Solid Waste	35	34	0	0	0	0
Tax Collection	24	25	0	0	0	0
Water/Sewer	4	4	0	0	0	0
Garbage	18	14	7	4	4	4
Nonessential						
Library	38	32	1	1	32	33
Planning/Zoning	25	4	0	2	0	0
Park/Recreation	3	3	1	2	37	37
Drainage/Wetlands	1	1	1	0	0	0
Ambulance/EMS	30	6	0	0	0	0
Building Inspection	11	2	4	4	0	0
Elderly Services	0	0	0	0	13	12

Florida TIF Survey (1988), N=49; 132 city subsample
Florida Needs Analysis Survey Update (1992), N=63; 132 city subsample

and micropolitan counties. They found that there were disparities, including one-third of the rural small town households were not connected to any modern method of sewage disposal (community system). Moreover, rural communities were less likely to have adequate levels of fire protection or garbage collection. However, under subjective measures of satisfaction, these rural residents were willing to "get by" with lower levels of services, provided that taxes remained low. In an investigation of households within two fast-growing rural Northern Michigan retirement counties, Marans and Rodgers (1978)discovered adequacy perception of municipal services was tied to place of residence. Small towns facing rapid growth and the influx of former city dwellers were more likely to be dissatisfied with public service levels. When asked if they were "willing to raise taxes for at least one additional service," only one in ten property owners responded affirmatively. The researchers found that twice as many year-round homeowners as seasonal homeowners were "willing to give up" a public service if it meant a reduction in property taxes. In a nationwide survey of growing and declining communities with populations below 50,000 persons, Bryce (1979) found that smaller cities had lower tax rates and fewer public services, with many lacking sewer, water, fire and garbage disposal. Moreover, older Frostbelt cities located in rural regions were facing stagnation and economic decline. Although these stagnating cities could ill-afford to maintain public service levels, these small Frostbelt communities simply lacked the political will to eliminate or privatize such services.

Table 10.2 suggests that Traditional-Individualism is apparent in Florida's smaller cities. This table tells us that the public managers are more likely to apply "selective targeting." At the same time, many Floridians are willing to pick up the slack with co-production efforts. Amenity type policies (parks, libraries, swimming pools, etc.) have been on the cutting block during economic downturns (Mattson, 1986). This table tells us that smaller Florida towns had to make hard choices by adopting **load shedding** or **municipal service shedding** policy behavior to make up revenue shortfalls due to sprawl and state growth mandates. No wonder, when their legislators returned to Tallahassee in 1993, these state legislators were quite willing to remove such required mandates under **The Planning and Growth Management Act (1993).**

Table 10.3 tells the reader information pertaining to privatization behavior. The logit analysis explains 48.8 per cent of the privatization policy behavior among the communities under scrutiny. The dependent variable is the **willingness to adopt** a privatization policy strategy. This implies a willingness to shift the costs to the citizen. According to the Logit Model, a combination of independent factors when interacting with the 120 communities was not significant for the overall model. However, the positive intercept does imply a willingness to undertake a privatization policy behavior which was tied to the town's population size. The larger the city, the more willing the city was to undertake privatization activity. This makes sense, as larger cities are more likely to have a greater scope and range of public services. Overall, **Table 10.3** tells us that those Florida towns that would participate in privatization are the rapid growing, fiscally stressed, mayor-council towns who have access to a planner. Obviously, these towns are more likely to be located on the urban-rural fringe and facing sprawl. These towns may be fiscally stressed because of their inability to meet population growth demands while trying to comply with the 1985 Growth Management mandates. If so, these towns are likely shifting scarce "own source" tax dollars to meet Rule 9J5 requirements.

Table 10.3 Logistic Regression of Privatization Participation, Community Level Characteristics

Community Attributes	Est.	St. Dev.
INTERCEPT	9.9527	40.4737
BOND	-4.7884	25.7720
FORM	-0.4443	0.6548
MFI	-8.9106	2.4095
SCALE*	0.4083	0.3052
PLNG	0.9036	0.7443
MIN	0.0886	0.6358
DIST	-2.6139	3.9535
EDLERLY	0.1877	0.1455
CHMBER	0.1354	1.5606
LNPOP	0.1118	0.3169

Chi Sq (df) 7.534 (11)
P>Chi Sq 0.1010
RSQ=48.79%
**N=120

*Indicates significance at .05 level
**Of the 128 CDBG eligible communities, response is from the overall 120 sample communities associated with this policy issue.
Source: FI DCA CDBG Files (FY 1983–1992), University of North Florida Center for Local Government Surveys (1989, 1992).

Policy Implication

Stein (1990: 83) writes that smaller citied will trade off efficiency gains to fulfill the demands of their constituencies. With a narrow tax base, the political voice of small towns places challenges for local planners who must fulfill the demands tied to rapid popuation growth within the municipal boundaries. Faced with competition from other towns, these outer ring towns must devise policy choices that allow them to maintain existing service levels while accommodating additional public service demands as mandated by the growth management legislation. Grant getting may help. But competition is stiff. Since the state legislature is unlikely to provide additional financial assistance, local town adopt policy strategies that are least painful to their respective constituencies. Privatization is one such alternative. Overwhelmingly a majority of the towns have selected the harmful choice, reducing service levels rather than eliminating public services altogether. The benefit principle, with its long southern heritage, allows for this privatization behavior. Besides, there is always hope that residential sprawl will always pay for itself, regardless of what previous research claims.

Chapter 11
ଛଠ
Small Towns and Economic Development

Spatially fixed rural towns within Florida are finally enjoying a population boom. These rural communities were bypassed by the post-War boom. By 1980, these urban-rural fringe communities had begun to enjoy the fruits of Florida's popularity as a playground for retirees, requiring the need to pay for costly public utility and other municipal service improvements. In this chapter, we will focus on what economic policy strategies were adopted by Florida smaller towns to remain competitive.

Corporate City Planning

The vitality of a rural community cannot simply be explained by the community's population size, its downtown business district or its distance from other communities. Instead, a community's vibrant sense of place is defined by its composite attributes, including its built characteristics (architectural styles and street layouts), its civic character (churches, cafes, fraternal lodges and such), and its amenity structure (type and array of public services such as fire stations, post offices, parks and libraries). In other words, a community is not merely tied to its economic functions of the production, distribution and consumption of goods and services. Instead, a community's viability is also tied to town's ability to define its civic cultural fabric. By doing so, then a community's residents and civic leadership can define a town's perceptual orbit within the realm of economic possibilities (Lowry, 1964; Ladd, 1972; Gusfield, 1975; Troustine and Christensen, 1982; Powers, 1990; Kemmis, 1991; Pagano and Bowman, 1995; Mattson, 1996).

Every town acts as an economic engine within a given regional setting. Communities exist within a network of cities, with each region dominated by a premier city. Subsequently, an economic hierarchy of cities emerges. Yet no town is condemned to a permanent socio-economic position. Technology has a habit of either enhancing or inhibiting a town's status. The steam locomotive enhanced the position of Florida towns such as Kissimmee. As an in-land town, the railroad allowed it to gain prominence over river towns—Sanford or Deland (Marshall, 2000: Ch.1). Technology alone, however, was not the determining factor. Historic evidence suggests that the "political will" of the town's core leadership is equally important, especially the political astuteness by local officials to understand their respective city's place within the existing hierarchy. That is, communities must make public investment strategies. Therefore, the goal of small town economic development investment strategy is to create new jobs or sustain existing ones (See Ramsey, 1996).

Since communities are spatially fixed, a recurrent community development theme is that a city must improve its economic competitiveness (Bartik, 1991; Blair and Premus, 1993; Howland, 1993). This type of economic planning hopes to achieve two objectives: (1) to attract additional industry; and, (2) to improve the wage level of the work force. This strategy will hopefully improve local income levels by expanding the industrial base. Overtime, an improved tax base means a better chance for the expansion and revitalization of its existing municipal service tax package bundle (public services). Eventually, the benefits derived from both an improved economic base and tax base allows the community to gain a competitive edge over neighboring jurisdiction, becoming a premier regional community (Levy, 1981; Malizia, 1986; Howland, 1993).

Corporate City Planning is such a strategy. The underlying philosophy of this development model is that local government must subordinate its role when addressing the needs of the private sector. A key policy concern is that public monies ought to be spent for private sector investment. Corporate City Planning is associated with the **growth machine** perspective, a socio-political theory that implies that there is an interlocking agreement between locally elected public officials and the community's business elite. Based on power elite regime theory, the premise is that a town's land-based town elite (insurance agents, real estate brokers, merchants and bankers) establish political coalitions to attract outside investors to the community. Implicitly, as community stakeholders this land-based elite devise public policies for the local city council that will benefit principally their personal economic interests (Molotch, 1976; Vogel and Swanson, 1989; Rudel, 1989; Tauxe, 1993; Ramsey, 1995).

There are four underlying policy goals within the Corporate City model which allow for this pro-business dominance (Mattson, 1987).

1. Establish a non-partisan electoral system that allows the business elite to dominate municipal governance through so-called good government reform organizations.
2. Discourage the adoption of strong conflict of interest laws under the guise of civic boosterism.
3. Dilute citizen participation by establishing quasi-public agencies or special district so that public funds can flow to the private sector ventures. Of course, these quasi-public agencies are under the umbrella of being non-partisan, blue-ribbon governmental entities.
4. Foster the philosophy of municipal service privatization so that corporate taxes are kept low by shifting the cost of government directly onto the citizen-taxpayer.

Collectively these four principle goal elements would limit the typical Floridian from having any say on such planning issues as what type of municipal service ought to be provided, how land ought to be zoned, or even how projects ought to be financed. In Chapter 3, we noted that during the Bourbon Era this was a common practice. As a civic philosophy, Corporate City Planning has deep ideological roots in Florida. For Florida's small towns and cities, Corporate City Planning helps alleviate the problems imposed by the paradox of all spatially fixed towns. That is, the development options are limited to its most obvious asset (land area). Since public services are needed to improve the town's land area, publicly sponsored economic development policy is tied to enhancing this economic component, often to the benefit of the private sector (Peterson, 1981; Schumaker, 1991).

Two Economic Policy Strategies

Two economic policy planning strategies are presently being used by small towns: **Smokestack Chasing** and **Town Amenity** strategies. Both borrow from the toolbox of Corporate City Planning. Both strategies expect to improve the economic viability of the small town; but, each differs in policy planning focus.

Type 1(Smokestack Chasing) model has been quite popular since the 1950s. It implies that jobs, any type of jobs is the solution to economic downturns. That is, small town revitalization policies are aimed at job recruitment, regardless of the type of industry. By increasing private sector investment, the accompanied industrial base expansion will ensure the rise of local incomes. In turn, this expansion will allow for commercial spinoffs that will expand the town's tax base. The town is a "seller" of industrial sites. The town's chamber of commerce becomes the seller of the town's quality of life, of its location, and of its workforce. The chamber offers various tax and facility incentives "in the same way that a private company sells its products to consumers" (Watson, 1995: 7).

With cheap labor, cheap land and low taxes, small town's civic leadership assumes the role of "agent- seller." Thus, the town's leadership's job is "to reach the buyers, discover their needs, package the various incentives into a competitive deal, and make the sale" (Kutler, et. al. 1993: 78). Yet, such an approach can encourage the local business elite to strike a Faustian bargain by "trading off" the community's unique character for a short term economic gain (Malizia, 1986; Hibbard and Davis, 1986).

Type 2 (Town Amenity) Model is somewhat more elusive. By contrast, this model urges local planners to build on the city's civic character. Sometimes called the **New Wave** approach, this model stresses a diverse policy planning strategy, including tourism, downtown ventures and civic improvements (Goetz, 1990; Clarke, 1992; Reese,1992; Howland, l993). As a policy strategy **Type 2** directs the town's recruitment energies so that the town does not sacrifice its civic culture. Instead, **Type 2** policy urges the civic leadership to build on the town's human capital, institutions, and historic image. As an economic development model it doesn't give "the store away." The city will extract concessions from the developer or the firm, such as a job training program, minority hiring program or the possibility of a day care center (Goetz, 1990). Obviously, **Type 2** is beyond conventional policy incentives to attract economic activity into the community.

Of the two models, the "Smokestack Chasing" strategy is less difficult to establish benchmark standards. Under the "Smokestack Chasing" approach, the number of jobs created is easily quantified based on the specific investment. For instance, the cost of the tax abatement divided by the number of jobs created for a specific manufacturing plant. However, a "Town Amenity" model may have a variety of "intangibles" spinoffs—an adult computer literacy course, improved building and housing code adoption, or a new playground. None of these program activities are readily quantified, and cannot be tied directly to job generation. For this reason **Type 2** is more difficult to sell to public officials as a viable alternative economic policy option.

Small Town Economic Policy Priorities

Traditional-Individualistic perspective is predominant within Florida. Above all, Traditional Individualistic politics seeks to avoid political conflicts in small towns that can easily become personal and generate a bitter animosity. With few political cleavages, an informal civic leadership pattern has emerged in such small towns. The subsequent policy choices tended to be highly selective, rarely establishing distinct winners or losers and often dominated by the growth machine faction (Wolensky and Groves, 1977; Exoo, 1984; Rudel, 1989; Schumaker,1991; Wikstrom, 1993).

Survey Findings

The following information is based on the two surveys conducted by The University of North Florida's center for Local Government Administration. The original sample group consisted of at least one community from each of Florida's 67 counties, with specific sub-group analysis on the 31 micropolitan counties and 10 urban-rural fringe counties (see **Table 9.1**).

Because Florida cities are highly dependent upon tourism and consumption taxes (MacManus, 1995; Grizzle and Trogen, 1994; Simmonds, 1990), the nationwide recession in early 1990s had an adverse impact of the fiscal health of Florida's local governments. **Table 11.1** tabulates the responses from all city planners when asked to rank what are the **critical issues facing their respective communities.** There are differences in priority rankings over the two time periods, with economic development as the principal focus for both time periods. There are three likely explanations for this impetus for policy planning stances. The most obvious are the increased fiscal problems encountered by the smaller cities was a motivational factor. Previous research has found that correlation exists between fiscal stress and the number and type policy strategies engaged by a city (Diaz and green, 2001; Pagano and Bowman, 1995; Mattson, 1991; Wolensky and Enright, 1991). No doubt, local officials faced with fiscal problems are expected to do something to change the community's plight. **Table 11.1** suggests that Florida's small town officials are rationally responding to economic priorities by selecting those policy choices that both will increase local job opportunities and will make the city's market position more attractive as a locale for economic activity.

Table 11.1 notes that there were subtle shifts in policy priorities in regards to economic development and fiscal policy activities. For instance, in 1988, among the five top concerns, crime was the only social issue of merit. In 1992, crime declined to seventh place, while drainage moved up form 14th to 3rd, and water/sewer moved from 6th to 2nd place. The table implies that public planners saw the provision of basic public services as the key to alleviating fiscal stress and attracting economic development while responding to the state's growth management mandates. At the same time, local officials appear to be ignoring the financial aspects of paying for such infrastructure development by ranking budget/financial management tools toward the bottom. It is quite possible that small town public managers and planners simply lack the fiscal policy knowledge and expertise beyond the capital budget and capital facilities planning.

Table 11.1 Priority Ranking Of Critical Issues Facing Florida Cities, As Perceived By Appointed Small Town Planners

Critical Issue	1988/89* Rank	Mean	1992/93** Rank	Mean
Downtown Revitalization	1	4.37	4	6.14
Street Repair	2	4.91	1	5.33
Planning/Zoning	3	5.47	6	6.30
Industrial Development	4	5.54	5	5.30
Crime	5	5.58	7	6.82
Water/Sewer	6	5.71	2	5.50
Housing	7	6.11	8	6.88
Solid Waste	8	6.77	9	7.04
Parks/Recreation	9	7.91	15	10.82
Education	10	7.97	10	7.83
Fire Protection	11	9.34	12	8.91
Health Care	12	9.37	11	8.02
Taxes/Budget Mngt	13	9.87	13	9.99
Drainage	14	10.77	3	5.02
Finance Growth	15	11.78	14	10.30

Sources:
*Florida TIF City Study (1989), N=49; 132 subsample
**UNF Center Update Survey (1992), N=62; 132 subsample

Table 11.2 provides additional insight into local economic development choices. This table asks public planners to rank the importance of those public services deemed most critical in sustaining and enhancing economic development in small towns. The policy choices of a town's leadership, according to Pagano and Bowman (1995), define whether a city will attempt to influence its policy environment or adapt to it. If we presume that planners are acting as surrogates for policy preferences for their city councils, then **caretaker and promoter type** municipal services are ranked quite high. These **essential type** municipal services, as indicated by (+), are known to be within the category of a basic municipal tax service package. In times of fiscal stress, as rational policy choices, planners are likely to look at this policy strategy as a selling point for competition in the marketplace. Indeed, the maintenance of a community's public safety and visual landscape are critical in attracting additional people and firms.

Economic planners often operate under conditions of uncertainty, making it risky to adopt innovative tools (Reese, 1993b; Schumaker, 1991). Consequently, there is a tendency to adopt "tried and true" policy choices. **Table 11.3** indicates whether this type of policy behavior exists. The public mobilization of capital according to Pagano and Bowman (1995: 23) refers

Table 11.2 Most Critical Municipal Services for Economic Development, As Perceived by Small Town Public Planners

	1988/89*		1992/93**	
	Rank	Mean	Rank	Mean
+Water/Sewer	1	3.38	2	3.39
+Street Repair	2	4.29	5	5.91
+Police Protection	3	4.46	1	3.23
Planning/Zoning	4	4.62	4	4.85
+Fire Protection	5	5.46	3	4.47
+Solid Waste	6	6.64	6	6.76
Parks/Recreation	7	6.98	9	7.93
+Trash Collection	8	7.59	8	7.42
+Tax Collection	9	8.15	13	9.85
Street Lighting	10	8.58	12	9.47
Building Inspection	11	9.35	7	7.41
EMS	12	9.77	10	8.37
Library	13	10.92	11	9.23
Elderly Care	14	11.64	14	12.18

*Florida TIF City Study (1989), N=49, 132 city subsample
**UNF Center Update Survey,(1992), N=62, 132 city subsample

to the process of "selection, packaging and utilization of financial resources" within the public realm for private purposes. In **Type 1** towns this is standard operating procedure (Reese, 1993a; Ramsey, 1995). The reason is obvious, the growth machine imperative suggests that downtown businesses are most likely to benefit from such publicly funded policies (Kantor and David, 1988; Rubin, 1988; Schumaker, 1991; Tauxe, 1993; Ramsey, 1996). No doubt, the local growth coalition, which is likely comprising these same beneficiaries, will exert considerable influence for such policy making. Or as Kantor and Savitch (1993: 234) note, fiscally stressed cities are often at a disadvantage and are faced with absorbing the cost of doing business, especially if they wish to remain competitive. Therefore some strong tendencies for tax abatements arise by member of the chamber of commerce (Bland, 1989; Rubin, 1988).

The community development game is highly unpredictable. With little knowledge of their real competitiveness, small towns usually offer an admixture of **Type 1 and Type 2** incentives (Goetz, 1990). By "cluster ranking" the responses of local planners and community development specialists, **Table 11.3** gives us some indication of the policy behavior among Florida's smaller cities at the time of this study when facing fiscal stress. We find that many communities in Florida are willing to modify existing land-use regulatory codes to attract business, contradicting state mandated **consistency clauses.** Although towns are expected to maintain a uniform threshold of public services, there is a bias toward **Type 1** policies. We saw a similar policy behavior with the CDBG program (Chapter 8). No doubt, **Type 1 or "nuts and bolts" economic activities will give a slight policy edge to local competition for industrial and commercial businesses**. Under the 1993/95 revisions, this form of policy behavior is more likely to continue into the 21st Century.

Table 11.3 note that small towns are quite conservative in the use of cost reduction incentives. They are quite willing to use traditional tax incentives such as loan guarantees or tax abatements, but quite reluctant to be involved in Tax Increment Financing, Business Incentive Districts or Local Option Sales Taxes to pay for needed upgrading of municipal services. Industrial Revenue Bonds appear to be a more likely policy choice. This policy behavior is understandable. If we presume that smaller towns lack the professional expertise, all three earlier policy strategies require some level of local fiscal management capabilities. The lack of skilled staff may be the explanation for the reluctance to adopt these innovative policy strategies (Baker, 1994; McGuire et.al., 1994; Mattson and Solano, 1986; Seroka, 1981; Wolensky and Groves, 1977; Hahn, 1970; Gamberg, 1966).

Under Smokestack Chasing, the traditional incentives identified such as land clearance, leaseback, infrastructure investment or loan guarantees are quite familiar to locally elected public officials. Moreover, small towns are expected to provide industrial parks, which favors the local civic elite (Levy, 1981; Watson, 1995). If we accept the growth machine thesis, the local civic elites, given the socio-political framework of the smaller community, are able to exert political influence within the economic development policy-making process, assuring that the conventional method of financing economic development prevails (Kanervo, 1994; Kantor and Savitch, 1993; Turner, 1993; Tauxe, 1993; Reese, 1993a; Powers, 1991; Rubin, 1988; Catanese, 1984).

Florida's Tax Increment Financing Program

Table 11.3 implied that smaller Florida cities are more likely to rely on conventional **Type 1** strategies because they lack the professional skills to undertake **Type 2** fiscal policy activities. The **Tax Increment Financing (TIF)** program illustrates this assertion. **TIF** is an economic development tool that attracts new industry to blighted areas of a city. It is used in more than thirty states. In this period of declining federal aid, it has become quyite attractive and a popular "creative financing tool" within the planner's repertoire. It is attractive because it does not impose a new tax on either the homeowner or the businessman. Derived from a **TIF** district the funds pay for public improvements within that district, which is classified as blighted. Moreover, the city can use existing tax dollars or federal funds (CDBG) to improve the existing infrastructure with the hope that such improvements will spur revitalization within this blighted area.

The general scheme is for the city to designate a redevelopment agency to oversee the development district. All property and sales taxes collected within the district are automatically placed into an "enterprise" account to "pay off" the funds allocated to improve the district. The "seed" or "up-front" money is designated to stimulate revitalization of the area by focusing on civic improvements that will attract private investment. Any new funds generated from the district beyond the "revenue baseline" are placed in a special revenue account or revolving fund that is earmarked for the **TIF** district. Over time, the new private sector businesses will raise existing property values and generate additional tax revenues for the special reserve account. The dollar amount of tax difference collected from the original assessed valuation [base-line year value prior to infrastructure improvement] and the assessed [increased property value assessments] goes directly into the **TIF** special reserve fund account. These additional monies are used by the TIF District Authority to defray the costs of civic improvements and to repay existing loans or bonds (Huddleston, 1984; Casella, 1984; Davis, 1989; Klemanki, 1989; Carlson, 1992). The idea is to establish a direct link between the publicly sponsored projects within the district and the benefits derived by the improved property within the district. At the same time, city tax revenues are not being squandered or being used for the benefit of a small business elite from the community.

Florida's **TIF** program has certain advantages. First, it is used to rehabilitate and improve designated blighted areas. The Florida statute restricts activities to nuts and bolts infrastructure improvements. It encourages a public/private partnership by the city for the funding of street, water/sewer and traffic circulation improvements. As an up-front cost for revitalization investment, the Florida **TIF** program acts as seed money for private reinvestment in commercial activities within such blighted areas. Jacksonville's

Table 11.3 Priority Ranking of Fiscal Policy Strategies for Economic Development

Fiscal Policy Technique	Priority Rank
Traditional Incentives	
Infrastructure Investment	1 (88%)
Land Clearing/Acquisition	6 (60%)
Leaseback/Leasehold	4 (71%)
Job Training Package*	5 (67%)
Modify Zoning/Subdivision	2 (86%)
Invest Municipal Services	3 (83%)
Financial Incentives	
Tax Abatements	2 (88%)
Ind. Rev. Bonds	3 (86%)
Deferred Tax Payment	4 (81%)
Tax Increment Financing	7 (55%)
Loan Guarantees	1 (92%)
Business Incentive Districts	5 (65%)
Impact Fee/ User Fee Deferral	6 (60%)
Local Option Tax	8 (54%)

N= 56 cities reporting, Priority rank is rounded to nearest decimal per cent.
* Type Two Policy Choice

Riverwalk is such an example. A **TIF** district is a potential tool for providing the spark to reverse the economic deterioration within a community. Through land assembly and civic infrastructure improvements, the local community development agency can increase economic competitiveness of an area that appears least desirable (Ponce and Mallison, 1978; Carlson, 1992).

A hindrance to a **TIF** district is that district is experiencing a totally flat or negative growth tax rate. The **TIF** redevelopment agency must float municipal bonds for infrastructure improvements. Therefore, the city must have a free hand in seeking outside revenue sources without being hampered by internal politics. Under state law, **Industrial Revenue Bonds (IRBs)** can be issued without a referendum by the tax payers, avoiding such potential political pitfalls. Once improvements are made, all anticipated revenue increases derived from tax assessments beyond the base line are tied to a revolving fund. A potential abuse is that the bonds are used to "bail out" slum speculators (Davis, 1989). Moreover, where real estate markets are weak, gross tax receipts may not outpace the initial investment costs (Williams, 1996; Stinson, 1992; Hood, 1992) With many firms and businesses having voted with their feet, the **TIF** district may not be a windfall but a white elephant to the city and its taxpayers (Huddleston, 1984; Casella, 1984; Stinson, 1992).

TIF Findings

The **Tax Incremental Finance (TIF)** policy strategy is perhaps the most popular newer form to be adopted by state and local governments. In this analysis we utilized a Logistic Regression analysis to evaluate and investigate whether certain town characteristics influence the policy behavior of smaller Florida communities. The measure for success was the implementation of implied stated goals as passed by the 1977 Florida legislature. As Casella (1984: 15-16) noted, certain factors were likely to influence participation success, including skill of community development specialists. This suggests that the following questions ought to be asked?

(1) Was there widespread participation among Florida towns?
(2) If not, what factor or factors inhibited participation?

Hopefully, **Table 11.4** will provide a response for this above inquiry. The data for the table was derived in the following manner.

First, from the list provided by the Florida League of Cities, we included all 155 eligible cities in our **Logistic Regression** analysis. Since we hoped to ascertain what community traits played a role, the analysis is based on the returned questionnaires. In our analysis, given Palm Beach's extreme MFI level, the city was considered a statistical anomaly that was distorting the findings. As a sample case "outlier," Palm Beach was removed from the analysis.

Who Participates

Among the surveyed communities, the survey found that population growth was a factor in participation rate. According to the negative intercept (-0.4833) and the negative sign for the population variable (-0.7862), we can conclude that towns within the smaller city category are participating in the program. In examining all the independent variables, however, the following scenario for a participation rate emerges. **Equation 1** within the table tells us that those Florida cities most likely to take an advantage of the **TIF program** are mayor-council cities, in the middle population range of 25,000 to 49,999. These towns should have better bond rating, higher median family income levels, and proportionately fewer elderly and minority population levels. This implies that these towns, which are beyond the metropolitan core, had been facing growth pressures during the previous decade.

If we presume that the responding communities are indicators of professional management capacity as well as local policy behavior, then **Table 11.3**, **Equation 2** can provide the reader with greater insight to this policy choice as a Main Street economic revitalization tool. The data from this table tells us that a city with fewer minority and elderly residents is likely to utilize the technique. Two other variables—MFI and Bond rating—fell between .05 and .08 level. The statistical rigor of Logit Analysis requires the rejection of both factors. If we included Palm Beach, Median Family Income (MFI) would have been a factor. Due to the high rental space, the city utilizes TIF to offset cost for marginal type businesses. Yet, it was felt that a distorting effect still was at play.

The Florida **TIF** program does not properly conform to the state legislature's original intent. In fact, it may not be accomplishing its original intent to revitalize the blighted "Main Streets" of marginal communities. Panama City in the mid-1990s plans to utilize TIF program to give its very viable downtown a "face lift." Our survey found that among the 155 eligible towns, those most likely to utilize the program are better off, with a higher bond rating and with fewer minorities. These smaller towns, within middle range of population, tend to have access to professional expertise, making it easier to pass TIF policies.

Table 11.4 Logistic Regression of TIF Participation, Community Level Characteristics

Community Attributes	EQ 1 Full Sample Participation		EQ 2 Without Palm Beach Participation	
	Est.	St. Dev.	Est.	St. Dev.
INTERCEPT	-0.4833	2.0014	-2.8149	2.8508
LNPOP	-0.7862**	0.3125	-0.5193	0.3907
FORM	-0.1413	0.5831	0.2899	0.8203
MFI	1.5001	0.0004	2.3004	1.4004
BOND	0.7174	0.6178	1.8345	0.9854
PLNG	0.2105	0.7180	-0.6807	1.1431
MIN	-0.0323	0.2183	-0.0648*	0.0341
ELD	-0.0194	0.0315	-0.0204	0.0392
Chi. Sq.	82.34 (67 df)		44.93 (37 df)	
p>Chi. Sq.	0.06583		0.0085	
R.SQ.	9.8%		17.31%	
N=	155		65	

Source: UNF TIF Survey (1989); Please note that Palm Beach, FL is considered an outlier and was dropped from the analysis. However, it was a significant model [Chi. Sq. 45.03 (37 df), p>.006; R. Sq. 17.11%], with negative Minority and Bond Rating both indicating significance at the .05 level.
*Significance at the 0.05 level
**Significance at the 0.01 level

Policy Implications

The survey findings in this chapter tells us something of the policy behavior of Florida's smaller towns. Among these communities the "nuts and bolts" policy choices appear to be of chief concern, supporting earlier research of municipal service and grant selection priorities. Some may say this focus is largely due to the need to conform to state growth management mandates. This was supported by the top rankings on **Table 11.1, which is highly suggestive of this assertion. Table 11.1** seems to support this assertion with the following strong rankings of: (1) street repair, (2) water/sewer service and (3) drainage. All three policy choices fall within the growth management act infrastructure requirements. But it may simply be a rational response to the high population growth rates experienced by these smaller communities over the past two decades.

It is possible that the "land use, physical development" orientation is a bias of the survey. Town officials are key policy actors for project priorities. These essential types, "nuts and bolts" projects tend to have a "distributive" character, spreading the benefits to all residents, not only to the community's business elite. Therefore, an essential type project makes all the residents "winners" in public service delivery policy game. If this is the reason for their selections, then this policy-making activity is in keeping with the Traditional-Individualistic tendency to avoid local controversy and spread the benefits in a distributive fashion.

Field trip investigations to Sebring, Boca Raton, Jacksonville Beach, Pensacola, and Lakeland found that **TIF districts** had a tendency to spend funds for distributive type, growth oriented municipal services (water/sewer, street repair, police and fire protection, and solid waste disposal). This suggests that small town officials are focusing on growth related, nuts and bolts concerns anyway. Faced with the need to upgrade infrastructure requirements, local officials were simply responding to **Rule 9J5 and other growth management mandates.**

Chapter 12
ಸಂಞ
Thinking Regionally, Acting Locally

For the past three decades there have been state legislative efforts to influence land use development patterns in Florida. As early as 1972, the review of local commercial, industrial and housing projects had become a state public policy matter. Unfortunately, the early state growth initiative had no funding and lacked regulatory teeth. In the mid-1980s, two new state growth management initiatives were passed to rectify past deficiencies. Both legislative acts—State Comprehensive Plan Act and the 1985 Growth Management Act—required the state, its 67 counties and 362 municipalities to prepare "functional plans" in specific areas ranging from transportation to health planning. Unlike the 1970s, these legislative acts appropriated funds for local comprehensive planning endeavors, but with strings attached. Under the 1985 Growth Management Act, local governments were required to tie local comprehensive plans to capital improvement projects, forcing each community to come to terms with how it would pay for its population growth within a regional context.

Florida has been in the forefront of this contentious battle over private versus public land use management values. Throughout the 1960s, the issue of sprawl had shattered political alignments that were decades old. Before 1960, like other Sunbelt states, there was a sharp delineation between the city and the countryside, with the socio-political alignments mirroring this delineation. Since then, the dynamics in technology (transportation and communications) and in demographics has caused shifting of local policy choices (Ch. 3; Ch. 4), making it difficult to justify the old-style of county courthouse politics. Indeed, even the influx of Midwest and Northeast social conservatives had rejected the extreme views when it came to sprawl ("Growth Management Survey," www.dca.state.fl.us/fdcp).

Sprawl and Florida's Policy Shift

One issue that is seldom discussed but is quite critical to growth management is land ownership. In this book, I have asserted that an understanding of the political cultural core values of land ownership is quite helpful in the formulation and implementation of land use plans. Traditional-Individualism with its view of land as a private commodity to be bought and sold with little government interference is a key civic core value, especially among Florida's small town officials. Often invoking a John Locke philosophical stance, Traditional-Individualists praise the value of the free market and its mechanism for land use resource allocation. Traditional-Individualists see no contradiction in how h/she manages h/her land as long as it does not infringe on a neighbor's similar held property rights (Ladd, 1972; Popper, 1981; Rudel,1989). Local jurisdictional politics with its tendencies toward avoiding unnecessary social conflicts assures the adoption of the least effective land use planning tools (Ch. 6). Sprawl has many faces, and has been blamed for a host of social issues—the degradation of the natural landscape, the rise of congested roads, the crowding of schools, and the increase in air and water pollution. Generally characterized as low density, poorly planned land developmental patterns, sprawl favors the automobile lifestyle. Sprawl, in terms of density, is neither located within the urban core or the countryside. Instead, it lies between the two, among the small towns on the urban-rural fringe (Gilliam, 2002:5). Historically, this is the political geography of the coalition of wealthy landowners, merchants, bankers and lawyers. For decades this county courthouse crowd had successfully set up and ran Florida's state and municipal governments. Their main priority was to make money and to keep political power out of the hands of the ordinary folk. Government functions were limited to a few basic essential services (Kirstein, 1995; Robinowitz, 1992; Scher, 1992; Buttton, 1989).

Sectionalism, an expression of social, economic and political cultural differences, has long been part of the Southern civic culture. Its civic cultural root has strong links to southern ruralism since before the Civil War. This local parochialism has always placed a political premium on Jeffersonian pastoral values—limited government, private entrepreneurship, rugged individualism and sanctity of private property (Ch.6; Ch.7). Sadly, for decades, Jim Crow was its principal form of expression in towns like St. Augustine, Gretna, Pensacola, or Daytona Beach. However, once the federal courts asserted themselves, Traditional-Individualism pragmatically adjusted, still retaining its spirit of the private marketplace. Demographics have aided in this policy shift. Prior to World War II, most Florida communities were somewhat homogeneous, with a small politically active population. The lack of a diverse manufacturing base assured few foreign immigrants. And, the disenfranchisement of the African-American solidified the lack of political opposition to this civic-commercial county courthouse elite. Even the early Twentieth Century reform efforts [The Progressive Era and the New Deal] had little impact on the alteration of this coalition's power base (Ch.3; Ch.4).

Sprawl determined by the diversity in population growth and the improvement of technology has altered the political equation. Jim Crow is no longer the driving force behind county courthouse politics. Instead, it is the "quality of life" issue (Ch. 5). As a recent Department of Community Affairs' "Growth Management Survey," (February 2001) testifies, more than 60 per cent of Floridians believe that the quality of life has deteriorated, with 48 per cent believing it is sprawl that is the culprit. In a state known for its natural beauty, sprawl-type activities are becoming less acceptable by residents. However, a majority of the respondents cannot agree at which level of government should there be intervention to correct the problem. Apparently, sprawl as an issue has a political fault line. Throughout the nation, most anti-sprawl political support is derived from relatively affluent, urban middle-class residents, and most pro-sprawl support is derived from the poorer, lower-middle class residents beyond the urban-rural fringe (Dowell, 1984; Baldassare, 1986; Eastbrook, "Suburban Myth" *The New Republic*, March 15, 1999; *Planning*, December 2000:20-23). Florida seems to mirror this fault line. By geography and temperament, Panhandle residents are least supportive of the state's anti-sprawl initiatives. In fact, Panhandle Floridians, as Traditional-Individualists, are more likely to seek a "local-parochial" solution (Ch. 4; Ch.5; Florida DCA Growth Management Survey, February 2001). With land being a valuable commercial resource, especially along its bays, rivers and lakes, political disputes are inevitable. Even with land use regulations in place, quality of life issues has remained a contentious political issue, causing a reexamination of the state's growth management activities ("Who will regulate growth? *The Florida Times-Union*, March 12, 2000; "Legislature to protect property rights," *The Florida Times-Union*, March 27, 2000; "Growth reform faces challenge from developers," *The Florida*

Times-Union, April 15, 2001;"State bill revisits Manatee zones, *Florida Today,* February 24, 2002; "Sebastian council candidates field growth topics," *Florida Today,* March 4, 2002).

A Southern Strategy, A Southern Solution

Bish and Ostrom (1973:19) write that there is an expectation that state government will assure "free market conditions," and resolve political disputes "between individuals participating in [such] market transactions." To fail in this expectation can easily question a state government's legitimacy. No issue has evoked more emotional and psychic energy than effort to foster an accommodation between the two land use camps—growth management and private property rights advocates ("Growth debate has Lawmakers pressured," *Florida Times-Union,* April 30, 2000). Under Florida's 1985 land management rules, local officials had to enforce growth management mandates or face Florida DCA moratoriums. Many local landowners saw growth management mandates as nothing more than "taking of private property" without compensation, which is a direct assault on a key Traditional-Individualistic core value. Local officials have little desire to enter into such property disputes, knowing it is a "no-win" situation. Thus, geography plays a critical role in the political support of Florida's growth management initiatives, with semi-suburban and rural counties less sympathetic toward Florida's growth management initiatives (DCA Growth Management Survey, February 2001). Nationally, distance from urban centers makes the benefits of sprawl and land use development quite attractive (Baldassare, 1981; 1986; Dowell, 1984; Rudel, 1989; King and Harris, 1989; Gale and Hart, 1992; Leo, et.al. 1998).

Earlier (Ch. 1; Ch. 5) we noted that besides the diversity in lifestyle preferences, fragmented regional planning and local parochialism were two additional factors that apparently contribute to sprawl. All three—civic core values, shifting demographics and fragmented regional planning—are intertwined to establish a set of conflicting land use planning rules that do aid homeowners to have a rural lifestyle within an urbanizing setting. For decades, without strong regional guidance, local governments have determined their land use regulations based on improving local tax base and avoiding internal jurisdictional squabbles. Southern Traditional-Individualism (Ch.3), local parochialism meant a community could shape its own destiny. Unfortunately, Florida communities in an effort to gain both worlds—maintaining a rural setting and achieving the suburban lifestyle—have made decisions that have brought about the sprawl.

Since 1985, Florida has taken a strong top-down land use planning approach (Ch.5), hoping to rectify the shortcomings of a splintered local planning process. At times its lead agency—Florida DCA—has overly micro managed the planning process, causing difficulty for the Regional Planning Councils and the various local governments to implement innovative planning. In *The Ecology of Place*, Beatley and Manning (1997:79) note that cities and state governments have a better chance of achieving the sustainable goals of growth management by educating and by cultivating strategies of regional cooperation from the local key stakeholders. Jeb Bush's growth management study commission urged the Florida DCA to acknowledge this reality. One strategy solution voiced was to give the 11 Regional Planning Councils greater responsibility. With each council's leadership board comprising an admixture of private and public stakeholders, the Regional Planning Councils can serve as the principal coordinators and mediators between local governments and the various state agencies as needed. Moreover, Bush's growth management commission believes that is where local and inter-local governmental disputes arise. The Regional Planning Councils have the professional capacity to mitigate such disputes ("A Liveable Florida For Today and Tomorrow," Florida Growth Management Study Commission, 2001:31-36). I tend to agree. Unless a compelling state interest is identified, knowing that Traditional-Individualism is still a factor, Floridians are better served by the Regional Planning Councils, which are sensitive to local political nuances and are less likely to be perceived for being heavy-handed. However, the Florida DCA can still act as the principal coordinator for resource allocation of the CDBG program, as the principal mitigator of environmentally sensitive policy disputes, and as the technical advisor for Main Street, PDR and other planning related state programs. The Regional Planning Councils, when funded properly, have demonstrated the technical capacity to assist the local governments in their efforts to implement workable solutions to stem urban sprawl (Catlin, 1997). It is in this context that the following recommended solutions are being made.

Smart Growth and the Local Community Options

The late Kevin Lynch claimed that a suburban town dweller needed a mental map to give meaning to h/her community. The automobile, free-market aspects of land consumption, and modern telecommunications have all contributed to the destruction of such mental maps. The late J. B. Jackson believed that Main Street, the County House Square, the old Mill, or Elm

Street were **sacred symbols** that defined a community's Sense of Place. The spatial arrangement of these symbolic landmarks helped forge a community's social interaction. As spatial mental maps, these sacred symbols became the historic anchors for the community. Sacred symbols helped identify why a citizen belonged and why h/her civic institutions are deemed important (Ch.6). Sprawl has placed each of these—Main Street, the County Court House, the old Swimming Hole and the Drive-in Theater—at peril.

Since the late 1950s, subdivision rules suggest that shopping centers are placed in one pod, residential units in another, and office parks yet in another. Rather than encouraging social integration, such decision rules have encouraged a highly segmented society where node activities are distant from one another, and are only accessible by the automobile (Duany, et.al. 2000; Gillham, 2002). The New Urbanism claims this to be inefficient land use planning, making our suburban society highly dependent upon an unsustainable infrastructure (Duany, et. el. 2000; Langdon, 1994: Ch. 2;). Sprawl with its love affair of the automobile has made it quite costly to the local citizens, both in terms of dollars and cultural roots.

Advocates of Smart Growth presume that existing traditional Euclidean-based zoning is also a culprit. It simply doesn't work, placing the quality of life at risk (Gratz and Mintz, 1998:146). Although zoning's original intent was "to keep factories away from houses, [and] to create separate zones for industry to carry on its noisy and dirty activities." Zoning laws have become inflexible, decision-rules that insist on the separation of human activity so that "the only acceptable connecting device is the car and its expensive infrastructure." (Kunstler, 1996:129). By standards of human scale, such zoning rules are incompatible with the small town ("Sprawl Cost Us All," Sierra Club, 2000; "Getting to Smart Growth, " International City Management Association, 2000; Sutro, 1990). High density and compact development does not mean congestion; rather, Smart Growth advocates insist that compact development will ensure both aesthetic human scale values and human civic engagement (Porter, 1997:153-161). Mixed-use developments, town centers, shared green or public spaces, and pedestrian friendly streets are all elements of this Neo-traditional planning style for combating sprawl (*Urban Ecology*, Spring 2001:27). A "Genius Loci" is the outcome of this unique spirit of place. That is, people of all walks of life will begin to mingle and to share a common experience of shopping, working and recreating (Garnham ,1985:7-12). Or as Robert Yaro (1993:104), the Director of the Center for Rural Massachusetts writes, the Genius Loci assures a town's social commonality of its sense of place.

Town character encompasses more than natural landforms and traditional buildings; it includes the town's social life as well. Whether people walk downtown, congregate at the post office or the corner store, sit on benches along the streets, or meet at the Town Hall, all these social activities contribute to the composite character of any town.

Until auto-oriented land use development emerged, every small town possessed such a Genius Loci. The dominance of the automobile has shattered this aspect of small town intimacy. "The car," declares Calthorpe (1993:27), "is now the defining technology of our built environment. It sets the form of our cities and town [s], dictating the scale of streets, the relationship between buildings, the need for vast parking areas, and the speed at which we experience our environment. " And, the automobile culture has become a prime initiator of sprawl with its low density of development and its out-of-home activities with minimal socially connected behavior.

Floridians have an impulse to fiddle with a town's sacred symbols for the benefit of the automobile. "If it can be moved, changed, rebuilt, reinvented, so much the better. This is, after all, a state where the Main Street is in Disney World rather than in an actual old town." (Dunlop, 1985:66). This impulse stresses the elimination of the familiar. It is highly disruptive to a town's sacred symbols. As architectural anchors, sacred symbols provide a certain intimacy and emotional attachment, reminding a town's residents of past cultural events (Hester, 1990). Tarpon Spring's Sponge Exchange or DeFuniak Spring's Chautauqua Building are good representatives of such symbolic cultural landmarks. In each case, for town residents, both structures are viewed to be quite ordinary. But, as sacred symbols, both structures are part of each town's respective cultural memory, a manifestation of the town's heritage. Sadly, in Florida where there is a constant rush to modernize its small towns, town governments are willing to sacrifice such sacred symbols. Garnham (1985:10) claims that our neglect for preserving such sacred symbols is placing a serious strain upon a town's collective consciousness. Over time, it has become increasingly difficult to retain a town's "character, scale and other attributes" which made so many small towns so special. For Floridians, as Dunlop (1985: Ch.4) notes, our love affair with the automobile has created the "Age of Bland." For Generation X, this plea to save such "funky"and "idiosyncratic" symbols from Florida's Golden Age may seem a bit hokey or whimsical; but, these sacred symbols—roadside attractions, period gas stations and resort motels—gives Florida its special charm. When we lose them, as Dunlop (1985:39) observes, "we'll lose a lot."

Social Solution—Pedestrian Friendly Communities

America's Main Street of yesteryear is not prepared for the vagaries of contemporary zoning. As New Urbanism declares, you can't rebuild Main Street, even if you want to. You can't remodel Elm Street if you so desire to. Under the automobile oriented zoning it is not legal. The automobile's impact has altered our sensitivities to what is our natural human scale. Older towns built prior to modern zoning codes were in balance between what was natural and what was man-made. Pre-automobile towns are now considered quaint tourist attractions. Historic towns such as Portsmouth, New Hampshire or Apalachicola, Florida cannot be replicated under the dictates of contemporary zoning. Any effort to reclaim the small town requires the complete revision of existing site design standards (Sutro, 1990; Calthorpe, 1993; Porter, 1997). Interestingly, Main Street is not a new idea. Thirty years ago planning schools taught the student that a neighborhood will whither away without an adjoining commercial district as its heart. HUD recognizes this rule. Its CDBG regulations require the targeting, the restoring and the revitalizing of Main Street.

Florida's Main Street program has tried to actively regenerate Elm Street and/or Main Street in 70 communities within 32 counties. Utilizing all three design elements, the Florida Department of State' Main Street Program has helped Mariana, Florida revamp its local ordinances so that three unique eateries could be built within its downtown district. In Sanford, the Main Street program has help revitalized two historic districts—downtown and lake front. Both revitalization efforts are at a human scale thanks to zoning changes. By doing so, Sanford has stabilized its local tax base and protected its town center's unique charm. Often tied to the Governor's Office of Tourism, Trade and Economic Development (OTTED), the Main Street Program helps connect the "ambience of place" to a "city's self identification." **Flex Zoning** is the key. Under Flex Zoning, a building owner can change the use of a building without undergoing some lengthy variance approval requirements. This solution allows for better capitalization on fluctuating market demands, assuring new opportunities to capture the retail dynamics associated with changing demographics within a community ("Getting to Smart Growth, ICMA, 2000:6). Governor Bush's Growth Management Study Commission has urged Flex Zoning [Recommendation #77] to fit local circumstances (*A Liveable Florida for Today and Tomorrow*, February 2001:39).

Town Centers and Mixed Development

Main Street's town center endures because it is part of America's spatial and social consciousness (Stilgoe, 1998:138). The small town represents a different era, when the pace of life was much quieter and slower (Powers, 1990; Tarrant, 1976). Even at noon, Stilgoe (1999:139) writes, "automobile traffic moves slowly, almost sedately, so children can move quickly, safely, sometimes running from late twentieth century into a past so remote it aches, as when a rare grade school still adjourns for lunch, and at least some children sprint home for hot soup." The town center is a reminder of when its community's streets and its public and commercial buildings were at a human scale. For generations, Main Street was where "the Fourth of July Parade was held, and later on it was where young people kill time at the drug store and the movie theater, and cruise around the weekend nights." (Kostoff, 1987:166). Unlike the shopping mall, Main Street played a vital social and cultural role within the community. It connected the town to its residents. It is a manifestation of what the community was, is and can be. Main Street is America's "visual icon." It defines our Sense of Place. Main Street's visual image persists because of its distinctive architecture. The height, bulk and placement of Main Street buildings give a sense of permanence. The architecture allows Main Street to give the impression that it has "changed less than its surroundings," and "all this helps explain why [Main Street] seems to be [a] haven from change." (Francaviglia, 1996: Ch.3).

Built before the automobile, the traditional Main Street was designed to promote foot traffic (Kenyon, 1989; Brooks and Searcy, 1995). Its scale makes for lots of light and air. Above all, the human scale allows for the shopper to admire the buildings within their vertical context (Stilgoe, 1999:141). In the South, Main Street had brought people together who were of different ages and social circumstances (Craycroft, 1981). The **town center**, a new term for Main Street, promoted human activity by enhancing a citizen's sense of civic public space. During the horse and buggy era, town leaders were keenly aware that mix uses would promote social interaction. Town councils encouraged design schemes that allowed each merchant-entrepreneur to lend his name and his fortune to a building. At street level there was commercial use, and on the second floor there was residential use. In fact, these design schemes were the very first public-private ventures, with town councils providing certain public amenities as incentives to the merchant who built such a monument to commerce.

Today, this pedestrian orientation has been blurred. The nature of automobile traffic prevents Main Street's greatest assets—its mix use—from being appreciated (Kern, 1994; Ewing, 1996: Ch. 3). In contrast to being confined to the slow speed of a buggy, the automobile quite literally requires Main Street to adapt to a more "streamlined, and horizontal perspective" (Francaviglia, 1996:46-51). Main Street has become display windows for the automobile passenger, and second floors are simply storage areas. Residential use is discouraged by building and housing code requirements. Today, the concept of foot traffic tied to mix use is viewed as a hindrance to auto traffic flow. Typically, First and Main Street, which are the town's historic heart, has succumbed to patterns of vehicular volume and flow. Over time, Main Street's walkways have been narrowed, impeding pedestrian circulation space (Kern, 1994; *The Village Handbook*, 1990:21-23). While street widening may solve traffic flows, this solution has ruined Main Street's commercial, historic and visual integrity.

Within southern small towns, today's design solutions ought not to be based on an urban design methodology. Pedestrian traffic is the key to the renovation of Main Street. Design choices ought to be within a "framework of common sense and forethought" (Craycroft, 1981). Across the state border, two Georgia design studies have emphasized the need to refocus the small town, downtown visioning process. If southern small towns wish to commercially revitalize their Main Street (Kenyon, 1989; Brooks and Searcy, 1995), both studies suggest a "visioning" strategy that is both a "social-cultural" as well as a "commercial-economic" focus. Not only are the physical attributes (building conditions, historic character and street scape appearance) of important design; but also, the social activity aspects (the pedestrian activators) are critical. In both studies, a master scheme that will generate foot traffic is the principal goal of any local activity. The local town chamber or planning department ought to be equally attentive about the location of a new coffee shop or the renovation of the local movie as they are likely to be about free parking spaces or tax abatements. Ewing's (1996) analysis of traditional Florida towns with population levels below 25,000 has come to the same conclusion. In his study to the Florida DCA, he urges good pedestrian accessibility. Pedestrian friendly, mixed land uses appear to have a positive impact on residential as well as commercial property values. A common denominator in his recommendations is accessible mixed-used development, which has become increasingly rare within Florida, as he reported from his survey of county planning agencies.

Craycroft (1981) urges that southern Main Street redevelopment should focus on the goal of converting the automobile driver into a shopping pedestrian. In the past, the quick fix was highly simplistic, more curbside parking on both sides of Main Street. This has sacrificed existing sidewalk space, and shade trees, causing the downtown to represent the parking lot of a Mall. Francaviglia (1996:76) claims to make the automobile owner a true Main Street pedestrian, we must design walkways and street-widths that are in proportion to Main Street's height and bulk. As Kern (1994) suggests, the pedestrian experience can work only if a town's Main Street is easy to reach and compact enough to walk from one end to another. A simple design solution is to make Main Street a one-way, and to reroute heavy thru-traffic in a loop around the commercial center, preserving the overall visual integrity of Main Street's spine (Sutro, 1990). For the shopper, Crankshaw (1998) suggests that a visitation to Main Street ought to be a three dimensional walking experience, where paths pleasantly lead the shopper to a variety of shopping destinations. Parking ought be within small lots strategically placed on the streets perpendicular to Main Street or on alternate sides of its spine. Fewer parking spaces on Main Street will allow for additional shade trees, benches and natural areas. Tree shaded alleyways and tree shaded perpendicular streets can become a pedestrian's complimentary pathway for Main Street shopping. Pocket parks will only add value to local property values, and remove unsightly vacant lots. Collectively, these design solutions will allow the walker-shopper to linger and enjoy the architectural embellishments of Main Street.

Main Street will never likely regain its prominence as a regional, commercial hub. The little rituals of commerce from a yesteryear—the bakery, the candy store, the butchers' shop—has succumb to the outlying commercial strip. With Big Box Stores, few drug stores or hardware stores are going to have grand openings on Main Street anyway. But, Main Street is still a place of mixed use—commercial, office and residential space—that can sustain noonday foot traffic. And, with intelligent adaptive reuse, a downtown's civic, commercial, and residential architecture can be a shoppers' delight. Mizner Park in Boca Raton emphasizes such pedestrian internal accessibility. Developed on the site of a former shopping center, it is to be the new town center for Boca Raton. It has its limitations, with its Main Street stopping at the ends of the project, causing Mizner Park to be somewhat isolated. The key is architectural compatibility with Main Street, and in that context Mizner Park works. Not all towns are the same, nor should they be a colonial Williamsburg. Sebring, Florida has a Main Street that works because it reflects the town's era, a 1920s commercial style period. On the other hand, Cedar Key's galvanized roofs and wooden textured buildings is representative of this town's 19th Century fishing/lumber port era. In both cases, community design guidelines fit the town's historic sense of place. And, when you are in Apalachicola, you know that you are in an old 19th Century panhandle fishing, lumber and cotton port (Dunlap, 1987:20-31). Sadly, Fernadina Beach has lost much of its fishing village charm of the 1970s. As a revitalized town center, its old downtown seems to work, but has lost its cultural past. In a rush to cash-in on historic renovation, Fernadina Beach's local officials simply tried to boiler plate ordinances of other communities, creating a "Disneyfied" Florida Main Street (Marshall, 2000: Ch 1; Farncaviglia, 1996:51-57, 145-192; Mattson, "Fernadina Beach Commercial Functional Analysis," UNF Center for Local Government, Summer 1990).

Civic Public Space

Common civic public spaces—parks, plazas and courtyards—are really "transition zones" between public and private space (Danzer, 1987:111). As a design element, civic public space expresses "the value we assign to community." (Calthorpe, 1993:23). Common civic public spaces are expected to compliment the town center. Public space ought to guide residents to the overall focal point—the town center, with public buildings complimenting this commercial center. Civic public space—the town library, the post office, or the county courthouse—have been paid for "by us and, in a fundamental sense, belong to us." (Kostof, 1987:246). Underutilized public parking lots can be transformed into public vest-pocket parks. Miami Lakes reportedly has more pocket parks than any other community in Florida, with one pocket park per one thousand people, providing residents with greenspace, well-defined edges and social focal points (Ewing, 1996:32). Parks, plazas and public buildings are places for informal social linkage points, and not simply inert "things" in the public domain. A town's visual setting—its parks, plazas, street patterns and public buildings—will tell the visitor "how the town unfolds, revealing itself and its character." (Garnham, 1985:28). The public realms' spatial arrangement is a basis for community life, for a sense of place. A charity pancake breakfast under a tent on the town green tells the visitor a lot about a particular community.

The Pedestrian Neighborhood

In 1950 southern small towns were predominantly residential with a central commercial district. Served by local water/sewer systems, residential lots were likely narrowly platted to be 30 to 75 feet wide and up to 175 feet long, with a minimum lot size of 4375 square feet. Given a one to four ratios for a residential dwelling unit, these pre-1960 Florida towns were both charming and pedestrian oriented. The 1960s brought uniformity in lot sizes and setbacks that was tied to large tract development. During this pre-growth management era, new platted lots beyond the town's original boundary were served by public drinking water but required on-site septic systems, negating lots smaller than a quarter acre. With larger lots, most subdivision standards mandated curbs, cul-de-sac and curvilinear neighborhood street patterns, with no walkway to give an "in-the-county" feeling. Such subdivision design standards are simply not as remarkable as the earlier small town design scheme.

A combination of many physical attributes helps make up a town's image—sacred symbols, architectural styles, circulation patterns, and entryways. All these elements play a critical role in defining the town's spirit of place. Each by itself may not be memorable, but collectively they give character to a community. Of these elements, it is the street layout that plays a "subtle underlying feature" to a town's character. It establishes order and hierarchy between the pedestrian and the automobile (Daenzer, 2001). The network of streets should guide the flow of automobile and pedestrian traffic. Moreover, the street provides a town's entry point, and provides the right of way for public utilities. But, equally important, the network of streets provides the visitor with their only lasting impression of a community (Hall and Porterfield, 2001:79).

Except in extreme topographical conditions, the typical small town street layout is interconnected. That is, the street layout and its walkways ought to be interconnected. To ignore these basic principles places the community's sense of place in jeopardy (Arendt, 1999:58). Therefore, a town's new street networks and lot-size layouts ought to be gracefully integrated (Sutro, 1990: 9-11). Interconnectedness means that the entire local street network should be meshing (Calthorpe, 1993). Under Smart Growth, local streets ought to be narrow, with tree-lined sidewalks, often "fronted by porches, balconies and entries rather than garage doors and driveways." Such streets are rarely thirty feet wide, and have sidewalks. Because of public utilities, the dwelling units are on smaller lots, creating human intimacy (Calthorpe,

1993:21). Smart Growth communities are known as pedestrian communities. Thus, such walkable communities give access to services "for one-third of the population that is too old, too young or too poor to drive" (Getting to Smart growth," International City Management Association, 2000:26).

Trees give a street a cohesiveness by acting as a shade canopy for sidewalks, front yards and the street. Before air conditioning, shade trees was something to be considered in 90 degree heat and 80 per cent humidity. Porches were quite functional by serving as a place to visit and restore oneself, especially during those sweltering southern summers. Neo-Traditional Planning suggests sidewalk on a grid street pattern. This street pattern is functional for two reasons. First, sidewalks connects the pedestrian to his neighbors. Second, the street grid system will evenly distribute traffic, and act as a calming effect (Porterfield and Hall, 1995:72). The grid system, as the alternative to cul-de-sacs or curvilinear pods, is not a street pattern that simply crosses at right angles; but rather, it helps calm automobile traffic (Langdon, 1994:123-25). Furthermore, the street grid system is far less costly for municipal infrastructure placement and installment. If cul-de sacs are necessary, Randall Arendt (1999) suggests that they be adapted to an existing street network by joining them in pairs, forming street loops that extend into the existing grid street pattern.

A town's overall street layout should be treated in a cohesive manner so that the pedestrian and bicyclist feel comfortable enough to share the neighborhood with the automobile. Foot traffic should be dispersed by the techniques of Traditional Neighborhood Development. Curbs, sidewalks, common greens, and shade trees are all part of this design scheme, with buffers to shield the pedestrian from traffic. Streets, in particular, are critical for Traditional Neighborhood Development. In newly annexed subdivisions, the street pavement width ought to conform to existing residential streets. The rule-of-thumb is the belief that a secondary collector street is functional when it can accommodate one lane of on-street parking, and a travel lane for both directions. A turning radius of fifteen degrees is about the small town norm for such streets. By accepting these design standards, we are rejecting the notion that streets are principally dedicated to the automobile (Daenzer, 2001; Duany, et. al., 2000; Arendt, 1999).

Environmental Solution—
Crisp Edges and Greenbelts

First impressions are lasting impressions. A town's entryway is similar to the sidewalk leading up to your door. For visitors, it is the first glimpse into your house. A tidy house is an inviting house. Oliver Gillham (2002:163) writes that special views and vistas have a lot to say about a community's self image. "How a land is used also has a lot to do with the community's makeup and way of life." Therefore, the images one sees "upon entering a village are very important to the overall image of the village" (*Village Planning Handbook*, 1989:11-15). If you have a deteriorating entryway with scattered litter, pothole roads, and dilapidated buildings, this can only be interpreted to mean that the "town is in decline" (Sutro, 1990). **Crisp edges** according to Arendt (1999:43-49) means the town has adopted site design standards that will clearly delineate the town from its neighbors. It means the town's officials are sensitive to the insertion of buildings and streets into the existing settlement patterns, acknowledging that land use patterns define the town's landscape and overall image. Crisp edges also mean the establishment of "buffer-overlay" zone. A "buffer-overlay" zone is also known as **a viewshed**, which includes natural features that help give a positive visual impact to the community (*Village Planning Handbook*. 1989:17-19; Houston, 1988). The **viewshed** can be some geological feature or simply open space. Moreover, it can accent a **sacred symbol** such as the town's old Grist Mill and/or the Old Swimming Hole. Safeguarding the town's **viewshed** is critical for two reasons. First, it is critical for the maintenance of the community's Genius Loci. Second, it serves as the transition zone from country to town.

Crisp edges is a policy planning tool for safeguarding a community's unique spatial identity (Freilich,1999; Arendt, 1999; Knapp and Nelson, 1992). Crisp edges are associated with greenbelts, which is not a new concept. Over a century ago, Ebenezer Howard advocated such a policy planning tool to maintain the English countryside. In contemporary planning language the terms **Urban Growth Boundary or a Viewshed** comes to mind. Both imply order, discipline and rational land use. Florida's 1985 Growth Management Act merely suggests voluntary compliance for urban growth boundaries as the mechanism for crisp edges (Ewing, 1999). Many Florida towns appear to have such crisp edges. Both Port Charlotte and Cape Coral had incorporated visual open space within their land use plans (Ewing, 1999:19). In reality, both "visual open space" designated areas are in private land ownership and subdivided into "lot sale" parcels, defeating the purpose of the respective land use plans. As Dunlop (1985:58) quips, you may fly over Florida and see many acres of green space, dotted with lakes and scrub forests. Yet, as we drive along the back roads, we soon discover all this land is ready for the bulldozer. Between 1982 and 1992, Florida land owners subdivided and developed an average of 116,310 acres per year. By the mid-1990s, the average number of acres rose to 189,060 acres per year (*Audubon*, March 2000:69).

An Urban Growth Boundary (UGB) is confronted by a host of technical and legal implications. All are tied to how the types of future development are to be procedurally administered by the local government. To merely draw a line on a map does not mean that open space will remain for perpetuity or sprawl will be confined (Caves, 1992: Ch. 6; Porter, 1997:62-69; Beatley and Manning, 1997:42-53). We must have some mechanism that preserves the greespace forever. Sarasota County, Florida is a case in point. In its 1981 Comprehensive Plan, it had adopted a three-tiered open space land use intensity system, with little regard as to how it would assure preservation beyond regulatory policy. After a decade of political controversy and lawsuits, the county was a hodgepodge of low density, singly dimensional developmental sprawl. Moreover, a serious infrastructure backlog had emerged. Even with a revised UGB, Sarasota County's grand land use scheme has meant a costly infrastructure backlog and no true public viewshed (Porter, 1996: 88-93).

Greenbelts, Taxes and Trigger Levels

Most small town dwellers do not want a shopping mall or a sprawling subdivision at their door step. Faced with the rise of **trigger levels** on his orchard or farmland, the adjacent land owner may have no choice, forcing him to sell part of his land to offset property tax increases tied to sprawl. The **trigger level** is defined as the temporal point within the development process whereby a combination of declining agricultural prices, rising public service costs, increased local property tax assessments, and the inflationary price of land forces a an urban-rural fringe property owner to sell (*New York Times*, June 23, 2001:A-14). Or as the Florida Growth Management Study Commission (February 2001:43) reports, it is the trigger point on the Florida landscape where rural land ownership retention has become a personal crisis. Under sprawl conditions, the **trigger level** creates conditions for **leapfrog development**.

Growth management initiatives are often expensive, and thereby raise the issue of implementation feasibility ("Smart Money" *Planning*, November 2001:14-17; "Stemming the Tide," *American Farmland*, Fall, 2001:10-13). For rural folk there is hostility toward proposed growth control strategies, who tend to believe that such regulatory schemes without compensation is design to benefit only the urban folks. For the rural small towner, there is a perception that land use preservation schemes will be a tax burdens for two reasons. First, open space preservation means that there will be a reduction of the overall tax base within a community or the county, and thereby shifting the tax burden onto existing property owners. Second, the loss of the potential land development tax base is likely to mean the loss of tax revenues to pay for public services, jeopardizing the quality of life for all residents. Subsequently, any local policy debate pertaining to open space preservation must focus on whether such a policy choice is a wise tax investment for the community or the county.

Under the free market principles, land use policy is evaluated by its highest potential use, with open space conservation not being viewed as an attractive economic policy option. For decades, as noted (Ch.11), rural local officials have seen land development as a means of improving a town's tax base to pay for public services. Under Smart Growth principles, a community is a finite place which distinguishes its fragile agrarian hinterland by distinct topographic and natural landscape features. A community's sense of place is then delineated by its compact, pedestrian-friendly, mixed land uses. Such a design policy strategy can be contradictory to those who wish to expand the tax base by converting the town's open space or farmland to commercial, industrial and residential uses. However, several land tax studies contradict this belief. For example, a Trust for Public Land study ("Community Choices," Ad Hoc Associates, 1999) discovered a positive tradeoff between land use conservation and local tax bills. In a comparison analysis of rural Massachusetts' communities, the TPL found that in the short run, development did raise the taxable value of land. However, this improved tax base did not sufficiently offset the cost of public services. On the average, over the long run, there was an increase cost in public services for those communities that converted farmland and open space to industrial, commercial and/or residential use. Overall, local property owners saw their taxes go up, and the very natural feature that attracted residential growth in the first place was likely to diminish.

Since the late 1980s, American Farmland Trust (AFT) has conducted more than 60 cost of community services studies for counties and towns facing sprawl on the urban-rural fringe. The following two southern studies are typical of the findings. Frederick, Maryland is still a county dominated by farmland, with approximately 1,350 family farms. Bisected by I-70 and I-270, its close proximity to the Washington/Baltimore metro region has assured a 110 per cent population growth over the past three decades, with much of it beyond the jurisdictional boundaries of its 11 small towns. Frederick County is the principal provider of public services. The American Farmland Trust ("The Cost of Community Services: Frederick County, Maryland," 1997) discovered that for every dollar raised from residential revenues, the county spent $1.14 in direct public services. By contrast, the farmland and open space had a ratio of 1:0.53, or for every dollar raise in taxes from farmland or open space, the county spent 53 cents in direct public services. Commercial and Industrial had a 1:0.50 ratio, making it this land use form more cost effective. Among the various Frederick County communities, farmland and open space was still cost effective when compared to residential use. The American Farmland Trust's joint cost of community services for Lexington-Fayette County, Kentucky (1999) also looked at the contribution of tax revenues by the three land types farmland/open space, residential and commercial/industrial. In this analysis, again farmland and open space did not raise the cost of services. Instead, for every dollar generated, Fayette County only spent $0.93 in public services for farmland and open space. In contrast, residential development quite expensive to city-county taxpayers, costing the county treasury $1.64 for every tax dollar collected. In its analysis of commercial and industrial land use public service costs, the AFT noted that a county's employee withholding tax paid the majority of the public service costs for both land uses. Thus, revenue collections were distorted, with the county spending only twenty-two cents for public services. Even so, this can be misleading. We cannot claim that commercial/industrial land use was cost effective because the individual tax-payer/employee was subsidizing the cost of public service provision by the wage tax. Overall, both studies did indicate that residentially, leapfrog development is least cost effective. In many respects, it is the local farmer or large landowner who was subsidizing sprawl.

Heritage Tourism and Open Space

Nationally, tourism is big business, with one 1995 study estimating that it generated $58 billion in tax revenues and supports almost 14 million locally-based jobs (Beatley and Manning, 1997:154). In a cost/benefit ratio study conducted by Utah State's Western Rural Development Center (1994) of northwestern United States communities, it was found that the measurable dollar benefit was 2.17; or, for every $1 tourist cost, the rate of return was $2.17 to the community. Moreover, a tourist dollar's "chain of spending" was quite positive in revenue tax capture, meaning for every $100 spent locally for goods and services from a tourist, a community could expect an increase in local tax revenues by an additional three to 5 per cent because of the multiplier effect ("The Impact of Visitor Expenditures on Local Revenues," WRDC Report #145; "Cost-Benefit Analysis of Local Tourism Development, WRDC, Report# 147).

In Florida, tourism is big business. Not everyone flies to Orlando or Miami. Much of Florida's tourism is small town heritage or nature-based. Many snowbirds are much happier to visit the antique shops in Milton, and then relax with an old fashion sundae at Milton's drug store. In fact, two out of every three Americans who visit Florida include a visit to a small town and have a nature-based experience (*Rural Florida: Opportunities for the Future*, Florida APA White Paper, November, 2001:6). In 1997, freshwater fishing, hunting and wildlife viewing generated $339 million annually in sales tax revenues, providing jobs for about 60,000 Floridians. Saltwater recreational activities, which depend on undisturbed estuaries and coast ecosystems, was responsible for an annual expenditure of $1.3 billion, which supported more than 23,500 retail and service jobs, generating about $235 million in wages. During that same year, beach tourism pumped another $7.9 billion into the state's economy, with the ripple effect of creating 359,450 jobs, and establishing a multiplier of dollars spent equivalent to $15.4 billion ("The Florida Preservation 2000 Program: Needs and Priority Study," www.P2000.dep.state.fl.us./economic.htm.). Since natural areas and the countryside which are a key pull factor for Florida tourism, it appears to makes dollar sense to recommend preservation of such landscapes. The Republican dominated blue-ribbon panel Florida Growth Management Study Commission agrees. It saw a linkage between the natural landscape and tourist dollars and had urged the state legislature to devise a policy incentive plan to pay local land owners to maintain and/or enhance their natural landscape and wildlife habitat areas (*A Liveable Florida for Today and Tomorrow*, February 2001:46).

Saving Countryside, Saving the Aquifer

The Florida Growth Management Study Commission (2001) noted that those who reside in urbanizing counties were more likely to support some form of urban growth boundary strategy. These UGB supporters were better educated and had incomes between $50,000and $70,000. Another recent poll for Collier County indicated that 75% of its residents want preservation of the natural areas ("A Lesson in Growing Pains, *St Petersburg Times*, June 6, 1999). In a 1998 Florida Trust for Public Land statewide poll showed that 70 of the respondents supported a programs that would create more parks, greenways and open space, believing such a policy will enhance tax base, protect the local aquifer and enhance the quality of life ("Florida Forever Initiative," Florida Trust for Public Land, June 16, 2001). Indeed, throughout the 1990s, Florida polls noted that the cohort most likely to support the curbing of sprawl is likely to comprise former Frostbelt Republicans or Independents residing on the urban-rural fringe, a critical swing group on other wedge issues (Ch. 3; Ch. 4). In the FY 2002 Budget, Jeb Bush obviously understood the political mood. Facing an apparent tough reelection race against Janet Reno, Bush had replaced more than $100 million within the Forever Florida program, over riding the wishes of many Republican legislators ("Bush Shields Fund for Land, *The St. Petersburg Times* June 6, 2002).

Tourism alone is not a reason to protect Florida's natural habitants and watersheds. In 1994 the Florida Fish and Wildlife Conservation Commission estimated that 4.82 million acres or 13% of Florida's land area should be designated as part of a Strategic Groundwater Preserve (*Rural Florida: Opportunities for the Future*, Florida APA Working White Paper, November 2001:6). By the Summer of 2000, Florida was experiencing a water crisis. With a twenty-one inch below normal rainfall for the previous year, Lake Jackson near Tallahassee was dry. From January to May 2001, the state had more than 2600 wildfires. In 2001, after three years of state drought, this designation seemed to make sense. As the drought persisted, the price for treating fresh drinking groundwater began to get expensive. In 1997, the cost of drinking water in Melbourne or Cocoa was between $1 and $1.50 per 1000 gallons. By 2001, this price rose to $3.70 per 1000 gallons. As ground water got saltier, both jurisdictions had to look elsewhere, with Melbourne looking to Lake Washington and Cocoa looking to Taylor Creek Reservoir. Both drinking water sources require additional treatment, driving up the cost per gallon ("Population lead to spike in water rates, *Florida Today*, March 2, 2001). Nor is treating drinking water the only cost issue, the construction of additional and the replacement of aging water pipes due to the demands of population growth and land utilization is plaguing many "boom-boom" communities. In FY2000 Annual Legislative Session, there were 261 municipal relief requests for financial help to revamp existing wastewater and surface water utility systems to the tune of $400 million. As Florida Stormwater Utility Association President Pat Collins had testified before the legislature, there was statewide a 50 per cent backlog of improvement projects of existing systems and it will only get worse ("Politics decides Florida's crucial water matters," *The Florida Times Union*, April 24, 2000). As the conservative James Madison Institute (*Water Management Policy in Florida,* January 2002) recently reported, the water crisis is tied to the failure by the politically independent watershed districts to acknowledge that water is a "precious commodity." Most subtropical Florida residents, who simply anticipate the daily four o'clock monsoons, are not prepared or politically willing to pay the true market price for such green lawns. For most Floridians, low-cost water is an expected right and not a lucky privilege. When the stakes are high, water politics can be conflict ridden, with few Floridians acknowledging the interrelationship among the needs for pure drinking water, the loss of natural landscape to sprawl, and the aging its infrastructure.

Conservation Easements and Heritage Tourism

There are many land preservation schemes—scenic easements, cluster zoning, agricultural protective zoning, and tax roll back agreements. Yet, without some sort of compensatory scheme, most are found to be inadequate, failing to curtail sprawl or to protect farmland or groundwater supplies permanently. All of these conventional tools have political pitfalls tied to private property ownership. The key policy objective is to minimize the **trigger level** of land. Under the conditions of sprawl, the demand for moderately priced residential and commercial land will foster **leapfrog development**. To minimize the impact, a land policy must accomplish three objectives: (1) formalize property rights of the land owner, (2) encourage mixed diversity of land use that values open space preservation, and (3) avoids costly litigation (Mattson, 1978, 1983).

Former Republican Governor Bob Martinez devised a such a strategy. Faced with a drought, he hoped that a conservation easement program could be adopted that would save both critical natural habitat and dwindling groundwater supplies. In 1989, Governor Bob Martinez created a blue-ribbon commission to evaluate Florida's freshwater resources. This blue-ribbon commission warned that state's natural aquifer recharge areas would be converted to other uses by 2020, endangering the state's drinking water resources. Governor Martinez proposed a typical Traditional-Individualistic policy solution to fund a conservation easement program. He proposed a $3 billion land preservation bond fund, with the bonds being paid by taxes derived from every real estate transaction in Florida. The **conservation easement** is a legal agreement between the landowner and the state/local government that permanently limits a property's uses in order to protect the state's aquifer. As part of the land trust agreement, the state pays for the easement, avoiding costly litigation.

This program known as **Preservation 2000** has funded one million acres of watershed and critical wildlife habitat within 60 Florida counties by 1998. Moreover, 20 local governments have matched state funds to purchase urban growth boundaries and/or greenbelt easements (www.p2000.dep.state. fl.us.). For instance, on November 5, 1996, 67 per cent of Miami-Dade County voters approved $200 million for the acquisition and improvement of Dade County greenspace and parks. Floridians have derived considerable economic benefit from the Preservation 2000 program. For instance, recreational activities tied to the program generated for 1995/95 about $201 million into the local economies. The Office of Greenways and Trails reported that three greenbelt trails alone (Pinellas, Withlacooche and St.Marks) had generated $17.9 million in visitor expenditures and more than $1.33 million in sales tax revenues, as well as the creation of 570 new jobs (www. P2000.dep.state.fl.us/economic.htm.).

The Preservation 2000 program was successful because it defused the trigger level of land value by voluntary compliance. It did not regulate but rather sought outright purchase of land. The state agency had a clear mission and had established criteria for land selection. The program's cost was paid by newcomers who were imposing an impact on the existing watershed within the respective regions. In many ways, it could be viewed similar to an Impact Fee program (Art VIII. SS 1 or 2). Thus, for Florida residents, there was a reasonable connection of future population growth, sprawl and the impact on existing natural resources. The state legislature established criteria that showed this reasonable connection between expenditure of funds collected and benefits derived to newcomers—the protection of greenspace, natural habitat and groundwater supply.

The success of the P2000 program paved the way for the **Florida Forever** program (S 259.105, F.S.). **Forever Florida** was passed by the state legislature in April 1999 to replace Preservation 2000, doubling state funding for urban parks and open space acquisition. Moreover, it should meet the water crisis, with more money allocated for water resource protection and urbanizing wildlife habitat areas. This is especially important for an urban state, where the U.S. census indicates that 90 per cent of Floridians reside in or near cities ("Florida Forever Initiative," Florida Trust for Public Land, June 26, 2001). The **Florida Forever** program distributes an annual allocation under a formula that provides a bulk of the money (92%) to three state-sponsored trusts—The Conservation and Recreation Lands (CARL), the Water Management Districts land acquisition program, and the Florida Communities Trust. Under specific criteria, which can be interpreted as assisting the funding of urban growth boundaries, the Florida Communities Trust governing board can select projects. In November 2001, it selected 74 projects for funding, with another 10 projects under contingent funding status, for a total award of about $122 million (www.dca.state.fl.us/ffct.).

The Florida 2001 Legislature approved the **Florida Rural and Family Lands Protection Act. (Ss. 570.70 and 201.15,F.S.).** The purpose of this program is to prevent agricultural land, especially on the urban-rural fringe to be converted to urban type uses. It is a state-level voluntary program aimed at providing financial payments for conservation easements. These easements may restrict the construction of buildings, roads and the subdivision of the property under the terms of the easement. There are three time categories: in perpetuity, a 30-year protection easement or a 5-10 year easement. The Department of Agriculture and Consumer Services is the lead agency. However, due to the state's fiscal crisis it has not been funded (*Rural Florida*, Florida APA White Working Paper, November 2001:12).

Saving the Countryside—Local Incentives

Governor Bush's Growth Management Study Group understood the linkage between land markets, infrastructure and rural communities. It urged a revamping of infrastructure financing and planning that included a definable geographic area that would promote infilling. It also urged the establishment of greenspace and definable natural boundaries (*A Liveable Florida Today and Tomorrow*, February 2001: 22-23; 45). Both require money and careful planning.

There are, but two local workable mechanisms are—**Purchase of Development Rights** and **Transfer of Development Rights**. Both are voluntary tools that provide compensation to the landowner, helping to avoid costly litigation for land preservation purposes. The underlying legal concept is the notion that all land has a bundle of property rights, each one of which may be severed from the rest, and transferred to someone else, leaving the owner with all other rights of property ownership. One of the component rights is the right to improve and develop one's own property. Based on the concept of an easement, the easement holder pays the landowner for the legal right to make limited use of the landowner's property. As a leasehold, the easement is expressed in a formal document that sets down the conditions of use. In this case, it is the prevention of the conversion of natural wildlife habitat or farmland to more intensive residential, commercial or industrial developmental use. An easement cannot be revoked by a subsequent owner without consent a leaseholder agreement.

Purchase of Development Rights

The Purchase of Development Rights (PDRs) technique was first devised and implemented in 1974 in Republican dominated Suffolk County. At the time as the fastest growing New York State county, Suffolk County, located on the eastern end of Long Island, was faced with the loss of its farmland and natural aquifer recharge areas (Mattson, 1978:63-77). Then Suffolk County's planning director Lee Koppleman sought a means to preserve at least part of the county's farmland for green-space and for the curbing of sprawl. By doing so, Lee Koppleman hoped to preserve the integrity of Long Island's drinking water supply. Of the 2.7 million residents in the bi-county region, only a fraction was served by sewers; the remaining homeowners had sunk thousands of cesspools in the soil, which could potentially contaminate 95 per cent of Long Island's precious drinking water supply (Mattson, 1978:82).

The Purchase of Development Rights (PDRs) technique is one sure way to achieve an urban growth boundary, without local government purchasing the land outright. Based on the belief that all land has a bundle of rights, Suffolk County simply acquired all development easement rights except land ownership and its existing agricultural use. As a policy strategy **PDR** removes the land "trigger value" which so often plagues urban-rural fringe landowners. Under **Purchase of Development Rights (PDRs)** the price of the development rights is based on the highest fair market value of the land minus the land's value at its historic and/or existing property tax rate. **PDRs** are shown to have several advantages: **First,** the landowner benefits by having tax rate stability. In turn, the land retains its aesthetically pleasing character while it remains in productive use as an orchard or a cornfield. **Second**, the landowner can re-invest the purchase price of the development rights into farmland improvements or establish a personal retirement fund. **Third**, as a planning tool, the county government can protect the land from development, and it remains on the tax rolls, reducing the cost of public services associated with sprawl development. **Finally,** the program is voluntary. Fair market compensation precludes the possibility of legal and/or administrative problems associated with other land preservation tools (Mattson, 1978).

Its implementation, however, requires a long-term, well-integrated comprehensive planning scheme (Mattson, 1978). Also, the PDR plan requires a great deal of money. In 1975, Suffolk County taxpayers committed itself to a $25 million bond program at a high interest rate. Since the mid-1970s, New Jersey has spent $168 million preserving 234 farms, and Connecticut has spent $75 million to save 169 farms. (Mattson, 1982; *New York Times*, July 2, 1998:B8; *New York Times*. June 23, 2001:A-14). Besides Suffolk County, twenty-four other counties have adopted the tool. By 1997, Daniels and Bowers (1997:Ch. 9) reported that 345,746 acres of farmland and open space in semi-rural areas has been preserved in ten states. Even Big Sky country is not immune to a suburban sprawl, Gallatin County, Montana in the past decade has had more than 17,000 acres of farmland subdivided into hobby farms, threatening the county's agricultural heritage and quality of life. In November 2000, voters in this highly Traditional-Individualistic county broke new ground by passing with a 59 per cent margin the state's first countywide purchase of a development right program to the tune of $10 million. By doing so, the county hopes to protect 12,000 to 18,000 acres of farmland ("Gallatin County, Montana—Purchase of Development Rights," The Trust for Public Land, June 25, 2001).

In 1992, former Jacksonville Beach state representative Joe Arnall (R) introduced a PDR program. It failed to gain support, being considered too frivolous during a cash-strapped year. In 1995, the Legislature created a new section of the state law (S 163.3177, F.S.). Under the **Rural Land Stewardship Areas** program, the 2001Legislature had authorized the Florida DCA to conduct test cases for the possible implementation of a purchase of development rights strategy. The Florida APA (*Rural Florida*, Florida APA White Working Paper, November 2001:23) noted that the inherent problem caused by scattered development on the urban-rural fringe requires such a coherent policy. Through my intimate knowledge of the Purchase of Development Rights program, it is my belief that PDRs is such a public policy strategy that will assure that individual property rights will be respected, and that environmental areas of critical importance could be protected from the path of sprawl forever.

Transfer of Development Rights

Purchase of Development Rights (PDRs) is often confused with the **Transfer of Development Rights (TDRs)**. Unlike Purchase of Development Rights, a **TDR program** is associated with zoning densities and bonuses. The development rights of land are tied to the real estate market. A city or county government establishes a development zoning credit scheme, which encourages the voluntary shift in development from places where the local government would like to see land preservation and shift the development to areas it wishes to see greater intensity of development. Normally, if the intent is to protect ground water recharge areas or farmland on the periphery, the local government takes the development credit potential associated with these areas based on the zoning map. The landowner can sell these credits to developer, who can then apply these "credits" to existing urban vacant land served by utilities. In return, the landowner's parcel has development restrictions on his environmentally sensitive land (Mattson, 1978). Rick Pruetz has uncovered 112 TDR schemes in 25 states across the nation (Pruetz, "Putting Growth in its Place with TDRs," Plannersweb.com, Summer 1998).

In most cases, the developer pays the landowner directly. Overtime, the town is able to shift development away from farmland, wetlands, open space, and historic areas. Lee County, Florida is such a case study for the **TDR** approach. There are more than 240,000 platted vacant lots within the county, with many owned by Yankees who desire a piece of paradise. Unfortunately, many of these lots are located on wetlands and were platted and sold decades ago. Lee County established a **TDR** ordinance to reclaim these environmentally sensitive areas and establish a legal means "to provide compensation to landowners who are economically harmed by restrictive low density requirements." Under the ordinance, an owner of any vacant lot and/or undeveloped parcel of land in a designated resource protection zone is eligible to participate in the **TDR** program. The landowner must agree to draw up a conservation easement for permanent protection of h/her environmentally sensitive land. Once filed and certified, the landowner has "the right to sell, trade, barter, negotiate or transfer those rights" using a simple deed of transfer (Stroud, 1992:15-17). A **TDR** program is "a compromise between outright acquisition and regulations of sensitive lands..." (Stroud, 1992:18). The program has limitations. **First,** it requires a very active real estate market. **Second,** it requires considerable land use data on a regional basis. Otherwise, the developer can leapfrog to the adjoining town, where there is no program (Mattson, 1978, 1983; Daniels, 1999:224-28). **Third,** without a solid, up-to-date comprehensive land use plan, there is unevenness in the land protection scheme. **TDRs** are least attractive to landowners with prime development property, and most attractive for people with low development prospects. The overall program may be an illusion to many participants who lack ideal location sites (Stroud, 1992:18).

Fiscal Solutions—Financing Public Services

As creatures of the state, small towns have limited revenue raising powers, with property and sales taxes being predominant. Under conditions of sprawl, the ability to raise revenues for needed public services can vary. Tax bites can become significant, accelerating the "voting with one's feet" of households and firms. Since tax burdens are important for location choices, local land use policymaking is tied to community tax differentials. The Florida Constitution is quite specific pertaining what taxes a community can impose. Moreover, the Florida Constitution has established the property tax caps on municipal millage rates. Finally, the state legislature has a strong say in the scope and range of tax funding sources for payment of public services (*Local Government Financial Information Handbook*, Florida Legislative Committee on Intergovernmental Relations, September 2001:4-9).

Sprawl and the Cost of Public Services

Discussions on sprawl-based development patterns inevitably lead to questions whether it pays for itself. The uncertainty of the land market lends to speculation and leap frog development. Home rule is said to assure that public investment decisions are made in a piecemeal fashion. Such parochialism with its independent, non-coordinated public investment behavior only adds to the confusion. Subsequently, for Smart Growth proponents, leapfrog development is cumulative consequence of home rule public polices, life style diversities and irresponsible private development practices. Inevitably, it is more than likely that the existing citizen-taxpayer and not the newcomer or the developer who will subsidize the cost of sprawl.

The improvement of public services is an integral part of sprawl debate. "Land cannot be successfully urbanized," according to Knapp and Nelson (1992:99), "until it offers essential services including access, shelter, water supplies, and waste-water disposal, often collectively referred to as infrastructure." As noted above, the American Farmland Trust (1997; 1999) cost of community service studies for Frederick Maryland and Lexington-Fayette County, Kentucky have argued that such scattered residential development doesn't pay for itself in tax revenues. Such public service cost studies are of particularly of interest to planners and local government officials because it is local government that will most likely be responsible for the provision such public services. As noted (Ch. 10), there is no predetermined municipal service package that the towns of the same size may offer, and citizens are free to pick and choose the community that may best fit their particular public service preferences. For local communities, (Ch. 11) the problem of fiscal correspondence—matching the municipal service package to the level of citizen tax payments—can lead to fiscal zoning and smoke stack chasing, causing greater uncertainty in the local land markets. Generally, the need for public service improvements is tied to population growth and density, with cost associated with user service levels and the scope or size of the service delivery network. Under conditions of sprawl, it is implied that population density and distance become a factor for cost, with compact development being more cost effective. That is, the research strongly suggests that less densely populated residential areas are less likely to pay for themselves, driving up taxes (Peiser, 1984; Frank, 1989; Duncan and Associates, 1989). Dane County, Wisconsin provides such an example. Between 1990–96, Dane County's population grew by almost 12 percent, but total property taxes in all communities in the county grew by almost 43 percent, or about 7 percent per year. Property taxes, which are the most visible of local taxes, grew 3.57 times faster than population, with most of this rise attributed to changing land use activities ("Cost of Sprawl: Dane County, WI," Sierra Club Sprawl Watch, *www.sierraclub.org/sprawl/article* April 18, 2002).

Closer to home, the Miami-Dade study evaluated the costs and benefits of alternative growth scenarios. This study estimated the cost of accommodating a projected growth of 2.4 million people in the South Florida region. If current sprawl patterns continue, the overall projected cost for accommodation—land use consumption, housing inflationary costs, infrastructure provision, and direct municipal service provision—is estimated to be 10.5 billion dollars over the next 20 years. However, there are significant overall savings of nearly 6.15 billion if an alternative "compact growth, building out" approach is followed. Under Smart Growth initiatives, Dr. Burchell of Rutgers University believed the area will be much greener, with a land savings of 67,725 acres, much of that being farmland. If the five-county region cooperatively followed compact development guideline agreements, there could be $157 million in water capital savings, $136.6 million in sewer capital costs, and $1.54 billion in local road costs (R. Burchell, et. al. "Eastward Ho! Development Futures," Florida Department of Community Affairs Report, February 1999). Given the many other needs of Southeastern Florida communities, and the limited tax resources available to meet such needs, it makes dollar sense, if not quality of life sense, to pursue the quality of life goals identified by the Smart Growth initiatives at a regional level.

It is obvious to anyone that population growth and land development creates spin-off cost, such as more classrooms and classroom teachers, more firefighters, more police officers, etc. Otherwise, existing public service staff is stretched too thin, placing the citizen-taxpayer in greater jeopardy. Many associated public service costs are off-site, and many are these costs tend to be classified under public service operation and maintenance, a hidden cost. For instance, in semi-urban Warren County, Ohio, which has grown 23 per cent in the past decade, tax payers had to hire six new deputies at an annual cost of $281,000 per year to maintain existing service levels. Monroe, Ohio, in Warren County, between 1998 and 1999, fire runs were up 41 per cent, emergency medical calls increased by 31 per cent and police responses increased by 11 per cent ("Sprawl Cost Us All," Sierra Club, 2000:12).These service level activities cannot be funded by debt finance, and cannot be shifted onto the next generation. Instead, these functional operations must then be paid out of taxes, and Floridians have few options (Ch. 9).

Most local officials play for time, hoping for the new development will generate sufficient taxes before the obligatory cost of upgrading service levels is required. As noted above, The Land for Public Trust (1998) study of small Massachusetts is not as optimistic, indicating that cost obligations often outstrip tax revenues derived. Another ticklish issue is who will subsidize growth. In examining the cost of sewer hookups, Florida State University Professor James Frank discovered that the actual hookup costs tend to vary, with inner-city Tallahassee residents actually subsidizing newer, upscale neighborhoods. In most cities, hookup costs are based on an average baseline fee. In Tallahassee it is $6000. For an inner-city neighborhood resident, where utilities have existed for some time, the actual cost is $4,447, allowing the city to make a tidy profit. On the other hand, for the homeowner in a newly built, upscale neighborhood on the city's northern edge, the actual hookup cost was $11,443, or nearly a five thousand-dollar loss to the city, suggesting that the inner city resident is subsidizing the cost for water and sewer utility extension. (B. Smith, "Accounting for Sprawl," *The Tampa Tribune*, April 2, 2001). Or as the Sierra Club "Sprawl Costs Us All" (1999:12) white paper notes, "And, since the true cost of extending these [public] services out to sprawling communities isn't paid by the new residents, this becomes one more hidden sprawl subsidy."

Fiscal Impact Analysis

Florida's Growth Management Study Commission (2001:20-21) recommended the adoption of a balanced full cost accounting system for local public service expenditures. The adoption of a fiscal impact analysis system at the local level would help the town or county to ascertain the full spectrum of revenues obtained and the full cost of public service expenditures paid out for any new land development project. Fiscal Impact Analysis is not a new planning tool. It was first utilized on a project-by-project basis during the late 1970 by Rutgers University Planning Professors Robert Burchell and David Listokin. It became increasingly popular in the mid-1980s for three reasons: first, Reagan's New Federalism policies shifted the bulk of infrastructure construction and fiscal responsibilities onto the states and their localities; second, the growing resistance by local taxpayers to simply pay for public service improvements without justification; and, third, the rise of court ordered fiscal analysis of large scale developments as a means of mitigating environmentally sensitive land use disputes.

Paul S. Tischler ("Fiscal Impact Analysis," *The Market Chronicle*, Spring 1980) claims that fiscal impact analysis is a critical planning tool within local government's repertoire because it provides municipal government with a general understanding of cost/revenue relationships that are generated by dramatic changes in population, housing units and employment activities due to shifting land use development patterns. Since local governments are the major providers of public services for new commercial, industrial and residential land developments, a fiscal impact analysis is normally conducted at the community level. Theoretically, it is presumed that a local government ought to have sufficient levels of revenues available to pay for public services prior to the approval of a land development project. For this reason, most early studies tended to be narrowly focused on a specific development site, assuring that the specific project was beneficial to the community in terms of the tax revenues and employment opportunities generated.

Rarely did these early studies look at the incremental nature of land use development beyond the specific project, ignoring the possible interrelationships between projects and their adverse impact on tax/expenditure revenue streams for the entire community ("Greece, New York's Fiscal Impact of Proposed Development," TMA Fiscal and Economic Newsletter, #19, 1984; "The Fiscal Impact Study of Carmel, New York," TMA Fiscal and Economic Newsletter, #20, 1984). As noted above, The American Farmland Trust's (1997; 1999) fiscal impact studies have been breakthroughs by demonstrating the interrelationship among local public service costs, tax revenues and land development activities. Thus, it makes dollar sense to require such fiscal analysis to be conducted either by the local jurisdiction or the regional planning councils.

Tax Increment Financing

TIF districts are intended to aid poorer cities in their Main Street revitalization efforts (Ch. 11). Our survey found that the wealthier, middle population range (25000-49,999) cities with fewer elderly and minority were most likely to participate. Field trip investigations to Sebring, Boca Raton, Jacksonville Beach, Pensacola and Lakeland discovered that in each TIF district paid for distributive-type (water/sewer, drainage, and solid waster disposal) municipal services. This suggests that town officials were responding to sprawl related issues. Obviously, much of this upgrading is a response to **9J5** and other growth mandated requirements. We noted that Florida's TIF program is quite limited. In these Florida case studies, it was indicated that to succeed, there must be a strong cooperative linkage between the planning department and the local chamber of commerce. Unfortunately, such a cooperation can lead to the crowding out of scarce dollars for other worthy projects. Overall, this linkage may explain for the policy performance success that each of these towns experienced in terms of job opportunities and Main Street revitalization.

Tax Base Sharing

A desire of each respective community to improve its tax base has fostered "checkerboard" sprawl. Fiscal zoning is a planning tool by which towns seek out expensive homes and premium commercial-industrial firms that require lost cost public services. This form of restrictive zoning is the key culprit for the fiscal disparities among communities within a metropolitan. Suburban enclaves such as Celebration, Florida or Laguna Beach, California are known to be culprits of fiscal disparities. Fiscal zoning does cause a transfer of tax base wealth and the uneven distribution of affordable housing (Marshall, 2000).

Tax Base Sharing is one fiscal policy tool that may assure tax relief for those communities who are not winners within the tax base competition game. The underlying premise to this policy tool is the elimination of the "winner-take-all" tendency of fiscal zoning. Property Tax Base Sharing severs the link between the cost of local public services and the need for a wealthy property tax base. Three states—Maryland, New Jersey and Minnesota—have utilized this policy tool for more than two decades (Beaton, 1980; Orfield, 1997:84-95). The Tax Base Sharing fiscal policy tool requires each participating community to contribute a portion of its growing tax base to a revenue pool. For instance, Minnesota law requires the taxing units to contribute 40 per cent of future tax base growth of their respective commercial-industrial base since 1971 to a common revenue pool, with more than 300 separate taxing units voluntarily participating. This money is then reallocated to pay for infrastructure improvements to those towns that have lost out in the competition. In the past quarter century, the tax base disparities within the Twin Cities Metroplex were reduced from 50 to one to roughly 12 to one. For smaller cities less than 10,000 people, this disparity was reduced from 18 to one to five to one (Orfield, 1997:87). Overall, the policy tool has given tax relief to communities throughout the Twin Cities Metroplex; and, thereby, has discouraged a "bidding" war, eliminating many of the fiscal problems associated with sprawl. Floridians may wish to consider such a strategy to offset the existing problems associated with fiscal zoning.

Local Option Sales Tax

Earlier (Ch. 11) it was noted that local option tax was low on the list of policy priorities. This is quite puzzling, given the heavy reliance on discretionary sales taxes within Florida (CH.9), with an estimated $2.173 billion disbursed to cities and counties. Overall, consumption type taxes have been a principal method to raise revenues. These taxes shift a part of the burden onto tourists and other outsiders. Indeed, in FY 2001, even with the state's downturn, the taxes derived from tourist rooms alone was estimated to $143 million. Administratively, local-option and state sales taxes are collected by holders of state sales tax permits at the point of sale and sent to Tallahassee, where they are processed and local proceeds are distributed back to the counties and cities quarterly. Known as Local Government Half Cent Sales Tax (Section 212.70 and Part VI, Ch. 28,F.S.), in FY 2002 almost $1.32 billion was collected. Often viewed as a painless tax, 51 counties and 59 per cent of Florida's population reside in jurisdictions that impose local option sales taxes. Therefore, it is quite puzzling that rural towns have not tapped into this tax as frequently as suburban communities.

Local option sales taxes can be highly regressive. The tax tends to hit lower income families harder as a percentage of their income. In Georgia, when controlling for intergovernmental revenues, it does not lead to dollar-for-dollar property tax reduction. However, the Local-Option Sales Tax did allow for greater spending priority flexibility and was quite effective in government revenue collections. Overtime, it was found that Georgia counties that adopted a LOST had lower property millage rates than non-LOST counties (Jung, 2001:85). For Local-Option Sales Tax (LOST) to be politically acceptable, it should be: (1) earmarked for a specific merit good purpose, such as a municipal pool, a library, a water tower or parks; and, it should not be: (2) designated for a vague public purpose such as the "catch all" phrases—economic development or economic revitalization. Furthermore, the local-option tax should be countywide, with each local entity specifying it intended use and a limited time-frame or common duration for the Local Option Sales Tax.

Impact Fees

Impact Fees is a unique financial instrument of local governmental home rule (Art VIII, S.2). As an exaction fee, it requires either the developer or the new homeowner to pay costs of the urban services required by the new development. Impact fees are collected formally through a set schedule or formula spelled out in the local city ordinance. It is not arbitrary and it is not a negotiated exaction. The impact fee must meet the " dual rational nexus" test . It requires the fees collected to pay for those services that directly commensurate with the increase levels of services due to the construction of the housing subdivision or commercial development (*Local Government Financial Handbook*, Florida Legislative Committee of Intergovernmental Relations, September 2001:33). It is popular among taxpayers for several reasons. First, impact fees are implemented to shift fiscal burdens from existing residents to the occupants of the new subdivision. Second, impact fees indirectly establish a pricing mechanism for the infrastructure costs of new developments. Third, impact fees if done properly synchronize the cost of public service delivery of capacity demands on existing infrastructures derived from the construction of new homeowner subdivisions and commercial development. It provides a market framework for the payment of urban growth and sprawl experienced by a community. Thus, by adopting impact fees, the locally elected officials are not being viewed as "growth curtailers"; but rather, they are viewed as "growth managers." Subsequently, they project an image of being sprawl managers by assuring that the negative social costs are being absorbed by the newcomers. For existing citizen-taxpayers, this approach is seen as a fair-minded policy choice. "If you desire to move into our town, then you pay (subsidize) the cost of those public services needed to maintain existing service levels." The impact fee is viewed by existing residents as a surcharge for the privilege of living within the community. In such fast growing areas, the Traditional-Individualistic notion of "paying your fair share" is politically attractive to local officials and taxpayer alike (Nicholas,1986, 1988; Juergensmeyer, 1986; Robert, 1986; Seimon, 1989; McKay, 1989).

At least 26 counties and sixty-two cities are using impact fees to pay for sewers, roads, parks and fire/police protection in Florida by 1990. Throughout the late 1980s about 345 million dollars each year are being raised to pay for needed infrastructure and other essential public services caused by the low density sprawl in Florida. A survey of a random sample of 213 water and sewer utility districts serving ten thousand or more people in nine southeastern counties found that at least 71 per cent of the districts had imposed an impact fee. Palm Beach County faced with an extensive capital improvement's requirement had imposed an impact fee system in mid-1980s, bringing in about 40 million dollars a year (Ryan, 1991:403). As sprawl creeps into the Panhandle, semi-rural counties and towns will likely adopt impact fees, as Nassau County had done in 1989 (UNF Center for Local Government Files).

Concluding Observations

This book has investigated the policy behavioral choices of locally appointed officials in smaller Florida towns. The survey found that population growth alone is not the issue, but also, what type of policy strategy ought to be undertaken to contain sprawl. Community scale is a factor, with Traditional-Individualistic political cultural attitudes persisting in contemporary Florida. Under Smart Growth, communities are urged to look at technology and other trends, and then adopt certain policy strategies that will encourage the community to acquire a vision that help it retain its small town values (Anderson, 1997:7). Yet, Florida's Vision 2000 Act (1986) has it limitations. Vogel and Swanson (1988) found that the business elite had dominated the visioning process in eleven Florida communities. This analysis (Ch. 10; Ch. 11) found similar results, with policy choices being highly selective, and with a decidedly pro-economic development focus.

Healy and Rosenberg (1979) had justified Florida's growth management initiatives for three reasons. First, growth management provided a framework for private and public land use priority disputes. Second, the state, as the primary source of police power, had the authority to establish priority distinction. Third, state initiated growth management was adopted because local controls were insufficient to handle the land consumption pressures due to population growth. Although Healy and Rosenberg justifications for state intervention were legitimate, several case studies have shown that there has been a tendency for prudent local parochial land use planning (DeGrove, 1984; Seimon, 1989; Stephenson,1997; Catlin, 1997). Tensions can arise when state government intrudes onto a policy area that local officials believe to be within their bailiwick (King and Harris, 1989; Rudel, 1989; Dalton, 1989; Chinitz, 1990; Leo, et. al. 1998). For three decades, the battle for rational land use management has been waged by local residential groups (environmental and homeowners' associations) against highly organized economic interest groups (homebuilders, chambers of commerce, etc.), causing the collective consensus of any Florida town to be muddled (Stephenson, 1997; DeHaven-Smith, 1991; Vogel and Swanson, 1988, 1989). Smart Growth on the surface seems to minimize land use tensions by appealing to a broad spectrum of stakeholders. Or as Anthony Down (2001:20) remarks, "Who can oppose Smart Growth—since the opposite is 'dumb growth'?" For many, Smart Growth's internal logic is quite appealing by suggesting that there are common sense solutions to sprawl (Salkin, 1999; Edlemen, 1999; Ewing, 1999; Shaw and Utt, 2000). Besides, Smart growth still means economic development. But, it means placing "development close to existing roads, sewers and infrastructure, rather than turning farmland into the next concentric ring of subdivisions" (*Governing* March, 2001:33). For Floridians, Smart Growth may be the better alternative, since the political dynamics suggest that other growth moratoriums have simply not worked as anticipated (Vogel and Swanson, 1989; Kerstein, 1991; Catlin, 1997).

In the South, before 1960, small towns were the heart and soul of Southern tradition. It was the place where residents shared gossip and forged the spirit of place (Carter, 2001; Wikstrom, 1993; McLaurin, 1987). Small towns, although regionally connected, saw themselves as arbitrators of local concerns. Of course, Jim Crow and local democratic elitism existed. This cannot be denied (Button, 1989; Rabinowitz, 1992; Wikstrom, 1993; Ramsey, 1996). The politics of the chamber of commerce had a local, self-serving perspective, with downtown merchants being the representatives on both the town council and the local planning board (Ch. 7). As town residents, they were also the sponsors of fund drives and the Fourth of July festivities. Today, it is unlikely to presume that the local store manager of the big box Walmart or Home Depot would ever undertake such a role.

From the nation's Founding, there has been a debate over political cultural styles (Ch. 6). A bipolar classification has emerged. This has allowed us to devise a neat and possibly a tidy framework to make sense out of the conflicts and contradictions in the American public policymaking tradition. This bipolar policy framework helps us categorize civic cultural values in terms of small town versus urban values, "planning with" versus "planning for," and top-down versus bottom-up policy management. Both sides embrace Jeffersonian agrarianism (Ch. 6, Ch.7). In this policy setting, each citizen-resident is civic minded, regardless of class, caste or income. Government policy choices have their limits, often defined by the capacity of these civic minded individuals to defend their private property and civil liberties. In many respects, Florida's political landscape, as a microcosm of America, has encompassed both of these faces of policymaking, with Florida's land use management politics simply being a reflection of the tensions between these two civic political cultural philosophies.

Bibliography

Books and Chapters

Abramson, P.R. 1983. *Political Attitudes in America*. New York: W.H. Freeman.
Abramson, P.R. et. al. 1998. *Change and Continuity in the 1996 Elections*. Washington, DC: Congressional Quarterly Press.
Abbott, C. 1981. *Boosters and Businessmen*. Westport: Greenwood Press.
Abbott, P. 1991. *Political Thought in America*. Itasca: Peacock Publishers.
Afifi, A. A. and V. Clark. 1984. *Computer Aided Multivariate Analysis*. Belmont, CA: Lifetime Publications.
Agger, R., D. Goldrich and B. Swanson. 1964. *The Rulers and the Ruled*. New York: John Wiley and Sons.
Aiesi, M and W. Rosenbaum. 1980. "Not Quite Like Yankees: The Diffusion of Partisan Competition in Two Southern Cities," in *Party Politics in the South*. R.P Steed, ed., New York: Praeger.
Alexander, E. R. 1992. *Approaches to Planning*. Philadelphia: Gordon and Breach Publishers.
Altshuler, A. A. 1965. *The City Planning Process*. Ithaca: Cornell University Press.
American Farmland Trust. 1997. *The Cost of Community Services: Frederick, Maryland*. Washington: D.C.: American Farmland Trust Foundation.
American Farmland Trust. 1999. *The Cost of Community Services: Lexington-Fayette County, KY*. Washington: D.C.: American Farmland Trust Foundation.
Anderson, G. 1998. *Why Smart Growth: A Primer*. Washington, D.C.: ICMA Press.
Anderson. J.E.,et. al. 1984. *Public Policy and Politics in America*. Boston: Duxbury Press.
Anderson, T.L. and P.J. Hill.1991.*Political Economy of the American West*. Lanham: Rowan and Littlefield.
Anderson, V. 1991. *New England Generation*. New York: Cambridge University Press.
Arendt, R. 1999. *Crossroads, Hamlet, Village, Town*. Chicago: Planners Press.
Arensberg,C. and S. Kimbell, 1965. *Culture and Community*. New York: Harcourt-Brace, Inc.

Arnold, D. 1980. *Congress and the Bureaucracy*. New Haven: Yale University Press.
Arsenault, R. and . G. Momino. 1988."From Dixie to Dreamland," In *Shades of the Sunbelt*. R.D. Miller and G.E. Pozzetta, eds., Boca Raton: Florida Atlantic University Press.
Atherton,L. 1954. *Main Street on the Middle Border*. Bloomington: Indiana University Press.
Ayers, E.L. 1992. *The Promise of the New South*. New York: Oxford University Press.
Bailyn, B. 1967. *Ideological Origins of the American Revolution*. Cambridge: Harvard University Press.
Baker, T. 1990. "The Impact of Urbanization on Party Coalition," in *Political Parties in Southern States*. New York: Praeger.
Baldassare, M. 1981. *The Growth Dilemma*. Berkeley: University of California Press.
Baldassare, M. 1986. *Trouble in Paradise*. New York: Columbia University Press.
Ball, T. and R. Dagger. 1995. *Political Ideologies and Democratic Ideal*. New York: Harper-Collins.
Baltzell, E. D. 1968. *The Search for Community in Modern America*. New York: Harper-Row.
Barnekov,T. , et. al.1989. *Privatism and Urban Policy in Britain and the United States*. New York: Oxford University Press.
Bartlett, R. 1998. *The Crisis of America's Cities*. Armonk: M.E. Sharp.
Bartlett, R. A. 1974. *The New Country*. New York: Oxford University Press.
Bartley, N. 1995. *The New South*. Baton Rouge: Louisiana State University Press.
Barro, S. 1989. "State Fiscal Capacity Measures," in *Measuring Fiscal Capacity*. H.C. Reeves, ed. Boston: Lincoln Institute of Land Policy.
Bass. J. and W. DeVries. 1976. *The Transformation of Southern Politics*. New York: Basic Books.
Baum, H. 1983. *Planners and Public Expectations*. Cambridge: Schenkman Publishers.
Beatley, T. and K. Manning. 1997. *The Ecology of Place*. Washington, DC: Island Press.
Beer. S. 1993. *To Make a Nation*. Cambridge: Harvard University Press.
Beitzinger, A. 1972. *A History of American Political Thought*. New York: Dodd, Meade and Company.
Bellah, R. et. al. 1985. *Habits of the Heart*. New York: Harper and Row.
Bender, T. 1975. *Toward an Urban Vision*. Lexington, KY: University of Kentucky Press.
Bender, T. 1978. *Community and Social Change in America*. Baltimore: Johns Hopkins University Press.
Benedict, M. L. 1996. *The Blessings of Liberty*. Lexington, MA.: D.C. Heath.
Bensel, R.F. 1984. *Sectionalism and American Political Development*. Madison: University of Wisconsin Press.
Benvensti, G. 1989. *Mastering the Politics of Planning*. SanFrancisco: Josey-Bass.

Bibliography

Bernard, J. 1973. *Sociology of the Urban Community*. Glenview: Scotts-Foresman.
Bigham, D. 1998. *Towns and Rivers of the Lower Ohio*. Lexington: University of Kentucky Press.
Biles, R. 1994. *The South and the New Deal*. Lexington: University of Kentucky Press.
Billington, L. 1971. *The American South*. New York: Scribner and Sons.
Billington, M. 1984. *Southern Politics Since The Civil War*. Malabar, FL: Krieger Publishing.
Billington, R. 1974. *America's Frontier Heritage*. Albuquerque: University of New Mexico Press.
Bish, R. and V. Ostrom. 1973. *Understanding Local Government*. Washington, DC: The American Enterprise Institute.
Black, M and E. Black. 1992. *The Vital South*. Cambridge: Harvard University Press.
Black, M. and E. Black. 1987. *Politics and Society in the South*. Cambridge: Harvard University Press.
Blackford, M. and K. Kerr. 1986. *Business Enterprise in American History*. Boston: Houghton-Mifflin.
Blair, J.P. and R. Premus. 1993. "Location Theory," in *Theories of Local Economic Development*. R.D. Bingham and R. Mier, eds. Newbury Park: Sage Publications.
Blakely, E.J. 1989. *Planning Local Economic Development*. Newbury Park: Sage Publications.
Blakely, E. J. and T.K. Bradshaw. 1981. "The Impact of Recent Migrants on Economic Development in Small Towns," in *Order and Image in the American Small Town*. M. Fazio and P.Prenshaw, eds., Jackson: University Press of Mississippi.
Bland, R. 1989. *Revenue Guide for Local Government*. Washington, D.C.: ICMA Press.
Boaz, D. 1997. *Libertarianism*. New York: The Free Press.
Bourgin, F. 1989. *The Great Challenge*. New York: George Braziller,Inc.
Bourke, P. and D. Debats. 1995. *Washington County*. Baltimore: Johns Hopkins Press.
Bowman, l. 1990. "Party Sorting at the Grassroots," in *The Disappearing South*. R. Steed , ed. Tuscaloosa, Al. : The University of Alabama Press.
Bowyer, R. 1993. *Capital Improvements Programs*. Chicago: Planners Press.
Boyer, M.C. 1983. *Dreaming the Rational City*. Boston: MIT Press.
Brady, D. 1988. *Critical Elections and Congressional Policy Making*. Stanford: Stanford University Press.
Branch, M.C. 1981. *Continuous City Planning*. New York: Wiley and Sons.
Breen,T.H. 1980. *Puritans and Adventurers*. New York: Oxford University Press.
Breen, T.H. 1985. *Tobacco Culture*. Princeton: Princeton University Press.
Brindenbaugh, C. 1981. *Early Americans*. New York: Oxford University Press.
Brodsky, D. 1988. "The Dynamics of Recent Southern Politics," in *The South's New Politics*. R. Swansborogh, ed. Jackson: University of South Carolina Press.
Brodsky D. and P. Cotter. 1998. "Political Issues and Political Parties," in *Party

Activists in Southern Politics. C. Hadley, ed. Knoxville: University of Tennessee Press.

Brower, D.J. et. al. 1984. *Managing Development in Small Towns*. Chicago: Planners Press.

Brown, R.E. and B.K. Brown. 1964. *Virginia: Democracy or Aristocracy?* East Lansing: Michigan State University Press.

Brownell, B.A. 1975. *The Urban Ethos in the South*. Baton Rouge: Louisianna State University Press.

Brownell, B.A. and D.R. Goldfield. 1979. *Urban America: From Downtown to No Town*. Boston: Houghton- Mifflin.

Bruchey, S. 1965. *The Roots of American Economic Growth*. New York: Harper and Row Publishers.

Bryan, F.M. 1981. *Politics in the Rural States*. Boulder: Westview Books.

Bryce, H. J. 1978. *Planning Smaller Cities*. New York: Lexington Books.

Bryce, J. L. 1888. *The American Commonwealth*. New York: AMS Press.

Buchanan, J. 1987. *Public Finance in Democratic Process*. Chapel Hill: University of North Carolina Press.

Bucks County Planning Department. 1989. *Village Planning Handbook*. Doylestown, PA: Bucks County Historical Society.

Bucholz, R.A. 1988. *Public Policy Issues in Management*. Englewood Cliffs: Prentice-Hall.

Bullock, C. and M. Rozell. 1998. "Southern Politics at Century's End," in *The New Poltics of the Old South*. C. Bullock and M. Rozell, eds. London: Rowman and Littlefield Publishers.

Burchell, R.W. and G. Sternlieb. 1978. *Planning Theory in the 1980s*. New Brunswick: Center For Urban Policy Research.

Burchell, R. et. al. 1999. *Eastward Ho! Development Futures*. Tallahassee, FL: Department of Community Affairs.

Burgess, P. 1996. "Of Swimming Pools and Slums," in *Planning the Twentieth Century American City*. M. Sies and C. Silver, ed., Baltimore: Johns Hopkins University Press.

Button, J. 1989. *Blacks and Social Change*. Gainesville: University of Florida Press.

Button, J and W. Rosenbaum. 1986. "Is there a Grey Peril?" in *The Egalitarian City*. J. Boles, ed. NY: Praeger.

Calthorpe, P. 1993. *The Next American Metropols*. Princeton, NJ: Princeton University.

Carlson, J. 1980. "Political Context and Black Participation," in *Party Politics in the South*. R. Steed, ed, New York: Praeger.

Carmines, E. and H. Stanley. 1990."Ideological Realignment in the Contemporary South," *The Disappearing South?* R. Steed, ed. Tascaloosa: University of Alabama Press.

Carter, J. 2001. *An Hour Before Dawn*. New York: Simon and Schuster.

Carter, L. J. 1974. *The Florida Experience*. Baltimore, MD.: Johns Hopkins University Press.

Cary, L. J. 1970. *Community Development as a Process.* Columbia: University of Missouri Press.
Castle, E.M. 1995. *The Changing American Countryside.* Lawrence: University of Kansas Press.
Catanese, A. J. 1984.*The Politics of Planning and Development.* Newbury Park: Sage Publications.
Catanese, A. J. 1974. *Planners and Local Politics.* Beverly Hills: Sage Publications.
Catlin, R. 1997. *Land Use Planning, Environmental Protection and Growth Management.* Chelsea, MI: Ann Arbor Press.
Caves, R. 1991. *Land Use Planning: The Ballot Box Revolution.* Newbury Park: Sage Publications.
Cayton, A.R.L. 1986. *The Frontier Republic.* Kent : Kent State University Press.
Chesteron, G.K. 1922. *What I Saw in America.* New York: Dodd, Meade and Company.
Chudacoff, H.P. and J.E. Smith. 1988. *The Evolution of American Urban Society.* Englewood Cliff: Prentice-Hall.
Chute, M. 1969. *The First Liberty.* New York: E.P. Dutton and Company.
Clark, J. 1976. *The Sanibel Report.* Washington, D.C.: The Conservation Foundation.
Clark, J. 1998. "Split Partisan Identification," in *Party Activistis in Southern Politics.* C. Hadley and L. Bowman, eds. Knoxville: University of Tennessee Press.
Clark, T. N. and L.C. Ferguson. 1983. *City Money.* New York: Columbia University Press.
Clarke, J. N. and D.C. McCool. 1996. *Staking Out the Terrain.* Albany: State University of New York Press.
Clawson, R.A. and J.Clark. 1988. "Party Activists as Agents of Change," in *Party Organization and Activism in the American South.* R. Steed, ed., Tuscaloosa: University of Alabama Press.
Cochran, T. 1981. *Frontiers of Change.* New York: Oxford University Press.
Conlin, T. 1988. *New Federalism.* Washington, D.C.: Brookings Institute.
Connery, D.S. 1972.*One American Town.* New York: Simon and Schuster.
Coulter, P. 1988. *Political Voice.* Tuscaloosa: University of Alabama Press.
Cox, K. 1999. "Ideology and the Growth Coalition," in *The Urban Growth Machine.* A. Jones and D. Wilson. eds. Albany: State University of New York Press.
Craycroft, R. 1981. "Small Town Public Policy: Strategies for Downtown Development," in *Order and Image in the Small Town.* M. Fazio and P. Prenshaw, eds. Jackson: University of Mississippi Press.
Cronon, W. 1983. *Changes in the Land.* New York: Hill-Wang.
Cullingworth, B. J. 1993. *The Political Culture of Planning.* New York: Routledge.
Dahl, R.A. 1982. *Dilemmas of Plural Democracy.* New Haven: Yale University Press.
Dahl. R.A. 1989. *Democracy and Its Critics.* New Haven: Yale University Press.
Danbom, D. 1995. *Born in the Country.* Baltimore: John Hopkins University Press.
Daniel, B. 1985. *Breaking the Land.* Urbana: University of Illinois Press.
Daniel, B. 1986. *Standing at the Crossroads.* New York: Hill and Wang.
Daniels, B. 1979. *Connecticut Towns.* Middletown: Wesleyan University Press.

Daniels, P. 1984. "The New Deal, Southern Agriculture and Economic Change," in *The New Deal and the South*. J. Cobb and M. Namorato, Jacksonville: University Press of Mississippi.
Daniels, T. 1999. *When City and Country Collide*. Washington, D.C.: Island Press.
Daniels, T and D. Bowers. 1997. *Holding Our Ground*. Washington, D.C.: Island Press.
Daniels, T. et. al. 1995. *The Small Town Handbook*. Chicago:Planners Press.
Danzer, G. 1987. *Public Places*. Nashville: AASL Historians Press.
DeGrove, J. 1984. *Land, Growth and Politics*. Chicago:Planners Press.
DeGrove, J. and R. Turner. 1991. "Local Government in Florida," *Government and Politics In Florida*. R. Huckshorn, ed. Gainesville: University of Florida Press.
DeGrove, J. and D. Miness. 1992. *New Frontier for Land Policy*. Cambridge: Lincoln Institute of Land Policy.
DeGrove, J. and P. Metzger. 1993. "Growth Management and Integrated Roles," in *Growth Management*. J. Stein, ed., Newbury Park: Sage Publications.
DeHaven-Smith, L. 1991. *Environmental Concern for Florida and the Nation*. Gainesville: University of Florida Press.
DeHaven-Smith, L. 1991. "Florida's Unfinished Agenda in Growth Management and Environmental Protection," in *Government and Politics in Florida*. R.Huckshorn, ed. Gainesville: University of Florida Press.
De La Garza, R. and L. DiSipio. 1996. *Ethnic Ironies*. Boulder: Westview Press.
DeSipio, L. 1996. *Counting on the Latino Vote*. Charlottesville: University of Virginia Press.
DeTocqueville, A. 1945 *Democracy in America* New York: A.A. Knopf.
Diamond, H. and P. Noonan. 1996. *Land Use in America*. Washington, D.C.: Island Press.
Dietrich, T.S. 1978. *Urbanization of Florida's Population*. Gainesville: Bureau of Economic and Business Research.
Doherty, J. 1991. *Growth Management in Countryfied Cities*. Alexandria: Vert Milon Press.
Dolbeare, K. M. and P.D. Medcalf. 1988. *American Ideologies*. New York: Random House.
Donohue, J. D. 1989. *The Privatization Decision*. New York: Basic Books.
Donohue, J.D. 1997. *Disunited States*. New York: Basic Books.
Douglas, M.S. 1967. *Florida: The Long Frontier*. New York: Harper and Row.
Dowell, D. 1984. *The Suburban Squeeze*. Berkeley: University of California Press.
Downs, A. 1994. *New Visions for Metropolitan America*. Washington: Brookings Institute.
Drukman, M. 1971. *Community and Purpose in America*. New York: McGraw-Hill.
Duany, A. et. al. 2000, *Suburban Nation*. New York: North Point Press.
Dunlop, B. 1987. *Florida's Vanishing Architecture*. Englewood, FL: Pineapple Press, Inc.

Bibliography

Dunlap, R.E. 1993. "Does Public Concern for the Environment Differ in the West?" in *Environmental Politics and Policy in the West*. Z.A. Smith, ed., Dubuque, IA: Kendall-Hunt Publishing.

Dunlop, B. 1987. *Florida's Vanishing Architecture*. Englewood, FL: Pineapple Press.

Dunn, C. and J.D. Woodard. 1991. *American Conservatism*. New York: Madison Books.

Dye, T. 1971. *The Politics of Equality*. Indianapolis: Bobbs-Merrill.

Dye, T. 1998. *Politics in Florida*. Upper Saddle River, NJ: Prentice-Hall.

Edleman, M. et. al. 1999. *Land Use Conflicts*. Washington, DC. Farm Foundation.

Eberly, D. 2000. *The Essential Civil Society*. Lanham, MD: Rowman and Littlefield.

Effrat, M.P. 1974. *The Community*. New York: The Free Press.

Elazar, D. 1970. *Cities of the Prairie*. New York: Basic Books.

Elazar, D. 1971. *The Politics of Belleville*. Philadelphia: Temple University Press.

Elazar, D. 1972. *American Federalism*. New York: Harper and Row.

Elazar, D. 1986. *Cities of the Prairie Revisited*. New York: Basic Books.

Elazar, D. 1994. *The American Mosiac*. Boulder: Westview Press.

Ellis, R. 1993. *American Political Cultures*. New York: Oxford University Press.

Ely, J. W. 1992. *The Guardian of Every Other Right: A Constitutional History of Property Rights*. New York: Oxford University Press.

Etcheson, N. 1996. *The Emerging Midwest*. Bloomington: Indiana Press.

Etzioni, A. 1993. *The Spirit of Community*. New York: Crown Publishers.

Etzioni, A. 1996. *The New Golden Rule*. New York: Basic Books.

Ewing, R. 1991. *Developing Successful New Communities*. Washington,DC: Urban Land Institute Press.

Ewing, R. 1996. *Best Development Practices*. Chicago: Planners Press.

Ewing, R. 1999. *Transportation and Land Use Innovations*. Chicago: Planners Press.

Faludi, A. 1986. *Critical Rationalism and Planning Methodology*. London: Pion Limited.

Faludi, A. 1987. *Decision Center View of Environmental Planning*. Oxford: Pergamon Press.

Feigert, F. and J. Todd. 1998. "Migration and Party Change," in *Party Activism in Southern Politics*. C. Hadley and L. Bowman, eds., Knoxville: University of Tennessee Press.

Fendrich, J. 1993. *Ideal Citizens: The Legacy of the Civil Rights Movement*. Albany: State University of New York Press.

Ferguson, R. and H. Ladd. 1986 "Measuring the Fiscal Capacity of U.S. Cities," in *Measuring Fiscal Capacity*. H.C. Reeves, ed. Boston: Lincoln Institute of Land Policy.

Fischer, D.H. 1989. *Albion's Seed*. New York: Oxford University Press.

Fitchen, J.M. 1991. *Endangered Spaces, Enduring Places*. Boulder: Westview Press.

Fishman, R. 1987. *Bourgeois Utopias*. New York: Basic Books.

Fodor, E. 1999. *Bigger Not Better*. Stony Creek, CT: New Society Press.

Flora, C.B.et. al. 1992. *Rural Communities*. Boulder: Westview Press.

Florida American Planning Association. 2001. *Rural Florida: Opportunities for the Future*. Tallahassee, FL: FAPA Press

Ford, K. 1990. *Planning Small Town America*. Chicago: Planners Press.

Forester,J. 1989. *Planning in the Face of Power*. Berkley: University Of Calaifornia Press.

Formisano. R.P.1983. *The Transformation of Political Culture*. New York: Oxford University Press.

Fowler, R.B. 1991. *The Dance With the Community*. Lawrence: University Press of Kansas.

Francaviglia, R.V. 1996. *Main Street Revisited*. Iowa City: University of Iowa Press.

Frank, J. 1989. *The Cost of Alternative Development Patterns*. Washington, D.C.: Urban Land Institute.

Frazer, W. and J. Guthrie. 1995. *The Florida Land Boom*. Westport, CT: Quorum Books.

Freie, J.F. 1998. *Counterfeit Community*. New York: Rowan and Littlefield.

Freilich, R. 1999. *From Sprawl to Smart Growth*. Washington: American Bar Association.

Freilich, R. and M. Shultz. 1995. *Model Subdivision Regulations*. Chicago: Planners Press,

Freund, R. J and W. J. Wilson. 1997. *Statistical Methods*. New York: Academic Press.

Friedmann, J. 1973. *Retracking America*. Garden City: Anchor Press.

Friedmann, J. 1987. *Planning in the Public Domain*. Princeton: Princeton University Press.

Fries, S. D. 1977. *The Urban Idea in Colonial America*. Philadelphia: Temple Press.

Fry, P. and F. Fry. 1995. *The History of Scotland*. New York: Barnes and Noble.

Gabris, G.T. 1992. "The Dynamics of Mississippi Local Government," in *Mississippi Government and Politics*. D. Krane and S. Shaffer eds. Lincoln: University of Nebraska Press.

Galston, W. and K. Baehler. 1995. *Rural Development in the United States*. Washington, DC: Island Press.

Garkovich,L. 1989. *Population and Community in Rural America*. New York: Praeger.

Garnham, H. 1985. *Maintaining the Spirit of Place*. Mesa, AZ: PDA Publishers.

Gilliam, O. 2002. *The Limitless City*. Washington, D.C.: Island Press.

Goggin, M.L. et. al. 1990. *Implementation Theory and Practice*. Glenview : Scott-Foresman.

Gold. S. 1989. "Measuring Fiscal Capacity Effort," in *Measuring Fiscal Capacity*. H.C. Reeves, ed., Boston: Lincoln Institute of Land Policy Press.

Gold, S. and J. Zelio. 1990. *State-Local Fiscal Indicators*. Washington: National Conference of State Legislatures.

Goldfield, D. 1987. *Promised Land*. Arlington Heights: Harlan-Davidson, Inc.

Goldfield, D. 1989. *Cottonfields and Skyscrapers*. Baltimore: Johns Hopkins University Press.

Bibliography

Goldfield, D. 1990. *Black, White and Southern*. Baton Rouge: Louisiana State University Press.

Goldfield, D. 1991. "Urbanization in a Rural Culture" in *The South For New Southerners*. P. Escott and D. Goldfield, eds., Chapel Hill: University of North Carolina Press.

Goldsmith, W. And E. Blakely. 1992. *Separate Societies*. Philadelphia: Temple Press.

Goodwin, . 1995. *A Resurrection of the Republican Ideal*. Lanham, MD:University Press of America.

Gottdiener, M. 1977. *Planned Sprawl*. Beverly Hills: Sage Publications.

Gratz R. and N. Mintz. 1998. *Cities From The Edge*. New York: Wiley and Sons.

Grathan, D. 1994. *The South in Modern America*. New York: Harper-Collins.

Green, A. 1974. *The Mayors Mandate*. Cambridge: Schenkman Publishing.

Green, C. 1965. *The Rise of Urban America*. New York: Harper and Row.

Greer, J. and J. Guth. 1990. "The Transformation of Political Elites," in *The Disappearing South*. R. Steed et.al.eds. Tusaculoosa: University of Alabama Press.

Greven, R. 1971. *Four Generations*. Cornell: Cornell University Press.

Gummer, B.1990. *The Politics of Social Administration*. Englewood Cliffs: Prenitice-Hall

Haas, E. 1977. "The Southern Metropolis, 1940-1976." in *The City in Southern History*. B. Brownell and D. Goldfield, eds., New York: Kennikat Press.

Hadley, C. and H. Stanley, 1998. "Race and Democratic Bi-Racial Coalitions," in *Party Activism in Southern Politics*. C. Hadley and L. Bowman, eds., Knoxville: University of Tennessee Press.

Hall, K. and G. Porterfield. 2001. *Community By Design*. New York: McGraw-Hill.

Harbour, W.R. 1982. *Foundation of Conservative Thought*. Notre Dame: University of Notre Dame Press.

Harmon, M.J. 1964. *Political Thought*. NY: McGraw-Hill.

Harris, B. 1972. "Forward," in *Decision-making in Urban Planning*. I.A. Robinson, ed. Beverly Hills: Sage Publications.

Harris, C. 1977. *Political Power in Birmingham*. Knoxville: University of Tennessee Press.

Harrison, A. 1991. *Black Exodus*. Jackson: University of Mississippi Press.

Hart, J. 1998. *The Rural Landscape*. Baltimore: Johns Hopkins University Press.

Hatch, E. 1979. *The Biography of a Small Town*. New York: Columbia University Press.

Hausheck, E.A. and J. Jackson. 1977. *Statistical Methods for Statistical Scientists*. New York: Academic Press.

Hays, S. 1957. *The Response to Industrialism*. Chicago: University of Chicago Press.

Hays, S. 1987. *Beauty, Health and Permanence: Environmental Politics in the United States*. New York: Cambridge University Press.

Healy, R. and J. Rosenberg. 1979. *Land Use and the States*. Baltimore: Johns Hopkins University Press.

Heilig, P. and R. Mundt. 1984. *Your Voice at City Hall*. Albany: State University Press of New York.
Hendler, S. 1995. *Planning Ethics*. New Brunswick: The Center for Urban Policy Research.
Herbers, J. 1986. *The New Heartland*. New York: Times Books.
Hicks, G. 1946. *Small Town*. New York: The MacMillan Company.
Himmelstine, J. 1990. *To The Right: The Transformation of American Conservatism*. Berkley: University of California Press.
Hine, R.V. 1980. *Community and the American Frontier*. Norman: University of Oklahoma Press.
Hoch, C. 1994. *What Planners Do*. Chicago: Planners Press.
Hofstadter, R. 1973. *America at 1750*. New York: Vintage Press.
Homman, M.1993. *City Planning In America*. Westport: Praeger.
Honadle, B. and A. Howitt. 1986. *Perspectives on Management Capacity Building*. Albany: State University of New York Press.
Hovey, H. 1986. "Interstate Tax Competition and Economic Development," in *Reforming the State Tax System*. S.Gold, ed. Denver: National Conference of State Legislatures.
Howe, E. 1994. *Acting on Ethics in City Planning*. New Brunswick, NJ: Center for Urban Policy Research.
Howell, J. and C. Stamm. 1979. *Urban Fiscal Stress*. Lexington,MA.: Lexington Press.
Howitt, A. 1984. *Managing Federalism*. Washington, D.C. : Congressional Quarterly.
Howland, M. 1993. "Applying Theory to Practice in Rural Economics," in *Theories of Local Economic Development*. R. Bingham and R. Mier, eds. Newbury Park: Sage Publications.
Hughes, J. 1990. *American Economic History*. New York: Harper-Collins.
Hummon, D. 1990. *Common Places*. Albany: State University of New York Press.
Hy, D. J. and W. Waugh. 1995. *State and Local Tax Policies*. Westport, CT: Greenwood.
Hyman., D. 1990. *Public Finance*. Chicago: Dryden Press.
Ingersoll, D. and R. Matthews. 1986. *The Philosophic Roots of Modern Ideology*. Englewood Cliffs: Prentice-Hall.
International City Management Association. 2000. *Getting to Smart Growth*. Washington, D.C.: ICMA Press
Isreal, G. and L. Beaulieu. 1990. "Community Leadership," in *American Rural Communities*. A.E. Luloff and L.E. Swanson. eds., Boulder: Westview Press.
Jackson, J. B. 1994. *A Sense of Place, A Sense of Time*. New Haven: Yale University Press.
Jackson, J. B. 1984. *Discovering the Vernacular Landscape*. New Haven: Yale University Press.
Jackson, K. 1985. *Crabgrass Frontier*. Oxford: Oxford University Press.
Johnson, C. 1992. *The Dynamics of Bureaucrats and Legislators*. New York: M.E. Sharpe.

Johnson, W. 1989. *The Politics of Urban Planning*. New York: Paragon House.
Jones, B.D. ,et.al. 1980. *Service Delivery in the City*. New York: Longman Press.
Judd, D. and R. Mendelson. 1973. *The Politics of Urban Planning*. Urbana: University Press of Illinois.
Juergenmeyer, J and T.Roberts. 1998.*Land Use Planning and Control Law*. St. Paul, MN: West Publishers.
Kammen, M. 1988. *Sovereignty and Liberty*. Madison: University of Wisconsin Press.
Kelley, E.D. 1993 *Managing Community Growth*. New York: Praeger.
Kelly, R. 1979. *The Cultural Patterns in American Politics*. New York: A.A. Knopf.
Kemmis, D. 1991. *Community and the Politics of Place*. Norman: Oklahoma Press.
Ketchum, R. 1993. *Framed for Prosperity*. Lawrence: University of Kansas Press.
Kettle, D. 1980. *Managing Community Development*. New York, : Praeger.
Key, V. O. 1984. *Southern Politics in the States and the Nation*. New York: A.A. Knopf
Klein, M. and H. Kantor, 1976. *Prisoners of Progress*. New York: MacMillan.
Knaap, G. and A.C. Nelson. 1992. *The Regulated Landscape*. Cambridge: Lincoln Institute of Land Policy.
Knoke, D. 1981. "Urban Political Cultures" in *Urban Policy Analysis*. T.N. Clark, ed. Beverly Hills: Sage Publications.
Kolankiewicz, L. and R. Beck. 2001. *Sprawl in Florida*. Washington, D.C.: Numbers USA, Inc.
Kostof, S. 1987. *America By Design*. New York: Oxford University Press.
Kotler, P. et. al. 1993. *Marketing Places*. New York: The Free Press.
Koven, S. 1988. *Ideological Budgeting*. New York: Praeger.
Kramer, P. 1970. " The River Cities:1800–1850," in *The City in American Life*. P. Kramer and F. Holborne, eds., New York: Capricorn Books.
Kramnick, I. 1987. *The Federalist Papers*. NY: Penquin Books.
Krane, D. 1992. "The Struggle Over Public Policy in a Tradtionalistic State," in *Mississippi Government and Politics*. D. Krane and S.D. Shaffer, eds., Lincoln: University of Nebraska Press.
Kunstler, J.H. 1993. *The Geography of Nowhere*. New York: Simon and Schuster.
Kunstler, J.H. 1996. *Home From Nowhere*. New York: Simon and Schuster.
Laboa, L. 1990. *Locality and Inequality*. Albany: State University of New York Press.
Ladd, E, C. 1999. *The Ladd Report*. New York: The Free Press.
Ladd, E. C. 1972. *Ideology in America*. New York: W.W. Norton.
Lamis, A. 1988. *The Two Party South*. New York: Oxford University Press.
Langdon, P. 1994. *A Better Place to Live*. Amherst: University of Massachusetts Press.
Lapping, M., T. Daniels and J. Keller. 1989. *Rural Planning and Development in the United States*. New York: Guilford Press.
Larsen, L. 1990. *The Urban South*. Lexington: University Press of Kentucky.

Leach, R. H. 1970. *American Federalism*. New York: W.W. Norton and Company.
Leyburn, J. G. 1963. *The Scotch-Irish*. Chapel Hill : Univesity of North Carolina Press.
Levin, M. 1987. *Planning in Government*. Chicago: Planners Press.
Levine, C.H., et. al. 1981. *The Politics of Retrenchment*. Newbury Park: Sage.
Levy, E. 1991. *Small Town America in Flim*. New York: Frederick Unger Press.
Levy, F. , et.al. 1974. *Urban Outcomes*. Berkeley: University of California Press.
Levy, J. 1981. *Economic Development for Cities, Counties and Towns*. Westport: Praeger.
Levy, J. 1994. *Contemporary Urban Planning*. Englewood Cliffs: Prentice-Hall.
Lienesch, M. 1988. *New Order of the Ages*. Princeton: Princeton University Press.
Lineberry, R. 1977. *Equality and Urban Policy*. Beverly Hills: Sage.
Lingeman, R. 1980. *Small Town America*. New York: Putnam and Sons.
Link, A. and R. McCormick. 1983. *Progressivism*. Arlington Heights: Harlan-Davidson.
Linowes, R. and D. Allensworth. *The Politics of Landuse*. New York: Praeger.
Lipsky, M. 1980. *Street Level Bureaucrats*. New York: Russell Sage Foundation.
Lockridge, K. A. 1985. *A New England Town*. New York: W. W. Norton.
Lowi, T. J. 1995. *The End of the Republican Era*. Norman: University of Oklahoma Press.
Lowi, T. J. 1969. *The End of Liberalism*. New York: W.W. Norton.
Lowry, R. 1964. *Who's Running This Town?* New York: Harper-Row.
Lucy, W. 1988. *Close to Power*. Chicago: Planners Press.
Lutz, D. 1988. *The Origins of American Constitutionalism*. Baton Rouge: Louisiana State University Press.
Lyon, L. 1989. *Community in Urban Society*. Lexington, MA.: D.C. Heath.
Lyson, T. and W. Falk. 1993. *Forgotten Places*. Lawrence: University of Kansas Press.
Lyons, W.E., et.al. 1992. *The Politics of Dissatisfaction*. Armonk,NY: M.E. Sharpe
MacManus, S. 1978. *Revenue Patterns in U.S. Cities and Suburbs*. New York: Praeger.
MacManus, S. 1991. "Financing Florida's Government," in *Government and Politics in Florida*. R. Huckshorn, ed. Gainesville, FL.: University of Florida Press.
MacManus, S. 1995. "Florida: Reinvention Derailed," in *The Fiscal Crisis of the States*. S. Gold, ed. Washington, D. C. : Georgetown University Press.
Macridis, R. 1989. *Contemporary Political Ideologies*. Boston: Scott-Foresman.
Mahoney, T. 1990. *River Towns of the Great West*. New York: Cambridge University Press.
Majchrzak, A. 1984. *Methods for Policy Research*. Beverly Hills: Sage Publications.
Marans, R. and J. Wellman. 1978. *The Quality of Nonmetropolitan Living*. Ann Arbor: University of Michigan Press.
Marcus, A.I. , 1991. *Plague of Strangers*. Columbus: Ohio State University Press
Marks, C. 1989. *Farewell—We're Good and Gone*. Bloomington, IN: Indiana University Press.

Marone, J. 1990. *The Democratic Wish*. New York: Basic Books.
Marshall, A. 2000. *How Cities Work*. Austin: University of Texas Press.
Martinez, M. 2001. *A Liveable Florida for Today and Tomorrow*. Tallahassee, FL: Florida's Growth Management Study Commission.
Matthews, R. 1995. *If Men Were Angles*. Lawrence, KS: University of Kansas Press.
Mattson, G. 1978. *Policy and Planning Implementation: Suffolk County Farmland Program*. Master Thesis, University of Rhode Island.
Mattson, G. 1986. *Perspectives on Small City Planning and Policy Making*. Lexington, MA: Ginn Press.
Mattson, G. 1987. "Corporate City Planning and the Traditional-Individualism Politics of Texas Cities," in *Texas Politics Today*. W. Maxwell and E. Crain, eds. New York: West Publishers.
Mayer, H. and C. Hayes. 1983. *Land Uses in American Cities*. Champaign: Park Press.
McClendon, B. and R. Quay. 1988, *Mastering Change*. Chicago: Planners Press.
McCoy, D. 1980. *The Elusive Republic*. Chapel Hill: University of North Carolina Press.
McClosky, H. And J. Zaller. 1984. *The American Ethos*. Boston: Harvard University Press.
McElvaine, R. 1984. *The Great Depression*. New York: Times Books.
McGlennon, J. 1998a. "Ideology and the Southern Party Activist," in C. Hadley and L. Bowman, eds., Knoxville: University of Tennessee Press.
McGlennon, J. 1998b. "Factions in the Politics of the New South," in *Party Organization and Activism in the American South*. R. Steed et. al. eds., Tuscaloosa: University of Alabama Press.
McMath, R.C. 1993. *American Populism*. New York: Hill and Wang.
McMath, R.C. 1975. *Populist Vanguard*. Chapel Hill: University of North Carolina Press.
Mehrhoff, W.A. 1998. *Community Design*. Newbury Park, CA: Sage Publications.
Melvoin, R.I. 1989. *New England Outpost*. New York: W.W. Norton.
Mikesell, J. 1986. *Fiscal Administration*. Homewood: Dorsey Press.
Miller, J.C. 1966. *The First Frontier*. Lanham: The University Press of America.
Mills, E. and W. Oates. 1975 *Fiscal Federalism and Land Use*. New York: Praeger.
Mills, W. and H.R. Davis. 1963. *Small City Government*. New York: Random House.
Mitchell, R. 1991. "From Conservation to Environmental Movement," in *Government and Environmental Politics*. R. Mitchell, ed. Baltimore: Johns Hopkins University Press.
Mohl, R. 1983. "Miami: Ethnic Cauldron," in *Sunbelt Cities*. R. Bernard and B. Rice, eds., Austin: University of Texas Press.
Mohl, R, 1985. *The New City*. Arlington Heights, IL: Harlan-Davidson.
Mohl, R. 1989. "Ethnic Politics in Miami: 1960-1986," in *Shades of the Sunbelt*. R. Miller and G. Pozzetta, eds., Boca Raton: Florida Atlantic University Press.
Monkkonen, E. 1988. *America Becomes Urban*. Berkeley: University of California Press.

Moore, A. 1957. *The Frontier Mind*. New York: McGraw-Hill.
Moreland, L. 1990. "The Impact of Immigration on the Composition of Party Coalitions," in *Political Parties in the Southern States*. T. Baker, et. al. eds., New York: Praeger.
Moreno, D. and C. Warren. 1996. "The Conservative Enclave Revisited: Cuban Americans in Florida," in *Ethnic Ironies*. R. De La Garza and L. DeSipio., eds. Boulder, CO: Westview Press.
Morgan,T. 1993. *Wilderness at Dawn*. New York: Simon and Schuster.
Mormino, G. 1993. "Peninsula Florida," *The Encyclopedia of Social History*. Chicago: Newmarket Press.
Mormino, G. 1983. "Tampa: From Hell Hole to the Good Life," in *Sunbelt Cities*. R. Bernard and B. Rice, eds., Austin: University of Texas Press.
Mosher, F. 1982. *Democracy and Public Service*. New York: Oxford University Press.
Muller, P. 1981. *Contemporary Suburban America*. Englewood Cliffs, NJ: Prentice-Hall.
Mumford, L. 1968. *The Urban Prospect*. New York: Harcourt-Brace.
Nagle, S. 1984. *Contemporary Public Policy Analysis*. Tuscaloosa: University of Alabama Press.
Nalbandian,J. 1991. *Professionalism in Local Government*. San Francisco, CA: Josey-Bass Press.
Norquist, J. 1998. *The Wealth of Cities*. New York: Addison-Wesley.
Oates, W. 1972. *Fiscal Federalism*. New York: Harcourt-Brace.
O'Rourke, T.G. 1988. "The Demographic and Economic Setting of Southern Politics," in *Contemporary Southern Politics*. J. Lea, ed. Baton Rouge: Louisiana State University.
Orfield, M. 1999. *Metro Politics*. Washington, D.C.: Brookings Institution Press.
Pagano, M. and A. Bowman. 1995. *Cityscapes and City Capital*. Baltimore: Johns Hopkins University Press.
Palumbo, D. 1988. *Public Policy in America*. New York: Harcourt-Brace.
Pammer, W.J. 1990. *Managing Fiscal Strain in Major American Cities*. New York: Greenwood Press.
Pardum, E.D. and J.R. Anderson.1988. *Florida Growth Atlas*. Tallahassee, FL: Florida Institute of Government.
Parker, S. 1988. "Shifting Party Tides in Florida," in *The South's New Poltics*. R. Swanesborogh ed . Jackson: University of South Carolina Press.
Parkes, H.B.1959. *The American Experience*. New York: Vintage Press.
Patton, C. and D.S. Sawicki. 1986. *Basic Methods of Policy Analysis and Planning*. Englewood Cliffs: Prentice-Hall.
Pattakos, A.and C. Morris. 1986. "The Maine Experience," in *From Nation to States*. E. Jennings, ed. Albany: State University of New York Press.
Pelham, T. 1979. *State Land Use Planning and Regulation*. Lexington,MA: D.C. Heath.

Pelham, T. 1995. "The Florida Experience," in *State and Regional Comprehensive Planning*. Buschbaum, P. and L. Smith, eds. Chicago, IL: ABA Publications.
Perin, C. 1977. *Everything In Its Place*. Princeton: Princeton University Press.
Perez-Stable, M. and M. Uriarte. 1993. "Cubans and and Changing Economy of Miami," in *Latinos in a Changing U.S. Economy*. R. Morales and F. Bonilla, eds. Newbury Park: Sage Publications.
Polster, B. and P. Patton. 1999. *Highway: America's Endless Dream*. New York: Stuart, Taylor and Chang Publishers.
Poplin, D.E. 1972. *Communities*. New York; MacMillan Press.
Portes, A. and A. Stepick. 1993. *City on the Edge: The Transformation of Miami*. Berkeley: University of California Press.
Porter, D. 1997. *Managing Growth in America's Communities*. Washington, D.C.: Island Press.
Porter, D. 1996. *Profiles in Growth Management*. Washington, DC: Urban Land Institute.
Potter, D. 1992. "American Individualism in the Twentieth Century," in *American Social Character*. R. Wilkinson, ed. New York: Icon Books.
Powell, S.C. 1963. *Puritan Village*. Garden City: Doubleday and Company, Inc.
Powers, R. 1991. *Far From Home*. New York: Random House.
Presthus, R. 1964. *Men At The Top*. New York: Oxford University Press.
Preston, H. 1991. "Will Dixie Disappear?" *The Future South* J.P. Dunn and H. Preston, eds., Urbana, IL: University of Illinois Press.
Price, E.T. 1995. *Dividing The Land*. Chicago: University of Chicago Press.
Prysby, C. 1990. "Realignment among Southern Political Activists," in *Political Parties in The Southern States*. T. Baker, ed, New York: Praeger.
Prysby, C. 1998. "Party Switchers and the Party System," in *Party Activiists in Southern Poltics*. C. Hadley and L. Bowman, eds., Knoxville: University of Tennessee Press.
Rabinovitz, F. 1969. *City Politics and Planning*. New York: Atherton Press.
Rabinowitz, H. 1992. *The First New South*. Arlington Heights: Harlan-Davidson.
Raimondo, H. 1992. *Economics of State and Local Government*. New York: Praeger.
Ramsey, M. 1996. *Community, Culture and Economic Development*. Albany: State University of New York Press.
Ranney, D.C. 1969. *Planning and Politics in the Metropolis*. Columbus: Charles E. Merrill.
Reed, B.J. and J. W. Swain. 1990. *Public Finance Administration*. Englewood Cliffs: Prentice-Hall.
Reed, J. S. 1986. *The Enduring South*. Chapel Hill: The University of North Carolina Press.
Reps, J. W. 1980. *Town Planning In Frontier America*. Columbia: University of Missouri Press.
Riley, R.B. 1977. "New Mexico Villages in the Landscape," in *Changing the Landscapes*. E. Zube and M.J. Zube. eds., Amherst: University of Massachusetts Press.

Robinson, W. S. 1979. *The Southern Colonial Frontier*. Albuquerque: University of New Mexico Press.
Roelofs, H.M. 1976. *Ideology and Myth in American Politics*. Boston: Little-Brown.
Rondinelli, D. 1975. *Urban and Regional Development Planning*. Ithaca: Cornell University Press.
Rose, R. 1978. *What is Governing?* Englewood Cliffs: Prentice-Hall.
Rosenbaum, W.A. 1975. *Political Culture*. New York: Praeger.
Rossiter, C. 1956. *First American Revolution*. New York: Harcourt-Brace
Rothman, J. and M. Hugentobler. 1986. "Planning Theory and Planning Practice," in *Interdisciplinary Planning*. M.J. Dluhy and K. Chen, eds., New Brunswick: Center for Urban Policy Research.
Rubin, I.S. 1983. *Running In The Red*. Albany: State University of New York Press.
Rubin, I.S. 1998. *Class, Tax and Power*. Chatham: Chatham House.
Rudel, T.K. 1989. *Situations and Strategies in American Land Use Planning*. New York: Cambridge University Press.
Rundquist, B. 1980. *Political Benefits*. Lexington, MA: Lexington Books.
Rusk, D. 1993. *Cities Without Suburbs*. Baltimore: Johns Hopkins University Press.
Savas. E.S. 1987. *Privatization*. Chatham: Chatham House.
Schaffer, D. 1988. *Two Centuries on American Planning*. Baltimore: Johns Hopkins University Press.
Scher. R. 1992. *Politics and the New South*. New York: Paragon House.
Schiffman, I. 1989. *Alternative Techniques for Managing Growth*. Berkeley: Institute of Government Studies.
Schneider, M. 1989. *The Competitive City*. Albany: State University of New York Press.
Schulman, B.J. 1991. *From Cotton Belt to Sunbelt*. New York: Oxford University Press.
Schultz, S. 1989. *Constructing Urban Culture*. Philadelphia: Temple University Press.
Schumaker, P. 1991. *Critical Pluralism, Democratic Performance and Community Power*. Lawrence: University of Kansas Press.
Scicchitano, M. and R. Scher. 1998. "Florida Political Change," in *The New Politics of the Old South*. C. Bullock and M. Rozell, eds., London: Rowman and Littlefield.
Seroka, J. 1986. *Rural Public Administration*. New York: Greewood Press.
Shalhope, R.E. 1991. *The Roots of Democracy*. Boston: Twayne Publishers.
Sharp, E. 1986. *Citizen Demand-Making in an Urban Context*. University, AL: University of Alabama Press.
Shaw, J. and R. Utt. 2000. *A Guide to Smart Growth*. Washington: Heritage Foundation.
Shermyen, A.H. 1991. *Florida Statistical Abstract*. Gainesville, FL: University of Florida Press.
Sierra Club Foundation. 2000. *Sprawl Costs Us All*. Washington, D.C.: Sierra Club Foundation Press.

Silver, C. 1984. *Twentieth-Century Richmond: Politics, Planning and Race.* Knoxvile, TN: University of Tennessee Press.
Simmons, A.. 1979. *Moral Principles and Political Obligations.* Princeton: Princeton University Press.
Sinopoli, R. . 1992. *The Foundations of American Citizenship.* New York: Oxford University Press.
Skidmore, M.. 1978. *American Political Thought.* New York: St. Martins Press.
Slater, D.. 1984. *Management of Local Planning.* Washington, D.C.: ICMA Press.
Smith, H. 1991. *Planning America's Communities.* Chicago: Planners Press.
Smith, P. 1966. *As A City Upon A Hill.* New York: Alfred A. Knopf.
Snell, R. 1993. *Financing State Government in the 1990s.* Washington, D.C.: National Conference of State Legislatures.
Sokolow, A. 1996. "Town and Township Government" in *Handbook of Local Government Administration.* J.J. Gargin, ed., New York: Marcel-Dekker, Inc.
Sokolow, A. 1990. "Leadership and Implementation in Rural Economic Development," in *American Rural Communities.* A. Luloff, ed., Boulder: Westview Press.
Sokolow, A. 1981. "Local Governments: Capacity and Will" in *Non-Metropolitan America in Transition.* A.H. Hawley. ed., Chapel Hill, NC.: University of North Carolina Press.
Starnes, E. 1993. "Substate Frameworks for Growth Management," in *Growth Management.* J.Stein, ed. Newbury Park: Sage Publications.
Starnes, E. 1988. "Suwanne River Land Acquisition Plan," in *Aesthetics of the Rural Renaissance.* E.J. Ward, ed. San Louis Obispo,CA.: California State University Press.
Steed. R. 1990. "Civil Rights Activists: Contribution to Party Transformation," in *Political Parties in the Southern States.* T. Baker, ed., New York: Praeger.
Steed, R. 1998. "Parties, Ideology and Issues," in *Party Organization and Activism in the American South* R. Steed, ed. Tuscaloosa: University of Alabama Press.
Steed, R. and L. Bowman. 1998. "Strength of Party Attachment," in *Party Organization and Activism in the American South.* R. Steed ed., Tuscaloosa: University of Alabama Press.
Stein, J. 1993. "Future Issues in Growth Management Planning," in *Growth Management.* J. Stein, ed. Newbury Park: Sage Publications.
Stein, L. 1991. *Holding Bureaucrats Accountable.* Tuscaloosa: University of Alabama Press.
Stein, R. 1990. *Urban Alternatives.* Pittsburgh: University of Pittsburgh Press.
Steinberger, P.J. 1985. *Ideology and the Urban Crisis.* Albany: State University of New York Press.
Steiss, A. 1975. *Local Government Finance.* Lexington, MA: Lexington Books.
Steiss, A. 1989. *Financial Management in Public Organization.* Pacific Grove: Brooks-Cole.
Stephenson, R. 1997. *Visions of Eden.* Columbus: Ohio State University Press.
Stern, R. 1986. *Pride of Place.* Boston: Houghton-Mifflin.

Stiverson, G. 1977. *Poverty in the Land of Plenty*. Baltimore: Johns Hopkins University Press.
Stock, C. 1996. *Rural Radicals*. New York: Penguin Press.
Stone, D. 1988. *Policy Paradox and Politics*. New York: Harper-Collins.
Sutro, S. 1990. *Reinventing the Village*. Chicago: Planners Press.
Swanson, B. 1970. *The Concern For Community in Urban America*. New York: Odyssey Press.
Swanson, B., et. al. 1979. *Small Town and Small Towners*. Beverly Hills: Sage Publications.
Sydnor, C.S. 1952. *American Revolutionaries in the Making*. New York: The Free Press.
Tauxe, C.S. 1993. *Farms, Mines and Main Streets*. Philadelphia: Temple University Press.
Thomas, H. And P. Healey. 1991. *Dilemmas of Planning Practice*. Brookfield: Avebury-Gower Publishing.
Tillson, A. 1991. *Gentry and Common Folk*. Lexington, KY: University of Kentucky Press.
Tindall, G. B. 1972. *The Disruption of the Solid South*. Athens: University of Georgia Press.
Tindall, G.B. 1989. "Mythology: A New Frontier in Southern History," in *Myth and Southern History*. P. Gerster and N. Cords, eds. Urbana: University of Illinois Press.
Toft, G.S. 1986. "Building Capacity to Govern," in *Perspectives on Management Capacity Building*. B.W. Honadle and A. Howitt., eds., Albany: State University of New York Press.
Tolbert, L.C. 1999. *Constructing Townscape*. Chapel Hill: University of North Carolina Press.
Troustine, P.J. and T. Christensen. 1982. *Movers and Shakers*. New York: St. Martins Press.
Turner, F.J. 1994. *Rereading Frederick Jackson Turner*. New York: Henry Holt.
Tweeten, l. and G. Brinkman. 1976. *Micropolitan Development*. Ames: Iowa State University Press.
Urofsky, M. I. 1988. *A March of Liberty*. New York: Alfred A. Knopf.
Van Wingen, J. and D. Valentine. 1988. *Contemporary Southern Politics*. Baton Rouge: Louisiana State University Press.
Vasu, M. L. 1979. *Politics and Planning*. Chapel Hill: University of North Carolina Press.
Verba, S. 1965. "Comparative Political Culture" in *Political Culture and Political Development*. L.W. Pye and S. Verba. eds., Princeton: Princeton University Press.
Verba, S. et.al., 1995. *Voice and Equality*. Cambridge: Harvard University Press.
Veri, A. et. al., 1975. *Environmental Quality By Design; South Florida*. Coral Gables: University of Miami Press.

Vidich, A.J. and J. Bensman. 1968. *Small Town in Mass Society*. 2ed. Princeton: Princeton University Press.
Vogel, R. 1992. *Urban Political Economy: Broward County, Florida*. Gainesville: University Press of Florida.
Waitley, D. 1997. *Florida*. Missoula, MT: Mountain Press.
Warner, S.B. 1995. *The Urban Wilderness*. Berkley: University of California Press.
Warren, R. 1987. *The Community in America*. Lanham: University Press of America.
Waterhouse, R. 1986. "Merchants, Planters and Lawyers" in *Power and Status*., B. Daniel, ed., Middletown: Wesleyan University Press.
Watson, D.J. 1995. *The New Civil War*. New York: Praeger.
Weiner, J. M. 1978. *The Social Origins of the New South*. Baton Rouge: Louisiana State University Press.
Weinstein, B., et. al. 1985. *Regional Growth and Decline in the United States*. New York: Praeger.
Wendel, 1986. "At the Pinnacle of Elective Success" in *Power and Status*. B. Daniels, ed., Middletown: Wesleyan University Press.
West, T.G. 1997. *Vindicating the Founders*. Oxford: Rowan and Littlefield.
Wheaton, W. and M. Wheaton. 1970. "Identifying the Public Interest," in *Urban Planning in Transition*. E.Erber,ed. New York: Grossman.
Wiebe, R.H. 1984. *The Opening of American Society*. New York: Vintage Press.
Wiebe, R. H. 1995. *Self-Rule*. Chicago: University of Chicago Press.
Winkle, K. J. 1988. *The Politics of Community*. New York: Cambridge University Press.
White, M. and L. White. 1962. *The Intellectual Versus the City*. New York: Mentor Books.
Wikstrom, N. 1993. *The Political World of a Small Town*. Westport: Greenwood Press.
Wildavsky, A. 1964. *Leadership in a Small Town*. Totowa: Bedminster Press.
Wilkinson, R. 1991. *The Community in Rural America*. Westport: Greenwood Press.
Wilkinson, R. P. 1988. *The Pursuit of American Character*. New York: Harper-Row.
Williamson, E. 1976. *Florida Politics in the Gilded Age*. Gainesville: University of Florida Press.
Wolf, S. 1976. *Urban Village*. Princeton: Princeton University Press.
Wolf, S. 1993. *As Various As Their Land*. New York: Harper-Collins.
Wright, G. 1986. *Old South, New South*. New York, NY: Basic Books.
Yaro, R. 1993. *Designing With Change in the Connecticut River Valley*. Cambridge: Lincoln Institute of Land Policy.
Young, F. 1999. *Small Towns in Multilevel Society*. Lanham, MD: University Press of America.
Zimmerman, J.F. 1992. *Contemporary American Federalism*. New York: Praeger.
Zimmerman, J.F. 1991. *Federal Preemption*. Ames: Iowa State University Press.
Zovanyi, G. 1998. *Growth Management for a Sustainable Future*. New York: Praeger.
Zuckerman, M. 1970. *Peaceable Kingdom*. New York: Vintage Press.

Journal and Monograph Articles

Anagnoson, T. 1983. "Bureaucratic Reaction to Political Pressure," *Administration and Society*. May): 97-118.
Anglin, R. 1990. "Diminishing Citizen Preferences for Local Growth," *Urban Affairs Quarterly*. (June): 684-696.
Audirac, I. et. al. 1990. "Ideal Urban Form and Visions of the Good Life,"*Journal of the American Planning Association*. (Autumn): 470-482.
Audirac, I and M. Smith. 1992. "Urban Form and Residential Choice," *Journal of Architectural and Planning Research*. (Spring): 19-32.
Audirac, I and A. Shermyen. 1994. "An Evaluation of Neotraditional Design's Social Prescription," *Journal of Education and Planning Research*. (13):161-173.
Baer, W. 1977. "Urban Planners: Doctors or Midwives," *Public Administration Review*. (November): 671-677.
Baker, J 1994. "Government in Twilight Zone" *State and Local Government Review*. (Spring):119-128.
Beaton, W. "Regional Tax Base Sharing," *Journal of the American Planning Association*. (Summer): 315-322.
Beck, P. 1982. "Realignment Begins? Republican Surge in Florida," *American Political Quarterly*. (October): 421-438.
Beck, P. and T. Dye, 1982. "Sources of Public Opinion on Taxes: The Florida Case," *Journal of Politics*. (Spring): 172-82.
Beck, P. et. al. 1987. "Citizen Views on Taxes and Services: A Tale of Three Cities," *Social Science Quarterly*. (Summer): 223-243.
Benton, J.E. and J.L. Daly. 1992. "The Paradox of Citizen Service Evaluations and Tax/Fee Preferences," *American Review of Administration*. (December): 271-285.
Blitz, L. and J. Pilegge. 1987. "Fiscal Stress and Response," *International Journal of Public Administration*. (Fall): 315-29.
Bloomquist, L. 1988. "Rural Manufacturing Gets Mixed Reviews," *Rural Development Perspective*. (4): 22-26.
Boeckelman, K. 1991. "Political Culture and State Development Policy," *Publius*. (Spring): 49-61.
Botner, S. 1991. "Trends and Development in Budgeting and Financial Management in Medium Sized Cities," *Public Budgeting and Financial Management*. (Special Issue): 443-456.
Bowman, A. 1988. "Competition for Economic Development Among Southeastern Cities," *Urban Affairs Quarterly*. (June):511-527.
Brooks, R. and C, Searcy. 1995. "Downtowns in Georgia," *Small Town*. (November):14-29.
Brown, A. and M. Daniels. 1988. "The Preservation of Federal Priorities," *International Journal of Public Administration*. (Winter): 155-172.
Browne, W. 1982. "Political Values in a Changing Rural Community," *Policy Studies Review*. (August): 55-64.

Bibliography

Buck, R. and R. Rath. 1970. "Planning for Institutional Innovation in Smaller Cities," *Journal of the American Institute of Planners*. (January): 59-64.

Button, J. et. al. 1998. "A Look at Second Generation of Black Officials in Florida," *State and Local Government Review*, (Fall): 181-189.

Calavita, N. and R. Caves. 1994. "Planners' Attitude Towards Growth," *Journal of the American Planning Association*. (Autumn): 483-500.

Chinitz, B. 1990. "Growth Management: Good for the Town, Bad for the Nation," *Journal of the American Planning Association*. (Winter): 3-8.

Clark, W. 1988. "Sources of Revenues and Growth Management," *Growth Management Innovations in Florida*. Boca Raton: Joint Center for Environmental and Urban Problems.88 (1).

Clarke, S. 1992. "The Next Wave: Post-Federal Local Economic Development," *Economic Development Quarterly*. (December):187-98.

Cothran, D. 1986. "Strategies for Enhancing Financial Management in Smaller Cities," *State and Local Government Review*. (Winter): 31-36.

Craig, S. 1992. "A Florida Income Tax," *Governing Florida*. (Spring):8-11.

Daenzer, R. 2001. "Changing Identity of a Small Town," *Small Town*. (January) : 14-23.

Dalton, L. 1989. "The Limits on Regulations," *Journal of the American Planning Association*. (Spring): 151-168.

Davis, D. 1989. "Tax Increment Financing," *Public Budgeting and Finance*. (Winter): 63-73.

Davis, J., et.al. 1994. "The 'New Burbs'" *Journal of the American Planning Association*. (Winter): 45-58.

Davidson, C. 1980. "The Importance of Small Business in Rural Development," *Texas Business Review*. (September): 283-288.

Decker, J. 1987. "Management and Organizational Capacity in Non-Metropolitan Florida" *Journal of Urban Affairs*. (Winter): 46-61.

Dewey, S. 1999. "Is This What We Came To Florida For?" *Florida Historical Quarterly*. (Spring): 503-31.

Diaz, D. and G. Green. 2001. "Fiscal Stress and Growth Management Efforts in Wisconsin Cites, Villages and Towns," *State and Local Government Review*. (Winter):7-22.

Donovan, T. 1993. "Community Controversy and Adoption of Economic Development Policies," *Social Science Quarterly*. (June): 386-401.

Doss, C.B. 1987. "The Use of Capital Budgeting Procedures in U.S. Cities," *Public Budgeting and Finance*. (Autumn): 57-69.

Downs, A. 2001. "What Does Smart Growth Really Mean?" *Planning*. (April):20-25.

Downing, P.B. 1992. "The Revenue Potential of User Charges in Municipal Finance," *Public Finance Quarterly*. (October):512-25.

Duncan, J. 1989. *The Search for Efficient Urban Growth Patterns*. Tallahassee: Florida DCA Technical Report.

Dye, R. and J. Sundberg. 1998. "A Model of Tax Increment Financing Adoption Incentives," *Growth and Change*. (Spring): 90-110.

Dzurik, A. 1984. "Water Use and Public Policy in Florida," *Journal of Water Resources Planning and Management.* (April): 167-179.

Ervin, O. 1985. "The State-Local Partnership and National Objectives," *Policy Studies.* (Fall):634-642.

Exoo, C. 1984. "Policy Attitudes of Rural Legislators," *Administration and Policy Journal.* (Spring): 151-172.

Farnham, P. 1981. "Targeting Federal Aid," *Public Policy.* (Winter):75-89.

Forrester, J. 1993. "Municipal Capital Budgeting: An Examination," *Public Finance and Budgeting.* (Summer): 85-91.

Feiock, R. and J. Clingermayer. 1986. "Municipal Representation, Executive Power and Economic Development Policy," *Policy Studies Journal.* (Summer): 211-229.

Feiock, R. and J. Clingermayer. 1992. "Development Policy Choices: Four Explanations," *American Review of Public Administration.* (Spring):49-63.

Fischel, W. 1991. "Good for the Town, Bad for the Nation: A Commentary," *Journal of the American Planning Association.* (Summer):9-13.

Fossett. J. 1987. "The Consequence of Shifting Control: Small Cities CDBG Funds in Four Southern States," *Publius.* (Fall): 65-80.

Fox, W. And J. Reid. 1987. "Targeting Federal Assistance to Local Governments ," *Publius.* (Fall): 33-51.

Fulton, W. 1990. "Addicted To Growth" *Governing* (October): 68-74.

Gabris, G.T. and B.J. Reed. 1978. "Responses of Cities to Federal Aid Decentralization" *Southern Review of Public Administration.* (December): 301-24.

Gale, D. 1992. "Eight Sponsored Growth Management Programs," *Journal of the American Planning Association.* (Autumn): 425-439.

Gale, D. and S. Hart. 1992. "Who Supports State-Sponsored Growth Management Programs?" *Journal of Planning Education and Research.* (Autumn): 101-114.

Gamberg, J. 1966 "The Professional and Policy Choices in Mid-Sized Cities," *The Journal of the American Institute of Planners.* (Spring): 171-178.

Garkovich, L. 1982. "Land Use Planning as a Response to Rapid Population Growth and Community Change," *Rural Sociology.* (Spring): 47-64.

Gargan, J. 1987. "The Knowledge-Interest Context of Public Finance: Judgements of City Finance Officers," *International Journal of Public Administration.* (Fall): 245-271.

Giventer,L. and W. Neely. 1984. "County Problems and Decision Making Perception" *Public Administration Quarterly.* (Winter): 498 - 517.

Goetz, E. 1990. "Type II Policy and Mandated Benefits" *Urban Affairs Quarterly.* (November):170-90.

Gottdiener, M. and M. Nieman. 1981. "Characteristics of Support For Local Growth Control," *Urban Affairs Quarterly.* (September): 55-73.

Grizzle, G. and P. Trogen. 1994. "Cutback Budgeting in Florida" *Southeastern Political Review.* (September):503-524.

Hahn, A. 1970. "Planning in Rural Areas," *Journal of the American Institute of Planners*. (Winter): 44-49.

Hall, J.1983. "Fitting the Community Development Block Grant Program to Local Politics," *Publius*. (Summer): 73- 84.

Halachmi, A. 1986. "Strategic Planning and Management? Not Necessarily," *Public Productivity Review*. (Winter):35-50.

Halachmi, A. and R. Boydston. 1991. "Strategic Management with Annual and Multi-Year Operating Budget," *Public Budgeting and Financial Management*. (Special Issue):296 - 317.

Hansen, R. 1991. "Political Culture Variations in State Economic Development Policy," *Publius*. (Spring): 63-81.

Hester, R.T. 1990. "The Sacred Structure in Small Town," *Small Town*. (January): 4-21.

Hibbarb, M. and L. Davis. 1986. "Economic and Cultural Myths of Small Town America," *Journal of the American Planning Association*. (Autumn): 419-27.

Hirsch. W.Z. 1964. "Local versus Areawide Urban Government Services," *National Tax Journal*. (December): 331-39.

Hood, L. 1992. "Nontraditional Sources of Funds in Tax Increment Financing Projects," *Economic Development Review*. (Spring): 38-40.

Houston, L. 1988. "Living Villages," *Small Town*. (November): 14-25.

Howe, E. 1992. "Professional Roles and the Public Interest in Planning," *Journal of Planning Literature*. (February): 230 - 247.

Huddleston, J. 1986. "Distribution of Development Costs Under Tax Increment Financing," *Journal of the American Planning Association*. (Summer): 194-198.

Innes, J. 1992. "Group Processes and Social Construction of Growth Management," *Journal of the American Planning Association*. (Autumn): 440-453.

Juergensmeyer, J. 1985. "Funding Infrastructure" *The Changing Structure of Infrastructure Finance*. Cambridge, MA: Lincoln Institute of Land Policy. 85 (5): 23-43.

Juergensmeyer, J. 1986. "Impact Fees After Growth Management," *Perspectives on Florida's Growth Management Act*. Cambridge, MA: Lincoln Institute of Land Policy. 86 (1): 183-91.

Jung, C. 2001. "Does the Local Option Sales tax Provide Property Tax Relief?" *Public Budgeting and Finance*. (Spring) 73-85.

Kanervo, D. 1994. "Economics Policy-making in Small Towns," *Southeast Political Review*. (December): 689-705.

Kantor.P. and H. Savitch. 1993. "Can Politicians Bargain With Business," *Urban Affairs Quarterly*. (December): 230-255.

Kelley, A. 1989. "Gender, Party and Political Ideology," *Journal of Political Science*. (Fall): 6-18.

Keller, L. and G. Wamsley. 1978. "Small Government as an Inter-Organizational Network," *Southern Review of Public Administration*. (December): 277-300.

Kenyon, J. 1989. "From Central Business District to Central Social District," *Small Town*. (March):5-8.
Kern, C. 1994. "Rethinking Main Street," *Small Town*. (November): 4-11.
Kerstein, R. (1991). "Growth Politics in Tampa and Hillsborough County," *Journal of Urban Affairs*. 13(1):55-75.
Kerstein, R. (1995). "Political Exceptionalism in the Sunbelt," *Journal of Urban Affairs*. 17(2):143-167.
King, L. and G.Harris. 1989. "Local Response to Rapid Rural Growth," *Journal of the American Planning Association*. (Spring): 181-191.
Klay, W. 1992. "Tax Reform in Florida," *Governing Florida*. (Spring): 12-17.
Klay, W. 1991. "Strategic Management, Policy Analysis and Budgeting," *Public Budgeting and Financial Management*. (Special Issue #2): 273-291.
Klay, W. 1977. "Budgeting in Rapid Local Growth," *Southern Review of Public Administration*. (December):303-313.
Klemanski, J. 1989. "Tax Increment Financing," *Policy Studies Journal*. (Fall): 656-670.
Klosterman, R. "Foundation of Normative Planning," *Journal of the American Planning Association*. (January): 37-45.
Klosterman, R. 1980. "A Public Interest Criterion," *Journal of the American Planning Association*. (July): 323- 340.
Krane, D. 1987. "Devolution of the Small Cities CDBG Program in Mississippi," *Publius*. (Fall): 81-96.
Krannich, R. and C. Humphrey. 1983. "Local Mobilization and Community Growth," *Rural Sociology*. (Spring): 60- 81.
Lamb, R. 1985."The Morphology and Vitality of Business Districts in Upstate New York Villages," *TheProfessional Geographer*. (May):162-72.
Landis, R. 1992. "Do Growth Controls Work?" *Journal of the American Planning Association*. (Autumn): 489-507.
Leistritz, L, et.al. 1989. "Why Do People Leave Town to Buy Goods and Services," *Small Town*. (July): 20-27.
Leo, C. et. al. 1998. "Is Urban Sprawl Back on the Political Agenda?" *Urban Affairs Quarterly*. (December): 199-212.
Lorentz, A. and K. Shaw. 2000. "Are You Ready to Bet on Smart Growth," *Planning* (January): 4-9.
Lynch,T. 1987. "Local Government Budget Strategy: A Case Study of South Florida," *Public Administration Quarterly*. (Fall): 361-78.
MacManus, S. and B. P. Grothe. 1989 "Fiscal Stress as a Stimulant to Better Forecasting and Productivity," *Public Productivity Review*. (Summer): 387-400.
MacManus, S. 1992. "Enough is Enough: Floridians' Support for Limiting State Mandates on Local Government, " *State and Local Government Review*. (Fall): 103-112.
Malizia, E. 1986. "Economic Development in Smaller Cities," *Journal of American Planning Association*. (Autumn): 489-499.

Mattson, G., et. al. 1993. "Planning Style, Grant Getting and Decision Rules, "*Journal of Architecture and Planning Research.* (Spring): 59-71.

Mattson, G. 1991."Fiscal Stress, Retrenchment and Small Cities," *Public Budgeting and Financial Management.* (Winter):119-150.

Mattson, G. and R. Twogood. 1991. "Retrenchment and Municipal Service Priorities," *National Civic Review.* (Spring): 183-197.

Mattson G. and P. Solano. 1986. "New Federalism and Small Towns," *Journal of Architecture and Planning Research.* (May): 133-147.

Mattson, G. 1982. "What Small Town Residents Should Know About Farmland Preservation Alternatives?" *Small Town.* (July):15-18.

McGowan, R. 1984. "Strategies of Productivity Improvement in Local Government," *Public Productivity Review.* (Winter): 314-32.

McGranahan, D. 1984. "Local Growth and the Outside Contacts of Influentials," *Rural Sociology.* (Winter): 530-540.

McGuire, M. et. al. 1994. "Building Development Capacity in Non-Metro Communities," *Public Administration Review.* (September): 426-33.

McKay, P. 1989. "Capital Improvement Planning in Florida," *Implementation and Growth Management.*

Ft. Lauderdale: Joint Center for Environmental Problems.

McKenna, F. et.al. 1990. "National Fiscal Policy Changes and the Impact on Rural Governments," *Public Affairs Quarterly.* (Fall): 324-351.

Miller, D. 1991. "The Impact of Political Culture on Patterns of State and Local Government Expenditures," *Publius.* (Spring): 83-100.

Molnar, J. and J. Smith. 1982. "Satisfaction with Rural Services," *Rural Sociology.* (Fall):496-511.

Molotch, H. 1976. "The City as a Growth Machine," *American Journal of Sociology.* (Summer): 309-332.

Moore, T.1978. "Why Allow Planners to Do What they Do?" *Journal of the American Planning Association.* (October):387-96.

Morgan, et. al. 1981. "Alternatives to Muncipal Service Delivery," *Public Administration Review.* (Summer): 184-199.

Morgan, D. and R. England. 1984. "The Small Cities Block Grant Program," *Public Administration Review.* (November/December):

Morgan, D. and W. Pammer. 1988. "Coping With Fiscal Stress,".*Urban Affairs Quarterly.* (September): 69-86.

Mullins, D. and M. Rosentraub. 1992. "Fiscal Pressure? The Impact of Elderly Recruitment on Local Expenditure," *Urban Affairs Quarterly.* (December): 337-354.

Nellis, L. 1980. "Planning with Rural Values," *Small Town.* (May): 20-24.

Nelson, A. 1992. "Characterizing Exurbia," *Journal of Planning Literature.* (May): 350-66.

Netzer, D. 1992. "Differences in Reliance on User Charges By American State and Local Governments" *Public Finance Quarterly.* (October): 499-512.

Nicholas, J. 1985. "Florida's Experience With Impact Fees," *The Changing Structure of Infrastructure Finance*. Cambridge: Lincoln Institute of Land Policy, 85 (2): 45-57.

Nicholas, J. 1986. "Capital Improvement Finance and Impact Fees," *Perspectives on the Florida Growth Management* Cambridge: Lincoln Institute of Land Policy. 86(5): 175-182.

Nicholas, J. 1988. "Impact Fees: A Fiscal Technique for Managing Growth," *Growth Management Innovations in Florida*. Ft. Lauderdale: Joint Center For Environmental and Urban Problems. 88 (1):109-132.

Nordheimer, J. 1986. "Florida Tries To Impose Some Order," *The New York Times.*, July 15,1986: pp. 5,16.

O'Grady, D. 1987. "State Economic Incentives: Why States Compete?" *State and Local Government Review*. (Fall): 86- 94.

O'Toole, L. and B. Stipak. 1991. "Strategic Planning and Budgeting in Local Government," *Public Budgeting and Financial Management*. (Special Issue):317-331.

Parker, S. 1990. "Florida Out of the 80s into the 90s," *Governing Florida*. (Winter):12-24.

Peiser, R. 1984. "Does it Pay to Plan Suburban Growth?" *Journal of the American Planning Association*. (Autumn):419- 432.

Peliserro,J. and Granato, J. 1989. "Local Officials' Evaluation of the State Community Development Program," *State and Local Government Review* . (Winter): 31-37.

Perry, T. and K. Kraemer. 1980. "Chief Executive Support and Innovation Adoption," *Administration and Society*. (August): 158-177.

Poister, T. and R. McGowan. 1984."The Contribution of Local Productivity Efforts in a Period of Fiscal Stress," *Public Productivity Review*. (Winter): 386-394.

Popper, F. 1988. "Understanding American Land Use Regulation Since 1970," *Journal of the American Planning Association*. (Summer): 291-300.

Price, W. 1980. "The Distribution of Public Works Services," *Southern Review of Public Administration*. (June):52-77.

Rainey, G. and R. Kline. 1979. "Administrative Resurgence and Policy Innovation," *Administration and Society*. (Fall): 307-34.

Reed, C., et. al. 1987. "Assessing Readiness for Economic Development Strategic Planning," *Journal of the American Planning Association*. (Autumn):521-30.

Reed, D. 1988. "Budgetary Retrenchment in Small Cities" Annual Meeting of the Southern Political Science Association Atlanta ,Georgia, November 3–5 1988.

Reese, L. 1990. "Decision Rules and Service Delivery in Small Cities," *International Journal of Public Administration*. 13(3): 435-458.

Reese, L. 1991. "Municipal Fiscal Health and Tax Abatement Policy," *Economic Development Quarterly*. (February):24-32.

Reese, L. 1993a. "Categories of Local Economic Development Techniques," *Policy Studies Journal*. (Fall): 492-506.

Reese, L. 1993b. "Decision Rules in Local Economic Development," *Urban Affairs Quarterly*. (March):501-513.

Reese, L. 1998. "Sharing the Benefits of Economic Development," *Urban Affairs Quarterly*. (May): 686-711.
Roberts, T. 1985. "Funding Public Facilities," *The Changing Structure of Infrastructure Finance*. Cambridge: Lincoln Institute of Land Policy. 85 (5): 1-22.
Roberts, T. 1986. "Capital Improvement Programming After the Growth Management Act," *Perspectives on Florida's Growth Management*. Cambridge: Lincoln Institute of Land Policy.86 (5):151-174.
Rubin, H. 1988. "Shoot anything that Flies, Claim anything that Falls," *Economic Development Quarterly*. (June): 236-251.
Ryan, J. 1991. "Impact Fees: A New Funding Source," *Journal of Planning Literature*. (May): 401-407.
Salkin, P. 1999. "Smart Growth at Century's End," *The Urban Lawyer* Vol 31 (3):601-648.
Seimon, C. 1989. "Carrying Capacity Planning," *Implementation of the 1985 Growth Management Act*. Ft. Lauderdale: Joint Center For Environmental and Urban Problems. 89(1): 9-38.
Seroka, J. 1986. "Attitudes of Rural County Leaders Towards Intergovernmental Cooperation," *Journal of the Community Development Society*. (Spring): 55-72.
Seroka, J. 1981. "Rural versus Urban Professional Public Administrators," *Southern Review of Public Administration*. (Spring): 34-50.
Simmonds, K.1990. "Local Taxation in Georgia and Florida," *Public Budgeting and Financial Management*. (Winter): 1-32.
Sokolow, A. 1982. "Population Growth and Administration Variation in Small Cities," *Policy Studies Review*. (August):72-85.
Sokolow, A. 1987. "Small Governments as Newcomers to American Federalism," *Publius*. (Fall):5-11.
Sokolow, A. and B. Honadle. 1984. "How Rural Governments Budget" *Public Administration Review*. (September): 373-382.
Starnes, E. 1986. "Florida's Minimum Criteria Rule," *Perspectives on Florida's Growth Management Act*. Lincoln Institute of Land Policy. 86 (5): 69-82.
Stillman, R. "The City Manager: Professional Helping Hand or Political Hired Hand," *Public Administration Review*. (November):659-670.
Stinsen, T. 1992. "Subsidizing Local Economic Development Through Tax Increment Financing," *Policy Studies Journal*. (Summer): 241-248.
Stroud, H. 1992. "Using Transfer Development Rights to Manage Growth and Development in Lee County, Florida,"*Small Town*. (March): 14-19.
Stround, N. and D. Connell. 1986. "Florida Toughens Up Its Landuse Laws," *Planning*. (January):12 - 14.
Tiebout, C. 1956. "A Pure Theory of Local Expenditures," *Journal of Political Economy*. (October): 416-24.
Tjersland, T. 1974. "Financial Management: The Small City," *Government Finance*. (February): 6-9.

Turner, R. 1992. "Growth Politics and Downtown Development," *Urban Affairs Quarterly.* (September): 3-21.

Turner, R. 1993. "Growth Management Decision Criteria: Do Technical Standards Determine Priorities?," *State and Local Government Review.* (Fall): 186-194.

Tyler, N. 1989. "Evaluating the Health of Downtown," *Small Town.* (September): 4-11.

Vogel, R. and B. Swanson. 1989. "Growth Machine versus the Anti-Growth Coalition," *Urban Affairs Quarterly.* (September): 63-85.

Vogel, R. and B. Swanson. 1988. "Setting Agendas for Community Change," *Journal of Urban Affairs.* 10(1):41-61.

Warner, P. and R. Burdge. 1979. "Perceived Adequacy of Community Services," *Rural Sociology.* (Summer): 392-400.

Watson, S. 1992. "Decentralizing Community Development Decisions," *Publius.* (Winter): 109-122.

Weinberg, M. 1984. "Budget Retrenchment in Small Cities" *Public Budgeting and Finance.* (Autumn): 46-57.

Williams, C. 1996. "Some Strength and Weaknesses of Tax Increment Financing," *Economic Development Review.* (Spring): 69-76.

Wolensky, R. and R. Enright. 1991. "Fiscal Stress Among Wisconsin's Small Governments" *Wisconsin Sociologist.* (Spring/Summer): 19-23.

Wolensky, R. and D. Groves. 1977. "Planning in the Smaller City," *Journal of Socio-Economic Policy Science.* (Spring): 37-41.

Index

Administrative Rules, 99-102, 110, 172
African-Americans, 31, 35, 50, 54-56, 76
Agricultural Adjustment Administration, 39
Apalachicola, FL, 29, 42, 202
Askew, R, 68, 138, 152

Baby Boomers, 57
Balanced Growth, 16-20
Benefit Principle, 137, 168
Black Officials, 51-52
Bloxham, W.D., 32-33
Bonita Springs, Fl, 77-78
Boulder, CO, 18
Bourbonism, 30-34
Boward County FL, 52
Broward, N.B, 34
Bush, Jeb, 46, 80, 127-34, 152

Caretaker Service, 176, 187
Cape Cod Plan, 17
Capital Budget, 144, 147
Capital Facilities Planning, 143, 145, 151
Carrying Capacity, 65
Carter, Jimmy, 21, 119
CDBG, Ch. 8, 52, 110, 117, 121-122
Cedar Key, FL, 29, 206
Charlotte County, FL, 5, 209
Checkerboard Sprawl, 19
Chiles, L, 73, 75, 126, 152

Churches and Politics, 27, 58-60
Civic Engagement, Ch. 6, 87, 169
Civic Public Space, 206
Civil Community, Ch. 6, 86-90
Civil Rights Act (1957), 51
Civil Voting Rights Act (1965), 51-52
Communalism, Ch. 6, 104
Comprehensive Planning, 100-02, 105-07
Concurrency/Consistency, 43, 72, 139
Corporate City Planning, Ch. 11, 182
Cost of Public Services, 63, 126, 170, 211-12, 221-24
County Courthouse Politics, 27, 31, 34, 46, 51
Crestview, FL, 36, 52, 119, 165
Crisp Edges, 209-10
Critical Realignment, 48
Cubans, 54, 76

Daytona Beach, FL, 33, 52, 119, 197
Decision Rules, 99-102, 110, 119-121, 200
Democrats, 30-39, 50, 56, 67, 132, 153
Dixiecrats, 50
DRIs, 69-70, 74

Economic Opportunity, 92
Eisenhower, D, 45, 51
Election 2000, 47-49
ELMS 1, 70

ELMS 2, 71,138
ELMS 3, 74
Entryways, 209-10
Environmental Land and Water Management Act (1972), 42
Environmentalism, 65-68
Essential Services, 158-61, 174-79, 187
Everglades, 68

Fernandina Beach, FL, 19, 25, 29, 165, 206
Feeney-McKay Dispute, 127-34
Fiscal Capacity, 124
Fiscal Equivalence, 160, 168
Fiscal Impact Analysis, 211-12, 221-225
Fiscal Policy Planning, 140
Fiscal Stress, 156-58
Fishkind Report, 130-34
Flagler, H, Ch.3; 32
Florida DCA, 69, 71, 82, 114-15, 117-22, 199
Florida Growth Management Study Commission, 75 81-82, 199, 201, 217
Florida Main Street Program, 202
Florida Tax Watch, 123, 131
Forever Florida, 216-17

Gainesville, FL, 173
Geni Loci (Sense of Place), 201
Gender Politics, 56-58
Generation X, 56-58, 201
Grant Spreading, 112, 120
Great Depression, 36-39
Greenbelts, 18, 209-12
Gretna, FL, 36, 119, 197
Growth Machine, 104-05, 182
Growth Management Act (1985), 13, 73, 114, 139, 145, 151
Growth Management, Ch.5, 12, 19

Heritage Tourism, 212-15
Historic Trend Analysis, 142

H. Hoover and A. Smith Contest, 36-39
Housing Trends, 7-8, 77-78

Ideology, 31, 53, 88
Impact Fees, 148-50, 227
Interchange Villages, 110
Internal Improvement Board, 32

Jacksonville, FL, 29, 34, 38, 41, 76, 117, 133, 136, 165, 166, 171, 191
James Madison Institute, 138, 215
Jeffersonian Agrarianism, 89-90
Jim Crow, 33, 50-52

Kirk, C, 46

Lake Okeechobee, 68, 77
Latinos, 48, 53, 76
Lamb Choppers, 31, 50
Leapfrog Development, 10-12, 64, 169
Lee County, Fl, 10, 75, 77, 220
Loadshedding Public Services, 174-79
Local Government Comprehensive Planning Act (1975) (LGCPA), 70, 106
Local Parochialism, 10, 70, 197
Local Option Sales Tax, 226-27

Main Street Assets, 20, 40, 42, 85, 186, 202-06
Martinez, Bob, 46, 138, 215-16
Marble Cake Federalism, 111
Miami-Dade, 27, 32, 44, 53-55, 76, 216, 222
Micropolitan Towns, 93, 115
Mizner Park, FL, 205
Municipal Services, Ch. 10, 161-64, 174-79

Negative Liberty, Ch.6, 28, 90
New Deal, 36-40
New South, 29-37, 161-64
Neo-Traditionalism, 19-23, 86-90

Index

New Urbanism, Ch.12
Non-Essential Public Services, 161

One Person, One Vote, 49
One Twenty Rule, 80

Palm Beach, FL, 34, 77, 119, 228
Panama City, FL, 27, 41, 129, 192
Pensacola, FL, 19, 25, 29, 31, 165, 194, 197
Picket Fence Federalism, 111, 121
Pinellas County, FL, 7, 41, 68, 79, 134
Planning and Growth Management Act (1993), 74
Plant, H., 15, 32
Plural Executive, 21, 31, 41, 49, 69
Policy Outputs, Ch.7, Ch.8, Ch. 10, 93-94
Policy Performance Rules, 99-102, 110
Policy Planning, 99-102, 111,
Political Culture, Ch.6, 87-89, 95
Political Efficacy, 52
Political Proximity, 135, 169
Ponte Vedra Beach, FL, 79
Pork Chop Gang, 15, 50
Population Trends, 3-7, 35, 41-42, 61-63
Populism, 33
Preservation 2000, 216
Privatization, 158, 174-79
Progressives, 34-36, 161-67
Property Taxes, 10-12, 135-36, 158-60, 169-70, 211-212, 221-224
Public Interest, 102-03,
Public Goods, 156
Purchase of Development Rights, 217-219

Quality of Life Issues, 66-68, 83, 133, 197, 214

Rational Nexus Test (Impact Fees), 149-50
Reagan, R., 112, 115, 136

Reconstruction, 29, 163
Regression Analysis (Logit), 113, 179, 191
Regional Planning Councils, 70-72, 82, 199
Republicans, 25, 45-49, 53, 59, 67, 127-34, 153, 214
Resource Allocators, 100-02
Retrenchment, 174-179
Roosevelt F. D, 39-40, 48
Rule 9J5, 43, 72, 75, 139, 141, 194
Rural Lot Splits, 9

Sacred Symbols, 87, 200-02
Sales Taxes, 124-25, 130-32, 135-37
Sanctity of Property, 91-92
Sanibel Island, FL, 10
Sarasota County, 3, 210
Seaside, FL, 23
Sebring, FL, 194, 205
Secular Realignment, 48
September 11th and the Budget Crisis, 127-134
Small Town Planning, Ch 7
Smart Growth, Ch.1, Ch.2, 174, 199-200, 229
Smokestack Chasing (Type I), Ch.11, 183-85, 188
Sprawl, Ch.1, 62-64, 78-80, 196-98, 221-24
St. Petersburg, FL, 32, 66, 79, 166
State Comprehensive Planning Act (1985), 72
Subdivision Codes, 13, 173, 207
Suffolk County, NY (PDR), 218-19
Swamp Lands Act (1850), 26

Tallahassee, 3, 29, 214, 223
Tampa Bay Area, 32-33, 41, 53, 55, 76, 79, 134, 165
Tarpon Springs, FL, 32, 201
Tax Abatements, 184, 191
Tax Base Sharing, 225

Tax Bite/Tax Burden, 123-25, 134-40
    159, 167
Tax Increment Finance, 189-93, 225.
Technocratic Planner, 103-05
Tiebout, C., 6-7, 12, 63, 159, 168-69
Traditional-Individualism, Ch.6, 26-
    29, 64, 198
Traditional Neighborhood
    Development, 207-08
Transfer of Development Rights, 116,
    220
Trigger Level (Price), 115, 210
Town Amenity (Type 2), Ch.11, 161,
    183-85, 188
Town Center, 203

User Fees/ User Charges, 146-48
Urban Growth Boundaries, 18, 209

View Sheds, 209
Volunteerism/Co-Production, 176

Water Quality Issues, 66-68, 214-15
Wedge Issues, Ch. 4, 66-68, 133
Works Progress Administration
    (WPA), 40

Yankee Newcomers, 53, 197, 214

Zoning Codes, 10-11, 63, 173, 200-02

BOCA RATON PUBLIC LIBRARY, FLORIDA

3 3656 0439746 9

Fla 307.7609759 Mat
Mattson, Gary Armes.
Small towns, sprawl and
 the politics of policy ch